The Culture of Cloth in Early Modern England
Textual Constructions of a National Identity

ROZE HENTSCHELL
Colorado State University, USA

Routledge
Taylor & Francis Group

LONDON AND NEW YORK

First published 2008 by Ashgate Publishing

2 Park Square, Milton Park, Abingdon, Oxon OX14 4RN
711 Third Avenue, New York, NY 10017, USA

Routledge is an imprint of the Taylor & Francis Group, an informa business

First issued in paperback 2016

British Library Cataloguing in Publication Data
Hentschell, Roze
The culture of cloth in early modern England: textual construction of a national identity
    1. Woolen goods industry – Social aspects – England 2. National characteristics, English 3. Industries in literature 4. Wool industry – Social aspects – England 5. Woolen goods industry – England – History 6. Wool industry – England – History 7. England – Civilization
    I. Title
    338.4'767731'0942'0903

Library of Congress Cataloging-in-Publication Data
Hentschell, Roze.
  The culture of cloth in early modern England: textual construction of a national identity / by Roze Hentschell.
    p. cm.
  Includes bibliographical references.
  ISBN-13: 978-0-7546-6301-0 (alk. paper)
  ISBN-10: 0-7546-6301-9 (alk. paper)
  1. Woolen goods industry—Social aspects—England. 2. National characteristics, English. 3. Industries in literature. 4. Wool industry—Social aspects—England. 5. England—Civilization. 6. Woolen goods industry—England—History. 7. Wool industry—England—History. I. Title.

  DA118.H55 2008
  338.4'767731094209031—dc22

                                    2007046691

ISBN 13: 978-0-7546-6301-0 (hbk)
ISBN 13: 978-1-138-25986-7 (pbk)

Contents

List of Figures

Acknowledgements

In a book about cloth, it is only fitting that I acknowledge those who helped in the weaving of this project. The writing of this book spanned several years and almost as many locations. I began the project in London and California, tried to keep it afloat in New Jersey and New York, and finally completed it in Colorado. Throughout these years, I made several sojourns to the Huntington Library in San Marino, California, where much of its research took place. I would like to extend my warmest gratitude to the librarians there for providing their able assistance. The bucolic setting and lunchtime conversations at the Huntington have been instrumental in sustaining my interest in and energy for seeing the project through to completion.

At the University of California, Santa Barbara, I had an exceptional group of friends and mentors that nurtured this project in its early years. Deepest gratitude is due to Patricia Fumerton and Richard Helgerson, whose guidance was especially central in helping me think through the connection between nationalism, material culture, and popular texts. They have followed my work tirelessly through the years and have cheered me on all the while. Their scholarly rigor, professionalism, and good humor have provided me with two amazing models for my own career. Thanks also to Mark Rose and the late Lee Bliss who read my work with generosity and a keen eye. Claire Busse, Jon Connolly, Patricia Marby Harrison, Simon Hunt, and Jessica Winston all read early chapters and I am grateful for their input and friendship. Jennifer Hellwarth and Kathy Lavezzo read and commented on countless drafts of my work in various stages of disarray and commented with appropriate adulation. Rachel Adams continues to be generous with advice, support, and good cheer. Jon Hegglund deserves a special acknowledgement for the many hours he has spent reading the various incarnations of this book and for what is now 15 years of friendship.

At William Paterson University, I had a wonderful group of colleagues whose support for my scholarship was instrumental in maintaining the momentum of the project despite many of life's pressures. Thanks especially to Catarina Feldmann, Linda Hamalian, Tony Jarrells, Timothy Liu, Donna Perry, Marge Ginsburg, and Barbara Seuss.

This book was completed at Colorado State University, where I have been lucky enough to find myself among exceptional, and exceptionally nice, people. My five years here have been among my happiest, due in no small part to my supportive and engaged colleagues and my wonderful students. Thanks to Ellen Brinks, Matthew Cooperman, Megan Palmer, and Debby Thompson at CSU and Scarlet Bowen, at the University of Colorado, for their valuable feedback on parts of the manuscript. I am especially indebted to Barbara Sebek and Catherine DiCesare for being my principal cheerleaders and for giving so generously of their time.

Thanks also to Erika Gaffney, my editor at Ashgate, for her encouragement, high professional standards, and patience. The writing of this book was enabled by financial support from UC Santa Barbara, William Paterson University, Colorado State University, and the Fletcher Jones Foundation at the Huntington Library.

I would like to acknowledge the many, many people whose love and support has personally sustained me, and by extension this project, over the years. I owe special thanks to my siblings, Felicia Bond, Paul Bond, and Celia Treamer, who have always understood and encouraged my bookish tendencies. My mother, Celia Hillings, and my late father, Bart Hentschell, gave me the freedom and encouragement to pursue my goals, even if they led me far away from home. I also want to express deep gratitude to my incredible friends, who have supported me through my life's journey and remain a constant reminder of joy in this world. You know who you are. Finally, I want to thank my husband, Thomas Cram, for bringing me so much happiness and for being my biggest fan. It is to him, and our amazing daughter Eleanor, that I dedicate this book.

Introduction

Ancient, Famous, and Decayed: The Culture of Cloth in Early Modern England

It is impossible to comprehend the development of English nationalism during the early modern period without also understanding the culture of cloth. Although wool had a prominent place in England's economy from the fifteenth to the early nineteenth century, from about 1550 to 1650 wool cloth occupied a position of centrality not seen before or after. Certainly we can look, as many economic and social historians have, to assize documents, county registers, or guild records to find evidence for such a claim. My purpose in this project, however, is not to revisit the already well-trod ground of cloth history. My argument begins with the assumption that the wool industry held a crucial place in early modern English economies. And while my primary object of inquiry is English cloth during the late sixteenth and early seventeenth centuries, I look beyond its role as a factor in England's economic development. To that end, I focus on wool cloth as an object of tremendous *cultural* importance. I argue that cloth reached far beyond its status as an object of production and commodity for exchange. It was also a locus for organizing sentiments of national solidarity across social and economic lines. Through the culture's textual output, we see that an ostensibly material, mundane, and economic topic is transformed into something larger, more symbolic, and more allegorical to contribute to an emerging and coalescing national identity.

The dominant perception of the wool industry in early modern England, at least for England's own writers, was that it was "ancient." In *A Quip for an Upstart Courtier* (1592), for example, Robert Greene asserts that wool goes back to the founding of the nation, "ever since Brute an inhabitant in this island" (294). In 1613, John May, the deputy wool examiner for James I, claimed that "[t]he antiquitie of Woll within this Kingdome hath beene, beyond the memorie of man" (1). The wool industry, then, was not merely historic; it claimed a sort of mythic status "beyond ... memory." Equally prevalent in the early modern mind was the image that the wool industry was "famous." In Thomas Deloney's, *Jack of Newbury* (1597), he articulates that "[a]mong all manuall Arts used in this Land, none is more famous for desert, or more beneficiall to the Commonwealth than is the most necessarie Art of Cloathing" (3). While the "art" of clothmaking was crucial in securing this acclaim, the source of the cloth was celebrated as well. According to William Lambarde, a London lawyer recording his observations of the Kentish landscape in 1576, England's sheep are "woorthy of great estimation, both for the exceeding fineness of the fleese ... and for the abundant store of flocks so increasing every where" (225–6). Many authors of the late sixteenth and early seventeenth centuries understood that England's wool was both "famous" and "ancient" and its esteem was largely due to its longstanding presence in England. In Richard Hakluyt the Younger's *Discourse of Western Planting* (1584), a promotional text for New World colonization, he notes that "for certen hundredth yeres ... by the peculiar commoditie of wolles, and of later yeres by clothinge of the same ... [England] raised it selfe from meaner state to greater wealthe and moche higher honour, might and power then before" (118). And the title alone of Anthony Munday's civic pageant commemorating the inauguration of London's Lord Mayor, *The Triumphs of Olde Draperie, or the Rich Cloathing of England* (1614), indicates the connection between fame and history: the clothing is "rich" because it is "olde."

While English wool enjoyed a positive reputation in the early modern period, almost as common was the understanding that the industry was in crisis; it, and thus England, was in a state of "decay." For instance, a proclamation "for the True Working and Dying of Cloth" (1613), asserts that "the Trade of Clothing hath been much discredited by the corrupt desires and practices" of some members of the clothmaking community (301). Here, blame for this dissolution was fixed on the manufacturers. Other times it was understood as caused by the consumers themselves. In 1583, Philip Stubbes attributed the degradation of English cloth to the desire to purchase foreign goods: "if we would contente our selves with such kinde of attire as our owne countrie doeth yeeld us, it were somewhat tollerable." Instead "we impoverish our selves in buying their trifling Merchandizes" (69–70). That the wool industry was in crisis was simply a well known fact: Robert Johnson, writing his *Nova Britannia* (1609) on behalf of the Virginia Company, hoped that a New World expansion of the cloth trade would "cause a mighty vent of English clothes, a great benefit to our Nation, and raising againe of that auncient trade of clothing, so much decayed in England" (245). In Johnson's argument, all three prevalent conceptions of the industry are at work: the "decay" in the industry may be rectified by a revision of the cloth trade, which will bring fame ("great benefit") *and* resurrect the "auncient" industry.

As this sampling of sentiments reveals, the ancient, famous, and decayed wool and woolen cloth industry was, importantly, England's own. Perhaps above all in the period's textual output, we see that for better or for worse wool manufacture and trade were largely considered to be national enterprises that affected nearly all subjects. Greene lauds wool's presence on "this island," and May "within this Kingdom." Deloney cites the benefit of clothmaking to "the Commonwealth," while Munday's "rich cloathing" belongs to "England." Writers also acknowledged that the state of decline into which wool had fallen was a problem of "our owne countrie." Wool was seen throughout the early modern period paradoxically as both England's pride *and* shame, that which brought glory and honor to the nation—and in many instances defined it—while simultaneously engendering contempt and ignominy for the nation. That interest in the national industry was held by such a wide swath of individuals should be apparent by the diversity of texts cited above. Greene's text is a satirical prose narrative, while May's document was officially commissioned by the crown. *Jack of Newbury*, a wildly popular romance in prose and verse, shares some of the same sentiments as Lambarde's text, a narrative about his "perambulations" in Kent. Hakluyt's *Discourse* and Johnson's *Nova Britannia* promote New World expansion, while Munday's Lord Mayor's pageant is a script describing spectacular tableaux involving mythical and historical figures. And Stubbes' text is famous as moralistic polemic, yet has much in common with proclamations issued by the Crown. Imaginative, propagandistic, fictional, polemical, satirical, and official, as I hope this study will show, almost all types of early modern writing engaged with issues of the English wool cloth industry.

The story of textile manufacturing and trade in the sixteenth and early seventeenth century is largely a story of wool cloth.[1] However, throughout the medieval period and up until the mid sixteenth century, raw wool dominated the English economy. Raw wool was exported to European nations to manufacture and finish it however they saw fit. England's raw wool came from sheep that produced a fine staple, less than two inches in length. The wool produced by England's sheep was considered superior because the country had several breeds of sheep that provided the carding wool necessary to make fine cloth.[2] This wool had fibers that were curly and serrated, allowing for substantial felting and shrinkage during fulling. The shrinkage was important to give the wool cloth a heavy, dense quality, which lent to its strength and cohesion (Munro, 45). The best wool came from sheep raised in Herefordshire and Shropshire in the Welsh marches, from the Cotswold region, from East Anglia, and from the Midlands. This English staple enjoyed a fine reputation among European nations and the ports of the north and east coasts dominated the market throughout the late fifteenth and early sixteenth centuries.

In the mid-sixteenth century, however, there was a rapid increase in the production of wool cloth. While the term "cloth" for us indicates an endless variety of textiles, for the early modern English, it generally designated textiles derived from sheep's wool. While I will discuss a variety of fabrics in the course of this book, I am primarily concerned with England's understanding of itself vis-à-vis the wool broadcloth industry. Broadcloth was a dense, tightly woven woolen, which was manufactured into large pieces, approximately 28 to 30 yards long and weighing up to 90 pounds (Ramsay, *English Woollen*, 13). In general, the process of manufacture was as follows:[3] the *shepherd*, usually an independent peasant or servant of a landowner, would sell the sheared raw wool to a wool *brogger* (broker), who would have the wool packed. It would be sold to a *clothier*, who then owned the product and saw to the rest of the manufacturing process.[4] It would be cleaned, oiled and

---

1 It is not my intention here to review the rise and fall of the wool cloth industry; historians of this topic have been doing this for the better part of the twentieth century far more comprehensively than I could. For an overview of the English cloth industry, see especially, Bowden; Kerridge, *Textile Manufactures*; Leggett; Lipson; Ponting; Ramsay, *The English Woollen Industry*; and Van der Wee.

2 For a discussion of sheep breeds in early modern England see Kerridge, *Textile Manufacturers*, especially Chapter 1.

3 See Ramsay, *The English Woollen Industry*, Chapter 1, and Zell, Chapter 6 of *Industry in the Countryside*, for a more thorough description of the process of manufacture.

4 In the medieval period and through the early sixteenth century, cloth was produced in a sort of a cottage industry system whereby each person responsible for a particular point in the process would own the cloth at that point, and then sell it to the next individual in the manufacturing process. An increase in exported cloth, and thus a more centralized selling at market, led to a significant change in the ownership system, which came to be known as the "putting out" system. See Van der Wee, p. 423; Zell, *Industry in the* Countryside, Chapter 7; and Bowden, Chapter 3, for a discussion of the rise of the clothier.

carded and sent to a *spinner*, who would spin it into yarn with either a distaff or a spinning wheel.[5] It was then given to the *weaver*, who would feed the yarn onto a loom to create the piece of cloth. The cloth would be given to the *fuller* or *tucker* who would scour it in a trough of water and then beat it. The cloth was then stretched out to dry on wooden racks, known as tenters, with iron hooks. The *rower* would raise the cloth's nap with teasels and then the *shearman* would clip off the rough wool nap to create a smooth surface. Rowing (or barbing) and shearing would have been repeated several times to achieve the desired quality. Since most cloth was exported undyed and undressed (also known as "unfinished"), the cloth would at this point have been wound or folded and sold at market, bound for either domestic customers or international shores.[6]

The mid-sixteenth century shift to cloth production was a watershed in the history of the English industry and allowed for an enormous expansion in exports. One reason behind this shift was that the government imposed large duties on exported raw wool while the export of wool cloth was hardly taxed at all, thus encouraging the Merchant Adventurers, the guild company that was primarily responsible for international trade, to focus their attention on the export of unfinished wool cloth (Van der Wee, 399). At mid-century, then, the overseas market for wool cloth— especially the market at Antwerp—expanded rapidly, leading to the great boom years in the cloth industry. The reasons for this expansion are several. First, the English Merchant Adventurers enjoyed a cooperative relationship with the city government in Antwerp as well as with those involved in the finishing trades. As the Merchant Adventurers were based in London, the capital became a much more prominent trading port than it previously had been.[7] The London merchants were given liberty to import cloth into the Netherlands with very few restrictions and the local cloth finishers in the Low Countries, particularly the dressers and dyers, benefited from an increase in demand for their expertise (Van der Wee, 412). Moreover, the English Crown gave the Merchant Adventurers a virtual monopoly over the export trade (Van der Wee, 413). Thus, by the mid sixteenth century, wool cloth surpassed raw wool as England's primary export and dominated the European market. By the 1570s, the export of raw wool was "no more than a trickle" (Ramsay, *The English Woollen Industry*, 19). Up until 1563, English wool cloth accounted for the "largest value of commodity" in Antwerp after silks and satins, which were produced elsewhere (Van der Wee, 418), and Antwerp alone took an astonishing 65 per cent of England's cloth exports (Croft, "English Commerce," 243).[8] While England's raw wool had always

---

5 The best quality yarn was produced by the distaff, a process known as rock spinning. See Alice Clark, Chapter 4, for the indispensable role women played in the cloth industry, particularly in spinning, which was largely the labor of women. See also Zell, pp. 166–8 of *Industry in the Countryside*.

6 By and large, the English had neither the labor skills for dressing nor the raw materials for dyeing to compete with dressers and dyers overseas.

7 The decline of the export of raw wool diminished the importance of the wool ports in the north and east of England. Wool cloth was principally traded through London, which handled 80 per cent of England cloth experts by the early sixteenth century (Wrightson, 107).

8 For a discussion of the important reciprocal relationship between London and Antwerp in the sixteenth century, see Keene. There were, of course, vicissitudes in the market and the

enjoyed a good reputation overseas, its wool cloth began to be perceived as the finest in the world. Importantly, the English recognized that with this product came a kind of national wealth and reputation that allowed England to emerge as a player on the world stage and became a focal point for emerging national solidarity.

Not long afterwards, however, English cloth suffered a grave setback when the Eighty-Years War between the 17 Dutch provinces and Spain interrupted the trade. More than any other episode, the unrest in the Low Countries created a crisis for the thriving cloth trade in England. In 1564, before any major conflicts erupted, Margaret of Parma, the governess of the Spanish Low Countries, temporarily banned the import of English wool cloth (Van der Wee, 420).[9] This and other measures to restrict the flow of English cloth caused a "violent contraction in the export market" (Bowden, xvii) and a sharp increase in domestic unemployment (Bowden, 158). After 1576 when the Spanish took the city, the port declined until it collapsed entirely in 1585 as the Dutch rebels closed off the Scheldt to traffic. The singular dependence on cloth as a commodity and the reliance on the port of Antwerp ultimately proved crippling to England.[10] And although the English set up new markets and shipped cloth to other ports, including those of Hamburg, Amsterdam, and Bremen, the loss of the Antwerp cloth market ushered in a years-long slump for the English cloth trade. While I will not discuss in great detail the mid-century crisis of trade, I want to underscore its prominence in the English imagination for the later years of the sixteenth century. The mid-century boom in the cloth century brought England so much prosperity and provided England with such a robust reputation, that this period was seen as a golden age, one which later generations strived to, but never could, recover.[11] There is, then, in the late sixteenth and early seventeenth centuries, a recurrent strain of loss and nostalgia in the writings about the industry.[12]

---

industry was by no means without challenges during this boom period. As Wrightson points out, "[t]he long upward trend in cloth exports had quickened in the 1540s as the price of English cloth fell in overseas markets. In 1549–50, however, it peaked and then collapsed as the market became glutted, precipitating widespread distress in the export-oriented clothing districts" (155).

9   According to Bowden, this restriction was "under the pretext of taking precaution against the plague raging in London" (158).

10 See Youings, p. 49, for a discussion of England's dependence on cloth and Davis, pp. 14–15, for a discussion of the decline of the Antwerp market.

11 Cloth remained a vital part of the English economy, but the high times of the mid-sixteenth century were never to be seen again. According to Van der Wee, "[b]y 1614, English cloth exports had achieved a new peak of 127, 215 cloths, which, however, was still well below the peak exports of the 1550s" (422).

12 The decline of the broadcloth industry led to innovations in cloth production in the late sixteenth and early seventeenth centuries. Worsteds, woolen produced from the longer hairs of the sheep, which was then combed instead of carded, were particularly prevalent. Worsteds were also lighter, using less wool per yard, and proved to be a popular fabric in warmer climes and also became a very important sector of the wool trade due primarily to the knitted stocking industry. See Thirsk, "'The Fantastical Folly of Fashion;'" Schneider; and Chapman for discussions of the worsted stocking knitting industry. Another important change in the cloth industry in England in the late sixteenth century was the advent of the so-called New Draperies. Lighter, often cheaper cloth derived from the long staple wool, the New

While the closure of the Antwerp market proved to be the most significant challenge to the English cloth trade in the late sixteenth century, and led to a number of other problems, there were also several other threats to the health of the industry throughout the period. First, in the mid-sixteenth century, complaints over land use, specifically the enclosure practices of landlords, led to an antagonism toward sheep farmers. Although land was enclosed for a number of reasons, in the popular imagination the proliferation of sheep pastures was blamed for impoverishing agrarian workers by turning them off lands. Anti-enclosure riots threatened landowners' livelihood and created a widespread sentiment that the unabated increase in sheep farming was deleterious to the nation. Second, crop failures of the sixteenth and early seventeenth century, and most significantly the weak harvests of 1595–97, devastated clothworkers who relied on the grain market for provisions. Rising prices for grain also decreased expendable income across the population, resulting in a severe drop in the purchase of cloth. Third, in the last quarter of the sixteenth century, immigrant weavers from the Netherlands seeking asylum from Spanish persecution flooded into English cloth producing towns, particularly Norwich and Colchester. While the native clothworkers initially welcomed the foreign weavers to help increase cloth production, the English came to regard the strangers as a serious threat. They were blamed for producing an inferior product, trading secretly and illegally with one another, not keeping their profits in England and, perhaps most grievous, not respecting the venerable English industry.

Fourth, after the closure of the Antwerp market, England struggled to reformulate its trading organization. The export of cloth through the Muscovy, Levant, and East India companies did not flourish as expected. Further, English traders complained about having to rely on trade arrangements involving the expanding Spanish empire just as Spain was becoming an increasing military danger to England. Finding suitable trading partners to expand or at least stabilize the trade proved to be an ongoing challenge. Fifth, the wool broadcloth industry was tested by the increasing popularity of luxury textiles that were imported from the continent. Silks and satins from Spain, France, and Italy were seen as creating a new kind of crisis for the wool industry whereby individuals across classes rejected wool in favor of luxury goods.[13] For the first time, wool cloth had real competition in the form of products

---

Draperies were originally produced in Flanders, but proliferated in England with the influx of Flemish immigrants. New manners of weaving diverse types of yarn allowed for seemingly endless combinations, and were reflected in the proliferation of cloth with new and unusual names, such as bays, says, serges, perpetuanas, calimancoes, mockadoes, and bombazines, just to name a few. For more on the New Draperies, see Coleman; Harte, p. 4; Holderness; Munro; Luc Martin; and Wrightson, p. 166–7. While the contribution of the New Draperies to the economy should not be underestimated, it is crucial to remember that these textiles did not replace wool broadcloth's place in England's economy or imagination. The broadcloth industry still accounted for a sizable portion of English exports through 1615, the year this present study concludes.

13 This was especially the case after 1603, the year that the sumptuary laws were repealed. Because these laws were notoriously difficult to enforce, however, there is reason to believe that a large portion of the population who could afford luxury goods did buy them even in the sixteenth century.

that were also seen as morally suspicious. Sixth, there was a perceived widespread corruption among wool manufacturers. Clothiers were charged with allowing and indeed encouraging the manufacture of a debased product that was too short, too stretched, or too light. Moreover, London drapers and merchants were accused of knowingly selling the fraudulent fabric, thus duping the unsuspecting customer and diminishing the reputation of wool. While these were not the only challenges to the wool broadcloth industry in the early modern period, they were the ones that figured most prominently in the English cultural imagination, contributed to the reputation that wool was in a state of "decay," and prompted the writers of the period to offer solutions to rectify the problems.

While obviously perceived of as problems, these challenges to the industry were crucial in defining the importance of cloth. As I argue, it is primarily through bringing the problems to light and imagining solutions to them that authors of the period were able to articulate how important wool broadcloth was to a national identity. While the study of material culture as a whole has gained significant attention in recent scholarship and new studies of physical objects have contributed to a greater understanding of the early modern world, this book is primarily a study of the culture of cloth and the singular importance that wool had in contributing to England's understanding of itself in the late sixteenth and early seventeenth centuries.[14] One reason cloth held such a prominent place in the early modern imagination was due to the personal relationship individuals had with textiles. Because so many individuals were involved in the production and trade of cloth, it was a material that became a focal point for thousands of laboring English men and women. Moreover, all English people wore clothing and most of them exclusively wore cloth that had been manufactured domestically. Ann Rosalind Jones and Peter Stallybrass have shown us the intimate connection early modern subjects had with the clothes that they wore. In their magisterial *Renaissance Clothing and the Materials of Memory*, the authors demonstrate the crucial and pervasive relationship between subjectivity and clothes, which possess the "power to constitute subjects" (2). As they eloquently assert, "[t]he material of cloth matters so much because it operates on and undoes, the margins of the self" (202). While Jones and Stallybrass's study is primarily one of finished cloth and its functions as clothing, their formulation is nevertheless helpful here. Cloth is important as an object in and of itself in serving a vital function in the lives of subjects; it "operates" as a source of clothing, an object of manufacture, a product for international trade and thus intersects with the subject at many turns. But because cloth is so socially complicated, it also deconstructs or "undoes" its

---

14 Criticism of the early modern period has given much attention to the study of material culture. While late twentieth century criticism of the period has been preoccupied with subjectivity, "self-fashioning," and the understanding of "the human," in the last 15 or so years scholars have paid increasing attention to the objects that constitute the subjects' world and indeed constitute the subjects themselves. For examples of recent work exploring material culture in the early modern period, see in particular, de Grazia, Quilligan, Stallybrass (eds), *Subject and Object in Renaissance Culture*; Fumerton and Hunt (eds), *Renaissance Culture and the Everyday*; Orlin (ed.), *Material London, ca. 1600*; Yates, *Error, Misuse, and Failure*; and the special issue of the *Journal of Medieval and Early Modern Studies* entitled "Renaissance Materialities" edited by Quilligan.

mere status as an object. Cloth comes to represent something more for the subject than its mere materiality. Indeed, it dismantles epistemological certainty for the subject. And it is this space of uncertainty that allows individuals to make meaning of cloth, to tell stories about it. This study hopes to expand on the work of Jones and Stallybrass to ask what happens when we investigate a national, rather than an individual relationship to cloth. We then may begin to understand that the identity of a people was just as bound to the materiality of their culture as that of individuals. The material commodity of cloth was so closely linked with the abstract idea of nation that England, in effect, became knowable through the cloth industry.

Because I am interested in exploring why cloth held such a prominent place in the English imagination, I look to textual productions—both fiction and non-fiction texts that often treat the cloth industry with mythic importance—to help explain how cloth comes to be a catalyst for nationalism.[15] My argument assumes that narratives, like nations, are cultural productions with specific agendas and ramifications.[16] Although "the nation" may be regarded as that which is always already in existence, handed down from generation to generation, the story of a nation can never be an essential or teleological one. The nation, and the sentiment of belief in that nation— nationalism—is always being refashioned, constructed, performed.[17] One important way in which nationalisms are continually created is through printed texts. Benedict Anderson argues that printed language is a fundamental aspect of the creation of nationalism because subjects understand that they are part of something larger than themselves once they can imagine others reading the same material: "these fellow- readers, to whom they were connected through print, formed ... the embryo of the nationally imagined community" (47). Printed matter allows for the nationalization of various regionalisms and assists in the inclusion of a wide number of readers. At the same time that print introduces new national epistemologies, it also creates tradition where none may have been: print "fixes" language, gives it permanence over time and space, which "helped to build that image of antiquity so central to the subjective idea of a nation" (Anderson, 47–8). The idea that the nation has always "been" is one that is constructed through a culture's various stories and metaphors. In this sense, texts can create a history of the nation. For early modern England, it was the collective belief in the antiquity of the cloth industry that allowed the culture to equate it with England itself. The texts that I discuss participate in the construction and reification of an ancient and venerable cloth industry that creates a past for England, thereby creating a sense of England as a nation.

The texts that I examine are largely topical in focus, informed by and participating in the contemporaneous debates surrounding the complexities of the cloth industry. And just as I am committed to rethinking canonical texts by looking at them in the

---

15 For Barthes, myth is necessarily "a mode of signification" (109), created by discourse, the "materials of myth" (110).

16 See Helgerson's remarks on the "four-way exchange" of texts, nations, authors, and discursive communities: "all are both produced and productive, productive of that by which they are produced" (*Forms of Nationhood*, 13).

17 See Bhabha's "DissemiNation," p. 299, for a discussion of performativity and nation formation.

context of the early modern cloth industry (Sidney's *Arcadia* in particular), I am also interested in examining texts on the margins of the literary canon, texts that have been given little critical attention despite the popularity with which they were often received in their own time. Agrarian verse, propaganda for New World expansion, religious polemic, ballads, and proclamations were among the types of writing that were crucial in contributing to an understanding of the national prominence of the cloth industry.[18] The pervasive sense in texts across genres is that the cloth industry is England's treasure, one to be promoted and protected.

The cloth-nation connection became legible through a vast array of texts. That a concern for the industry should appear in so many different sorts of textual modes shows a diversity of response befitting a complex industry. No one genre or mode could possibly attend to all the disparate elements of the trade, just as diverse genres could not attend to a particular element in an identical manner. Throughout this study, I argue that distinct genres perform particular kinds of cultural work; they make sense of unique cloth-related situations in unique ways. Despite this diversity of attention, I assert that authors working in a multiplicity of modes do possess a commonality in their concerns. What these texts all have in common—the traditionally literary as well as those usually considered to be historical documents—is their contribution to an understanding of how diverse sectors of the population perceived the cloth industry and its role in constructing England's nationhood. While the texts and issues on which my project focuses are wide-ranging—linking pastoral with issues surrounding land enclosure, prose narrative with cloth production, promotional literature with cloth exports, satire with foreign imports, drama with corrupt mercantilism, and civic pageants with an international trade crisis—I argue that they all help us to understand the interwoven relationship between literature and the cloth industry in early modern England. Attending carefully to the language of all of these texts, we see how poets, propagandists, and prose writers, satirists, sovereigns, and sermonists share a concern for the fate of the English cloth industry. Texts and textiles are inextricably tied in their power to materially articulate national identity.[19]

The Culture of Cloth in Early Modern England focuses specifically on texts from the late sixteenth and early seventeenth century (approximately 1575–1615). In these years the cloth industry was indispensable to England's economic vitality both at home and abroad. At the same time, it is in this forty-year period that the industry also faced challenges never before encountered on a major scale. Once

---

18 While recent critics have shown the complex and inextricable relationship between emerging nationalism and literary production during this period, they primarily focus on canonical texts and authors. See, for example, Baker, Escobedo, Hadfield, Helgerson, *Forms of Nationhood*; Howard and Rackin, Joughin, Maley, McEachern, and Schwyzer. I do not claim that texts that have been read and loved over time cannot help us to understand the emerging of English national identity during the early modern period; I am proposing, however, that we expand the body of literature that we study to complicate the important connections between nationhood and literature.

19 To be sure, not all sectors of the population necessarily would have cared to read all the texts I discuss in this book. However, with only one or two exceptions, all of the texts that I investigate were printed in their own time, and thus participate in a sort of public discourse in a way that archival manuscripts do not.

a booming and well-organized industry, the cloth trade had become damaged and broken under the pressure of so many challenges. In spite of these challenges, or likely because of them, the authors who were concerned with the cloth industry persisted in imagining a future thriving industry which, as it would resuscitate the economy, would also bind the nation's people. In Julian Yates's study of material objects in the early modern period, he asserts that "the success of these objects may be gauged by their relative invisibility. If they work well, no one notices them." However, "each is prone to error, misuse, and sometimes failure" and "it is with these lapses" that we may "recover the silent work of 'things' in the production of what we take to be human drama" (xix). This is a helpful formulation for thinking about woolen cloth. Although cloth is not just one "thing," having many forms and residing in many places, the writers of the early modern period notice it more when something is amiss: when the laborers are unhappy with their conditions, when the cloth itself is seen as adulterated and sold by corrupt merchants, when wool is threatened by silk. It is in these times of crisis, of "error, misuse, and failure," that discourse surrounding the industry speaks the loudest. I am interested in how texts engage with these moments of crisis, how authors, some who had little to do with the cloth industry, felt compelled to add their voices to the conversation and, importantly, how this often cacophonous conversation contributed to a national discourse. As Homi Bhabha has argued, "[t]he language of culture and community is poised on the fissures of the present becoming the rhetorical figures of a national past" (294). That is to say, the understanding of the nation is only possible in times of crisis; it is the moments of failure that enable and engender the texts that become a nation's story, which includes a narrative of its history. The writing of the nation is that which "turns that loss into the language of metaphor" (Bhabha, 291).

 The Culture of Cloth is divided into three sections, each comprising two chapters. The first section, "Resistance in the Flock: Labor Rebellion in Pastoral Literature and Prose Romance," focuses on the ways in which the romance, a traditional and celebrated literary form, becomes the unlikely vehicle for sentiments of social protest. In my first chapter, "Pasture and Pastoral: Sheep, Anti-Enclosure Literature, and Sidney's Seditious Peasants," I read pastoral literature against the backdrop of didactic agrarian texts and the land enclosure debates in the second half of the sixteenth century, focusing particularly on anti-enclosure literature and on the rebellion of the rustics in Sidney's *Arcadia*. The bucolic landscape dotted with grazing sheep and their shepherds is a mainstay of the pastoral mode and for years critics have seen pastoral as obfuscating agrarian labor in the interest of exploring more allegorical themes or reframing the classical eclogues of Virgil. However, many pastoral texts reveal an unlikely engagement with the material conditions of sheep and shepherding of the sixteenth century, and particularly with the hardships that this occupation entailed. The conversion of arable land to sheep pasture at a time when the cloth industry was shifting from the raw staple to woven cloth led to depopulation of agrarian laborers and a placing of blame on the enclosing landlords and their voracious sheep. Anti-enclosure sentiment written by poets, polemicists, and economic thinkers became a popular strain of literature and, as I argue, must share the textual landscape with pastoral literature. While pastoral seemingly erases the problems of the changing agrarian landscape by privileging the otiose life of shepherds and their benevolent sheep, the violent uprising of the peasants in *The Arcadia* reveals the extent to which the discontent of agrarian laborers was a concern for the landowners, including Sidney himself, in the late sixteenth century. The stable notion of the English countryside and thus the nation promoted in pastoral literature, is disrupted by the discontent among agricultural workers with shepherds and landowners. The decisive squelching of the rebellion in *The Arcadia* allows for the triumph of the landowner and his sheep. That Sidney includes the skirmish at all, however, reveals the dangers that the landowners faced during a time of changes in land use due in large part to the burgeoning cloth trade.

In Chapter 2, "Clothworkers and Social Protest: The Case of Thomas Deloney," I examine Deloney's *Jack of Newbury* in the context of his dual career as a silkweaver and balladeer during the difficult decade of the 1590s, a time of harvest failures at home and depressions in the cloth market abroad. Deloney was outspoken against what he saw as threats to his profession, particularly the challenges posed by successful immigrant weavers and government apathy to the plight of clothworkers in the face of grain shortages, and was twice in trouble with the authorities for his activism. Rather than seeing his popular prose romance, *Jack of Newbury*, as a departure from his activist writing, I argue that it too participates in a culture of social protest. The text's dedicatory epistle, the description of Jack's workshop, and especially Jack's dealings with the King and his advisors, show an ironic idealism that belies the calamity that besieged the cloth industry. Like pastoral, the genre of prose romance may seem to obfuscate the troubles afflicting the clothworkers in the text. However, I argue that the narrative presents a populist nationalism that imagines cloth laborers as vital to England's wealth and security at a time when the government was denying their existence as such. Both of these chapters engage with issues of resistance against what was perceived of as unfair treatment of rural laborers. But while Deloney's text takes up the cloth manufacturer's cause and celebrates his work as constitutive of a robust nation, Sidney's *Arcadia* shows that agricultural workers were sometimes violently at odds with, and vastly inferior to, their counterparts who contributed to sheep farming. In both instances, however, the cloth industry emerges as the victor and as central to a thriving and cohesive nation.

Part Two, "The Circulation of Subjectivity in the Cloth Trade," investigates how the overseas cloth trade both in imports and exports contributed to an increased sense of national identity among English subjects. To be sure, domestic manufacture was crucial in creating an epistemology of the industry because so many individuals were involved in wool production. However, as wool cloth exports became more and more important to England's economic well-being, international trade relations emerged as the focal point for many. Writers saw that slumps in the industry, then, would necessarily need to be rectified by a revision in trade arrangements with foreign nations. In Chapter 3, "'Vente for our English Clothes': Promoting Early New World Expansion," I focus on propaganda for exploration and colonization of the New World in the last quarter of the sixteenth century, showing how authors of promotional texts based their arguments for expansion in large part on the claim that the decayed cloth industry would be revived. Conflicts with Spain had proved challenging to England's European trade routes and exporting to lands further east had not panned out as the Merchant Adventurers had hoped. The voyages to the New World, still in their nascent stages, allowed the promoters to imagine the possibility of an abundant land, which would presumably provide the home industry with products once only available from foreign nations. Further, the colonizers would ostensibly find an eager new trading partner in the native Americans. While the desire to expand the English cloth industry was a benevolent form of colonialism when compared to what England regarded as Spain's tyrannical tactics, English ambition to clothe the naked natives reveals a complex dynamic of colonialism: promotional materials show how the English desired to convert the indigenous population from "savage" consumption to the "civilized" consumption of English cloth. Thus, the promise of a new outpost for the English textiles also served to consolidate a greater national unity.

In my fourth chapter, "Treasonous Textiles: Foreign Cloth and the Construction of Englishness," I look at the religious and satiric reaction to luxury textiles as they are imported into England. Foreign cloth was associated with the suspect morals of its country of origin and thus wearing it in England was regarded as a symbolically treasonous act. The English preoccupation with foreign fabrics was seen as disruptive to the national wool industry both because it detracted from the purchase of domestic wool and because it suggested that England's own were turning away from what was constructed as a morally superior product. Robert Greene's *A Quip for an Upstart Courtier*, a satirical prose narrative in which a homegrown cloth pair of breeches argues with an Italian pair of velvet breeches about his prerogative to be in England, demonstrates how thoroughly the debate over foreign cloth had seeped into the popular psyche. While the aim of these texts is to demonize foreign imports, or in the case of Greene to deride those who were obsessed with them, the authors cast their criticisms of the vice of foreign cloth in terms of the virtues of domestic cloth, and in so doing present a glorification of England itself. Cloth then emerges as the material through which early modern writers negotiated questions of national selfhood and foreign otherness. Both of the chapters in this section, then, show how English wool, as a commodity of exchange, was central to the definition of a national identity. This identity, though, could only truly be known through an engagement with the foreign other. Whether imagining trade relations with the little known New World or enduring the indignities brought on by the textiles from European nations, the English necessarily regarded their own product as superior in both quality and the moral integrity this quality represented.

The third section, "Staging the Cloth Crisis," examines the performance in both drama and civic pageantry of issues important to the cloth industry in the first quarter of the seventeenth century, a time of increasing threats to the cloth trade. Chapter 5, "The Fleecing of England, or the Drama of Corrupt Drapers: Thomas Middleton's *Michaelmas Term*," explores the early seventeenth-century perception that cloth manufacturing was in a state of grave decline. We see a widespread concern for the rampant degradation of domestic cloth manufacturing and marketing, which included shoddy production practices, fraudulence in the presentation and sale of cloth, and deliberate swindling of consumers on the part of the London drapers. Governmental publications, especially royal proclamations, as well as polemical texts expressed a deep concern for the decline. Despite the criminal practices with which the cloth producers were often charged, there seemed to be great difficulty in reining them in, even though there was a proliferation of legislation surrounding wool manufactures. Thomas Middleton's city comedy, *Michaelmas Term*, highlights this crisis through the character of Quomodo, a corrupt London draper who eventually receives his comeuppance. I argue that by attending closely to Quomodo's profession, something that previous critics have not done, we see how Middleton expresses his culture's stereotypes and fears about that occupation. Moreover, Middleton offers a corrective to the draper's behavior, thus publicly presenting a solution, something that government officials could not do.

The ineffectuality of government intervention in resolving crises in the cloth industry is the principal subject of the final chapter, "Politics on Parade: The Cockayne Project and Anthony Munday's Civic Pageants for the Drapers." In this chapter I outline the deep trouble that the English broadcloth industry found itself in after the disastrous Cockayne scheme, a government project meant to revive the industry by exporting only broadcloths that had been dyed and dressed in England. Cockayne's project, which was enthusiastically endorsed by the Crown, led to a collapse in cloth exports and an attendant crippling of domestic manufactures. I turn to Anthony Munday's two pageants for the Drapers' Company to commemorate the Lord Mayors' inaugurations of 1614 and 1615, written as the crisis was unfolding, and read them in the context of this depression in the cloth trade. In the pageants, Munday invokes the cloth industry's glorious medieval past as well as its mythical fame to celebrate the wool industry and the new Mayors' link to that venerable trade. For Munday the "decay" of the industry can only be rectified if the new Lord Mayors, and the thousands of spectators in attendance, also recall that it is "ancient" and "famous." As a member of the Drapers' Company, the Mayors' associations with English wool—the Golden Fleece—mark them as "London's Jason." But by connecting the challenges that await the Lord Mayors to the brave leader of the Argonauts, Munday is doing much more than celebrating the crest of the company; he is also reminding the Lord Mayor of the perilous journey that he must undergo if he is to claim the Fleece as his own. For the Lord Mayors, recovering the Fleece is akin to saving the cloth industry and the nation from its degenerative condition. The popular nature of the pageants also allowed for a public challenge to the King's policies, which had led to the dilapidated state of affairs. Distinct from other textual forms, texts for performance allowed for a wider exposure to the problems of the industry and thus contributed to a cultural understanding of an industry in crisis. Like *Michaelmas Term*, Munday's pageants not only envision but also stage solutions to crises in the industry and thus offer critiques of the King's policies at the same time as they celebrate the glory of the broadcloth industry.[20] Both of these

---

20 If the discussions of the texts in this study are not necessarily arranged chronologically, it is because the complex vicissitudes and difficulties of the cloth industry did not play themselves out in a linear fashion. For example, the cloth industry was a focal point for reaction to the harvest failures at home, propagandistic literature conceiving the New World, threats from foreign imports, and corrupt manufacturing practices, all during the 1590s. The historical backdrop of the issues, however, is much more episodic than teleological, telling a story of how the cloth industry continually faced challenges and setbacks. For instance, the enclosure debates over sheep farming have a notoriously long and sustained role in England, but I am primarily looking at those of the mid-to-late sixteenth century. And, while harvest failures tended to aversely affect cloth-producing regions in particular whenever they occurred, I am focusing on those of the late 1590s. The chapters are arranged with attention to

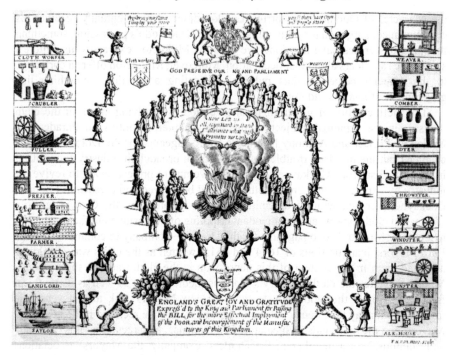

Fig. 1   F.H. Van Hove, *England's Great Joy and Gratitude*, c. 1690

chapters specifically highlight the important role that London merchants played in representing the nation's industry.

In a late seventeenth-century broadside illustration celebrating the passing of a bill "for the more Effectual Imployment of the Poor" and "Incouragement of the manufactures of this Kingdom" (see Figure 1), a group of laborers in modest, homespun clothes join hands around a bonfire.[21] Rising above the fire's smoke are the following words: "Now Lett us all joyn in Hand T'advance what most Promotes our Land." The clasping of hands in a unified ring demonstrates the men's solidarity with their fellow English workers: they recognize their common project to "promote" the "land" of England through employment and manufacture. The 14 illustrations along the side borders of the broadside depict images associated with such occupations as alehouse keeper (the interior of a tavern), sailor (a ship on the sea), and farmer (a horse pulling a plow). Significantly outnumbering the images representing these trades are those related to the many branches of the wool cloth industry: we see the

---

chronology, but with an understanding that chronological divisions are ultimately untenable when it comes to the complexities of the industry.

21 This image appears as the cover image and frontispiece to David Cressy's *Bonfire and Bells*. Although he does not discuss the image, it does suggest the importance of bonfires in political activism of the early modern period, a focus of his book.

weaver's loom, the spinner's wheel, the dyer's vats, the fuller's trough, and various other machines and instruments associated with cloth production.

Their sheer numbers suggest the primacy of occupations related to the wool industry as those which are crucial to defining "the manufactures of this Kingdom." The images themselves, however, are devoid of human figures, who seem to have stepped out of the frame and into the celebration around the fire. They stand behind the ring of men, holding up instruments of their trades, as if to give an offering and join in the festivities expressing "England's great joy and gratitude" for "our King and Parliament" and their passing of the bill. Further emphasizing the centrality of wool workers, three crests of guild companies are represented, those of the Weavers, Clothworkers, and Worsted Weavers. At the top of the broadside two male figures frame the Stuart coat of arms. The clothworker on the left says, "Preserve your fleece t'imploy your poore," as the weaver on the right concludes, "you'll then have coyn and people store." Together their verse indicates that if the government "preserves" or protects England's domestic cloth industry (the "fleece," which is represented by two standard-bearing sheep), then the country's poor will be working and England will be financially secure. While, as the broadside suggests, the relationship between government and laborer was a necessarily reciprocal one, the image—like so many texts of the early modern period—makes abundantly clear the continued importance of the cloth industry in defining the nation.

PART 1
Resistance in the Flock:
Labor Rebellion in Pastoral
Poetry and Prose Romance

Chapter 1

Pasture and Pastoral:
Sheep, Anti-Enclosure Literature,
and Sidney's Seditious Peasants

"It is meant therby, when any man hath taken away and enclosed any other mens common, or hath pulled down houses of husbandry, and converted the lands from tillage to pasture. This is the meaning of this word, and so we pray you remember it."
—*Instructions to the Enclosure Commissioners*, Appointed June 1548

"Is it then the Pastoral poem which is misliked? (For perchance where the hedge is lowest they will soonest leap over.) Is the poor pipe disdained, which sometime out of Meliboeus' mouth can show the misery of people under hard lords or ravening soldiers, and again, by Tityrus, what blessedness is derived to them that lie lowest from the goodness of them that sit highest; sometimes, under the pretty tales of wolves and sheep, can include the whole considerations of wrong-doing and patience; sometimes show that contentions for trifles can get but a trifling victory."
—Philip Sidney, *The Defence of Poesy* (c. 1582)

"It is not easy to forget that Sidney's *Arcadia*, which gives a continuing title to English neo-pastoral, was written in a park which had been made by enclosing a whole village and evicting the tenants."
—Raymond Williams, *The Country and the City*

In writing a book that argues for the centrality of the wool cloth industry in the early modern imagination and in forming England's nationalism, I would be remiss if I did not explore the role of England's sheep, the source of this venerable product. However obvious it may seem that sheep played a crucial part in England's economies, there has been no thorough study of the animal as the cultural icon that I argue it was in the sixteenth century. Perhaps it is the very omnipresence of sheep, both in the English countryside and in the textual production of the period, that allows them to be ignored. To critics interested in the rural landscape, the pervasiveness of sheep in pastoral and agrarian literature has rendered them as little more than background noise to the shepherd's song or the farmer's instruction. And while historians have long recognized the singular importance of wool and cloth in shaping England's economic structure in the Middle Ages and early modern period and literary critics have recently begun to acknowledge its crucial place in shaping an understanding of the culture, the source of the product has received curiously little attention. This chapter, then, is an attempt to carve out a space for sheep to be recognized. Once we see the significance of sheep in shaping both agrarian texts and pastoral literature, we may also begin to bring them to the forefront of the discussion of the cloth industry.

Indeed, I argue that these two endeavors are intimately tied. It is precisely because the wool broadcloth industry was so central in shaping England's image in the early modern period that texts concerning sheep proliferated.

In this chapter, I will first trace the role of sheep and sheep farming in the period's pastoral literature and in husbandry manuals, popular didactic texts that dispense advice on farm management, demonstrating that the presence of sheep is not merely part of an idyllic backdrop, but often a serious reminder of their importance in early modern economies. A hallmark of early modern pastoral literature is the idealized representation of sheep. The ovine became an emblem for an imaginative bucolic world, representing the otiose life of the lovelorn shepherd-poet. At the same time, the animal had significant material importance as the source of England's primary industry. The animal was valued above all others for its raw wool and therefore materially crucial to England's economic welfare.[1] The sixteenth and early seventeenth century saw two seemingly disparate worlds, the courtly and the agrarian, intersect in the figure of the sheep. Thus we have two competing images: On the one hand we find sheep as convenient props in a pastoral landscape of leisure. On the other hand, we see sheep as sources for human consumption and profit. These two representations, however, are not necessarily relegated to one type of text nor are they mutually exclusive. Just as we see the economic importance of sheep in pastoral literature, we also find an idealized portrait in many didactic texts. Although a study of sheep in these texts allows us to gain a greater understanding of how significant they were to the culture, by and large shepherds and their sheep emerge as agrarian heroes, central to engendering the image of the lauded cloth industry.

In a particular strain of literature in the sixteenth century, however, sheep and shepherds are presented not as innocent participants in an idyllic world, but rather as symbols of—and often key players in—the demise of an older, idealized social order. In texts that take up the issue of land usage in the sixteenth century, sheep are imbued with the power to destroy that landscape with their insatiability. In anti-enclosure literature of the sixteenth century in particular, the image of the greedy sheep takes shape. The second movement of this chapter, then, is an interrogation of the role of sheep in this popular mode of writing. For those who study early modern agrarian history, anti-enclosure literature holds a particularly important role, not only for the fine example of vitriolic polemic that it gives us, but also for how it reveals a preoccupation with the fate of the *nation's* land. In the mid-sixteenth century, just as England's wool broadcloth industry was flourishing as never before, there was an increasing concern with the deleterious effects this boom had for the agrarian communities, whose land had been turned into sheep pasture.

The study of enclosure in England in the early modern period is certainly well-trod ground; for decades, economic historians have been investigating both the reasons for and results of land enclosure, as well as the extent to which land

---

1   The wool provided by England's sheep was superior because the country had several breeds of sheep that provided carding wool, the wool necessary to make fine cloth. For a discussion of sheep breeds in early modern England see Kerridge, *Textile Manufactures*, especially Chapter 1. For a general discussion of sheep farming and wool production, see Bowden, Chapter 1.

was actually enclosed. Although property was enclosed for a number of reasons, it is clear that the writers of the invective against landlords who put up hedges or fences or dug trenches around their land, almost always focus on and decry the act of turning arable land into pasture for sheep grazing. In privileging sheep farming for wool production, landlords appeared willing to displace agricultural laborers, leading to depopulation of the countryside, widespread unemployment, and vagrancy. Although each of these serious social problems had several roots, enclosed pastures were regarded in the period as the primary cause. The landlord's sheep, then, became the symbol for the enclosure and a central object of derision. In anti-enclosure riots of the sixteenth century in particular, sheep become metonymic representations of the greedy landlords on whose land they grazed. Thus, at a time when England was organizing sentiments of national solidarity based on the burdgeoning cloth trade abroad, there was a simultaneous notion that the very source of this wealth was causing the impoverishment of the nation at home. The anti-enclosure riots that occurred in the mid-sixteenth century, then, became the logical result of the privileging of sheep farming. Those resistant to the proliferation of sheep farms, particularly agricultural laborers, saw their livelihood dwindle just as the booming cloth industry increased the wealth of the landlords.

The background of the sheep's role in pastoral texts, agrarian manuals, and anti-enclosure literature is the context for my re-reading of Philip Sidney's *The Countess of Pembroke's Arcadia* (1580), the chapter's final movement. My argument that much pastoral literature is concerned with the material conditions of sheep and shepherds opens up Sidney's text to a new interpretation where the literary mode can be seen in relation to the material world of wool production and the debates surrounding it. Taking seriously the fact that Sidney composed this text while at Wilton House, the seat of the Earls of Pembroke, I read the scenes in which a drunken group of rustics revolt against the Duke Basilius as an example of the fear of agrarian resistance that plagued landowners in the sixteenth century. The manorial lands of Sidney's brother-in-law's family, in the county of Wiltshire, a rich wool-producing part of England, were not only notoriously enclosed in the mid-sixteenth century, but were also the site of an agrarian rebellion. Furthermore, several members of Sidney's family were directly involved in suppressing mid-century enclosure riots. I argue that Sidney's *Arcadia* presents us with a full picture of the ovine. The sheep is conventionally situated in the pastoral landscape of the text, serving as an accessory by which we can identify the shepherds and shepherd-poets of the prose narrative. They also become, like the beasts of anti-enclosure literature, associated with the aristocratic world of the landowner. Throughout the prose romance, the figure of the shepherd coincides with traditional representations we see in other pastoral poetry and prose. However, when revisiting *The Arcadia* by looking at the context of debates over land use and agrarian discontent, we see that the scenes of the insurrection of the Phagonians appear strikingly similar to the literature chronicling anti-enclosure riots. In the text's suppression of the rebels we find a reassertion of the landlord's prominence and a triumph of the sheep. And in this victory, we see a reification of the crucial position that sheep had in shaping England's cloth industry and promoting the nation's wealth.

The Golden Fleece

In Leonard Mascall's popular husbandry manual, *The First Book of Cattell* (1587), the author interjects a verse in his didactic prose to emphasize the singular significance of the sheep in the daily life of the English:[2]

> These cattell sheepe among the rest,
> Is counted for man one of the best.
> No harmefull beast nor hurt at all,
> His fleece of wooll doth cloth us all. (Aa1v)

The author not only asserts that the ovine is gentle in his demeanor, showing the animal's kinship with man, he also makes clear the beast's importance to "all" in the utility of his fleece. Of all the cattle, the sheep is regarded as particularly beneficial "for man," indicating the crucial role that sheep play in the daily life of those who must be clothed. Mascall goes on to express that sheep

> ought to be the first cattell to be looked unto, if ye marke the great profite that cometh by them: for by these cattell wee are chiefely defended from colde, in serving many waies, in coverings for our bodies. They do not onely nourish the people of the villages, but also to serve the table with many sortes of delicate and pleasant meates. (Aa2v)

Providing the central needs of food and clothing, sheep are crucial to both rich and poor, city dweller and country denizen.[3] Lauded as useful and the source of "great profit," Mascall recognizes their key role in England's economy as well. In the form of wool and mutton, though, sheep are commodified and disassociated from the products they provide.[4] Circulating in the economy, sheep become sources for human consumption and financial gain, as the continuation of Mascall's poem makes clear:

> His flesh doth feed both yong and old.
> His tallow makes the candels white,
> To burne and serve us day and night.
> His skinne doth pleasure divers waies,

---

2   Mascall's text went through 13 editions between 1587 and 1662. McRae asserts that its popularity as well that of other husbandry manuals from the period was in part because the author sought to expand his audience to include farmers of lower classes, and not simply rich landowners, who had been the target of earlier tracts. See McRae's "Husbandry Manuals and Agrarian Improvement" in *God Speed the Plough*.

3   In Heresbach's *Four Books of Husbandry*, translated into English in 1577, the author demonstrates why sheep are to be "assigned" to "the cheefest place" among all other agrarian animals: "for as Oxen serve for the tylling of the ground, & necessary use of men, so is to this poore beast ascribed the safegard of the body, for the Sheepe dooth both with his fleese apparayle us, & with his milke, & holesome fleshe, nourish us" (S1v). Heresbach's text no doubt served as an important source for Mascall.

4   For a discussion of the several uses of sheep aside from wool, see Bowden, pp. 8–13.

To write, to weare at all assaies.[5]
His guts thereof doe make whele strings,[6]
They use his bones to other things.
His hornes some shepeheards will not loose,
Because therewith they patch their shooes.
His dung is chiefe I understand,
To helpe and dung the plowmans land. (Aa1v)

The sheep's body is parceled out in a sort of bestial blazon to show its variant uses. We move from a product recognizable even in pastoral literature—the value of the sheep's "fleece of wooll"—to the more mundane and perhaps abject uses of the animal: its "flesh," "tallow," "skinne," "guts," "bones," "hornes," and—finally—"dung" represent its material importance.[7] Here the sheep as animal is at once completely defamiliarized—disassembled into multiple commodities—while remaining whole; it is "his" body that is pieced apart.

At the same time as the sheep could be seen as the source of disparate products, the animal dotted the rural landscape, a pervasive visual symbol of its key economic role and the sum of its parts. The abundance of sheep was often of interest to countryside travelers who wrote about their observations. In his *Perambulation of Kent* (1570), William Lambarde, a London lawyer whose father was a master draper, describes the landscape of the Isle of Sheppey, a small island off the north Kent coast, which he regards as a microcosm of England when it comes to sheep farming.[8] The sheep are

> woorthy of great estimation, both for the exceeding fineness of the fleese (which passeth all other in Europe at this day, and is to be compared with the auncient, delicate wooll of Tarentum, or the Golden Fleese of Colchos, it selfe) and for the abundant store of flocks so increasing every where, that not only this litle Isle whiche we have now in hand, but the whole realme also, might rightly be called Shepey. (225–6)

---

5   Sheepskin as well as calfskin was used for vellum. In *2 Henry VI*, the rebel Jack Cade responds to the famous request by one of his followers to "kill all the lawyers": "Nay, that I mean to do. Is not this a lamentable thing, that the skin of an innocent lamb should be made parchment? that parchment, being so scribbled o'er, should undo a man?" (IV, ii, 76–81).

6   It is not entirely clear to what sort of wheel Mascall refers, although it is possible that he means the spinning wheel, whose spokes may have been made with offal from sheep intestines. Thus the sheep provides both the commodity and means of production. Sheep "guts" were also used to make the strings of various instruments. In *Much Ado About Nothing*, the cynical Benedick wonders at the curiosity of men who are moved by the sound of music: "Is it not strange that sheep's guts should hale souls out of men's bodies?" (II, iii, 59–60).

7   The movement from the "fleece" to the "dung," from the high to the low, also suggests a hierarchy of "parts" resonant with the blazon of early modern love poetry where a woman's body is scanned from her idealized hair and facial features to her breasts, often stopping before her genitalia, the unspeakable parts. Spenser's Sonnet 64 from the *Amoretti* and stanza 10 of the *Epithalamion* are examples of this.

8   Lambarde's text heads up the nascent genre of antiquarian writing, as the *Perambulation of Kent* is the first history of a British county. For an excellent study of English writers' understanding of their own history, see Daniel Woolf, *The Social Circulation of the Past*.

English sheep are so aggrandized that they are described as if they were members of the nobility, "worthy of great estimation," in their contribution to the nation. They are also ubiquitous and ever-increasing. As Paul Hentzner, a German traveler described in 1598, one only needs to see sheep grazing to be reminded of their material dominance:

> There are many hills without one tree or any spring, which produce a very short and tender grass, and supply plenty of food to sheep; upon these wander numerous flocks extremely white, and whether from the temperature of the air or goodness of the earth, bearing softer and finer fleeces than those of any country. This is the true Golden Fleece, in which consist the true riches of the inhabitants, great sums of money being brought into the island by merchants, chiefly for that article of trade. (109–10)[9]

Hentzer's description emphasizes the material "riches" that the sheep represent; their fleece, "soft," "fine," and "extremely white" are symbolic of the nation's wealth and superiority of wool manufacture. At the same time, the language with which he demonstrates this reveals the extent to which sheep had become idealized figures. The sheep "wander," as if roaming through the landscape of a pastoral poem. Their fine wool is possibly a result of the divine "goodness of the earth." In both of these observations, the sheep become mythologized as "the Golden Fleece," protected in the grove of England. As sacred as the object of Jason's quest, English sheep emerge as materially and symbolically valuable.

This idealized representation of sheep is of course an important component of pastoral literature, where the animals often take on the properties of the idyllic land or the amorous shepherd. We find sheep as obedient props in a pastoral landscape of leisure, completely evacuated of their material use, as in John Dickenson's *The Shepheardes Complaint* (c. 1594). In this poem, a shepherd falls asleep and dreams he is "transported into the blessed soile of heavenly Arcadia" (A3r) where

> Flockes of sheepe fed on the plaines,
> Harmlesse sheepe that rom'd at large:
> Here and there sate pensive Swaines,
> Waiting on their wandring charge. (A3v)

These "harmlesse" sheep play and "roam at large," without the boundaries of enclosing hedges and with very little supervision from their shepherds who sit "pensive[ly]." In Michael Drayton's eighth eclogue of his *Poemes Lyricke and Pastorall* (1606), we see that when the "shepheard pip'd a good," his flock "forsooke theyr foode, / to hear his melody" (E2v). These animals, nourished by their shepherd's song alone, serve to accompany their master on his ongoing search for idyllic love. Even in an influential agrarian manual of the sixteenth century, Conrad Heresbach's *Four Books of Husbandry* (1577), the practical instructions for caring for one's flock are consonant with the activities we see shepherds perform in pastoral literature: "The

---

9   In his libretto to the opera *King Arthur, Or England's Worthy* (1691), Dreyden expresses a similar sentiment: "*Though* Jasons *Office was Fam'd of old, / The* British *wool is growing Gold; / No Mines can more of Wealth supply*" (284). See my Chapter 6 for a further discussion of the myth of the Golden Fleece in the context of the cloth industry.

shepheard ... must deale gently, and lovingly with their flocke, and comforting, and cheering them with synging, and whistling: for ... this kind of cattell taketh great delight in musicke, and that it dooeth them as much good, as their pasture" (S5r). The shepherd here becomes less of a laborer who herds his flock for profit and primarily a courtly entertainer serving his noble audience who takes "delight" in his music. It is not, then, only in a pastoral fantasy that sheep can receive sustenance from music as well as from the "pasture" on which they feed. In this didactic text, the shepherds are encouraged to sing and whistle to the sheep, and indeed to attribute to them the human emotions of comfort, cheer, and delight. According to both didactic and poetic texts, the lyrical shepherd will undoubtedly be a successful tender of his flock.

In most pastoral literature, the low tones of the sheep's bleating suggest the melancholic state of the shepherd's mind. In Richard Barnfield's "Shepherd's Content," from *The Affectionate Shepherd* (1594), however, the flock literally accompanies the swain in song, providing the orchestral backdrop to his happy piping:

> He sits all Day lowd-piping on a Hill,
> The whilst his flocke about him daunce apace,
> His heart with joy, his eares with Musique fill:
> Anon a bleating Weather beares the Bace,
> A Lambe the Treble; and to his disgrace
> Another answers like a middle Meane:
> This every one to beare a Part are faine. (140–46)

In pastoral literature, sheep are important in large part because their grazing and bleating mirrors the life of the young swain who wanders the pastures playing his pipe, sustained by his love for a young shepherdess. In Thomas Lodge's pastoral sonnet cycle of 1593, the lovesick shepherd, Damon, reads the poems he has written to Phillis to his "ruthful sheepe" (4.6). Although Phillis calls the poems "trifles" (10), the words nevertheless "[h]ave made my Lambkins, lay them downe and sigh" (9). Like the shepherd who is often seen sprawled out under a tree, sighing and lost in a love-induced contemplative state, the sheep follow the lead of the shepherd. Here, though, the shepherd does not lead his flock through the pasture, but rather into a lyrical swoon.

The health of the sheep is so closely tied to the emotional state of the shepherd that they will suffer starvation if the swain remains in a forlorn state. In Philip Sidney's masque, *A Dialogue Between Two Shepherds* (1577?), one shepherd laments the despair that results from falling in love because it will affect his profession: "God shield us from such dames; if so our downs be sped, / The shepherds will grow lean, I trow, their sheep will ill be fed" (39–40). Just as the lovelorn shepherd is apt to neglect his herd, so too is the neglected sheep likely to become a metaphor for the love-starved shepherd. In a poem from Robert Greene's *Menaphon* (1589), the shepherd Melicertus (the disguised Maximus) begins his madrigal by asking "What are my Sheepe, without their wonted food? / What is my life, except I gain my love?" (134). The conflation of shepherd and sheep is most poetically expressed in Sidney's *The Countess of Pembroke's Arcadia*: The princely shepherd, Dorus, appealing to Pamela in verse tells her that

My sheep are thoughts, which I both guide and serve;
Their pasture is fair hills of fruitless love:
On barren sweets they feed, and feeding starve:
I wail their lot, but will not other prove.
My sheephook is wan hope which all upholds:
My weeds, desire, cut out in endless folds.
What wool my sheep shall bear, while thus they live,
In you it is, you must the judgment give. (94)

While sheep in pastoral literature often serve as physical stand-ins for the shepherd's mental state, here they become completely incorporated into Dorus's psyche as an elaborate conceit representing the cogitations of his lovesick mind. More fit to herd and "serve" his "thoughts" than actual sheep, the noble shepherd-poet gives over the fate of his flock—the quality of the wool they will "bear"/the outcome of his amorous "thoughts"—to Pamela. The practice of shepherding is so completely subordinated to the tortures of a lovesick mind, that it is Pamela, not the shepherd, who is in control of the flock. Absorbed into the shepherd-prince's mind, the sheep no longer need to be fed as they cease to be real animals. The shepherd then may devote his efforts to the pursuit of his lover rather than agrarian labors.

The erasure of rural work has long been regarded as a necessary component of pastoral literature.[10] Evacuated of signs of material labor, the landscape is able to become a space where fantasies of idealized love can be sown. The reaping of songs and sighs obfuscates the plowing of land or the harvesting of crops. And the presence of sheep signals the presence of the shepherd. But the shepherd in many cases is not a figure that labors in the landscape. Rather he is, as Paul Alpers has noted, "representative" of the poet himself, a shepherd-courtier or shepherd-poet (or, often, both) whose survival depends less on his labor than on his lover.[11] As Louis Montrose argues, the perceived conception of the shepherd's work as leisurely is well suited to the lyrical activities of the shepherd-poet:

> Literary celebrations of pastoral otium conventionalize the relative ease of the shepherd's labors. Compared to other agrarian tasks, sheepfarming requires very little investment in human resources. The fictional time-space of countless eclogues and other Elizabethan pastorals is structured by the diurnal rhythm of sheepherding: driving the flock out to pasture at daybreak and driving them back to fold at dusk. Within this frame, the literary shepherd's day is typically occupied by singing, piping, wooing, and other quaint indulgences of the pastoral life. ("Of Gentlemen and Shepherds," 427–8)

In *God Speed the Plough*, an excellent study of agrarian labor and culture in early modern England, Andrew McRae asserts that "pastoral was widely exploited as a mode particularly suited to the idealized representation of rural conditions from the perspective of the landed gentry and nobility" (263). Agrarian labor, if represented at all, is seemingly painted over with a courtly gild.

Despite the obvious absence of material labor in pastoral texts, shepherding remains prevalent and crucial. As Leo Marx has famously written, "[n]o shepherd, no pastoral."

---

10 See Montrose, "Of Gentlemen and Shepherds," p. 422.
11 See Alpers, *What is Pastoral?*, especially Chapter 4, "Representative Shepherds."

While Montrose argues that the material labor of agrarian life is erased in Elizabethan pastoral, he does concede that the "irrelevance of ... Elizabethan rural life ... to Elizabethan pastoral literature ... is nevertheless *conspicuous*" (422). I would argue that in several pastoral texts, we are made very aware of the tedious and sometimes treacherous life of the shepherd and the problems associated with the tending of sheep. While we may not find the kind of detail that we would need to get a complete picture of the quotidian life of the common shepherd, their labors are not entirely hidden. And despite the perceived absence of overt references to the wool or mutton industries, the work of the shepherd can never be fully obfuscated due to their prominence in agrarian England. They are idealized, to be sure. However, details of their work emerge even in the most poetic of landscapes. Ovine disease, threat of predators, exposure to harsh weather, and the tendency for shepherds to fall asleep on the job due to sheer exhaustion all infiltrate the bucolic landscape, revealing the extent to which the "real" world insinuates itself into the idyllic. Pastoral literature is a nostalgic, allegorical mode that subordinates contemporary agrarian problems to privilege aristocratic leisure. But it is also a mode largely in touch with and responding to issues that were crucial to English economic relations—the well-being of the sheep themselves.

Specific evidence of the material conditions of shepherds and other agrarian laborers in the period is hard to come by. Indeed, as Alan Everitt eloquently writes, "no one has written his signature more plainly across the countryside; but no one has left more scanty records of his achievements" (396).[12] However, if we look to husbandry manuals as well as pastoral literature, we may begin to see their relation to one another and come to understand the practices and worries of the shepherd in early modern England. Looking at these two types of texts together calls into question the notion that the labor of the shepherd is "irrelevant" to the imaginative world of pastoral. Rather, the husbandry manuals share, or perhaps provide, a sense of the "conspicuous" work of the laborers in the fictive texts.

Since keeping the flock intact was the shepherd's primary duty, the loss of any one member had serious consequences because it translated into a direct loss of raw wool or mutton. Vigilant watch over the sheep was thus crucial in keeping them protected from preying animals or immoral thieves, as we see in Heresbach's husbandry manual when he instructs that shepherds

> must be well ware in the driving of them, and rulyng of them, that they guide them with theyr voyce, and shaking of theyr staffe, not hurting, nor hurlyng any thing at them, nor that they be any time farre of from them, and that they neyther lye, nor sitte: for yf they goe not forwarde, they must stand: for it is the shepheards office to stand alwayes as hie as he can, that he may plaine and easely discerne, that neyther the slowe, nor the great bellyed in layning tyme, nor the quicke, nor the lively, whyle they roame, be severed from theyr felowes: and least some theefe, or wylde beast, beguile the necligent shepheard of his cattell. (S5r)

---

12 Of course, scholars have culled archives and private household documents to provide some details about shepherds. See Allison, "Flock Management;" Kussmaul, *Servants and Husbandry in Early Modern England*; and most recently, Everitt, "Farm Labourers." The majority of shepherds were landless laborers that tended their master's flock and perhaps had a few sheep of their own, given to them as gifts from their employers (Everitt, 415–16; Montrose, 423). They were generally hired annually and their wages varied dramatically.

Mascall, who likely used Heresbach's text as a source for his own, says that the shepherd should not "straie farre of from [the sheep], nor to sitte or lie downe. If he doe not goe, he ought to stand, and to sit very seldome. For the office of a shepheard is as a high watchman for his cattel, to the end that the slow sheep doe not slip from the other" (Aa8r). While in pastoral literature the supine, daydreaming shepherd is commonplace, we see here the dangers of such a posture. Indeed the "atmosphere of *otium*," one of "pastoral's defining characteristics" (Alpers, 22), is anathema in husbandry manuals because it engenders idleness and wastefulness—not to mention danger to the herd—rather than industry and thrift.

In Francis Sabie's *Pan's Pipe* (1595), a book of "Three Pastorall Eglogues, in English HEXAMETER," we see the perils associated with shepherding.[13] Thirsis complains to his fellow swain, Tyterus, about the shepherd's difficult existence and the unfortunate circumstances that might befall an attendant of sheep:

> I think we shepheards take greatest paines of all others,
> Sustaine greatest losses, we be tyred with daylie labour,
> With cold in winter, with heat in summer oppressed,
> To manie harmes our tender flockes, to manie diseases
> Our sheepe are subject, the thiefe praies over our heardlings,
> And worse than the thief, the Fox praies over our heardlings,
> Thus we poor heardsmen are pincht and plagu'd above others. (A4r)

Written in the meter of classical eclogues, Sabie's poem announces itself as a participant in a tradition associated with the learned and leisurely. Thirsis's grievances, though, are ones that would have been recognizable as the bane of the poor working shepherd. The primary activity of the shepherd is no longer singing to his flock. Rather, this shepherd takes "paines" and is exhausted from his "daylie labour." His sheep, too, have little cause for either comfort or cheer, as in Heresbach's husbandry manual; they, instead, are subject to disease—such as rot and murrain—as well as to thievery. In the guise of a lament, this particular section of Sabie's poem actually delineates the primary concerns of shepherds: the exhaustion and exposure to which the shepherd was subject and the disease and theft to which the sheep were vulnerable.

Pan's Pipe is perhaps the text that best reveals the material life of the shepherd, despite its associations with the conventions of pastoral verse. The First Eclogue follows a dialogue between two shepherds—a traditional trope of pastoral literature made famous by Virgil's *Eclogues*—one of whom is in despair:

> Ah, *Tyterus, Tyterus*, how can I cease to be pensive?
> One o'mine ewes last night, hard fortune, died in eaning,
> One o'mine ewes, a great ew, whose fruit I chiefly did hope of,
> Eaned a tidie lambe, which she no sooner had eaned,
> But the Foxe did it eat, whilst I slept under a thicket:
> Thus have I lost mine Ewe, my lamb the Fox thus hath eaten. (A4r)

---

13 The writings of Sabie were not particularly popular in his own day; indeed, none of his texts went into a second edition. He is barely known today at all, except as the writer of *Fisherman's Tale* and *Flora's Fortune*, both from 1595, two minor sources for Shakespeare's *Winter's Tale* (*Flora's Fortune* is a verse paraphrase of *Pandosto*). However, *Pan's Pipe* is important as the first attempt in English to write in Virgilian meter (Bright and Mustard, 436).

In this conventionally marked text,[14] leisure on the part of the shepherd does not simply result in amorous woes. The consequences of the otiose life are rendered in harsh terms, as the loss of a ewe in birthing and a lamb by the predatory fox were specific and real concerns of shepherds in the early modern period. The traditional loss of love is subordinated to the loss of members of the flock. To help distract Thirsis from the grief over this loss, Tyterus relates ancient stories of love. In introducing his tale, however, the grim world of shepherding enters again. Tyterus tells a story of falling asleep while tending his flock. Hunters come near and their dogs run to his cattle. After he wakes up, he discovers his sheep have been massacred: "and nought but a carcasse / Of my Wether I sawe, the clawes and skuls of an Ewe-lambe. / Out alasse I cride, I am undone, spoyled and undone" (A4v). Even in his attempt to recuperate the pastoral text by privileging the traditional romantic plot, Sabie allows the quotidian world of dangers associated with shepherding to reassert itself. Meanwhile Tyterus relates that Alexis, another shepherd, came to him and also complained that "seven of mine Ewes be devoured, / And the rest are strayed away" (B1r). In searching for their flocks, they run into Galatea, and Alexis, who is smitten with her, forgets about his sheep. Tyterus is clearly disturbed by this turn of events: "And unmindfull quite of his heardling, he wholly delighted / In talking of her, and passing by her, I wild him / To reject this love, which would bring beggary with it" (B1r). The "beggary" that Alexis will suffer is ambiguous here. In the context of a romantic plot, Alexis will surely suffer the pangs of lovesickness if he accepts Galatea's love. However, given that Sabie sets the First Eclogue of his text firmly in the realities of shepherding and its discontents, and Tyterus emphasizes that Alexis is "unmindfull" of his flock, it is difficult not to see that the "beggary" that he will suffer is that which will come from the loss of a herd. Indeed, in husbandry manuals, negligent shepherds emerge as degenerate villains:

> by their idlenes & long rest, they grow now to wax stubborn and are given (for the most part) to frowardnes and evill, more then to good profit to their maisters, and evil manered, whereof breedeth many theevish conditions, being pickers, lyers, and stealers, and runners about from place to place, with manie other infinite evils. (Mascall, Aa2r)

While Sabie's shepherds may not exhibit the scurrilous qualities of which Mascall warns, there is a sense in his poem that idleness, usually seen as a necessity for pastoral figures, has dire consequence for a shepherd's profession.[15]

One final text will serve to demonstrate the extent to which early modern pastoral literature engages in meaningful ways with the agrarian world. In *Taylors Pastorall* (1624), John Taylor the Water Poet frames a panegyric poem to shepherds and sheep as a conventional pastoral. Although Taylor acknowledges the "learned poets of all times" have sung of the "loves," "fortunes," and "felicitie" of "rurall shepheards Swaines," his

---

14 Thirsis and Tyterus are both stock names for shepherds in pastoral literature.

15 In addition to loss of sheep due to thieves and predators, disease was also a concern. Murrain, a fatal and contagious disease akin to anthrax, was the primary worry among animal husbandman; also hoof rot was (and still is) a serious concern. See Brathwait's poem, *The Shepheards' Tales* (1626), sig. O1v, and Sidney's *Old Arcadia*, p. 109, for examples of pastoral concerns with ovine disease.

poem does not repeat those tropes (C1r). Rather than presenting yet another tale of the lovelorn shepherd-poet, Taylor's text, as his subtitle indicates, is a poem about the "Noble Antiquitie of the Shepheards, with the *profitable use of Sheepe*" (A2r).[16] In this sense, Taylor's work shares more similarities with husbandry manuals than with idylls or eclogues. Echoing and expanding upon the sentiments put forth in Leonard Mascall's *The First Book of Cattell*, Taylor emphasizes the sheep's importance to the entire world:

> He with his flesh and fleece, doth feed and clad
> All languages and nations, good and bad:
> What can it more, but die, that we may live,
> And every yeare to us a liverie give?
> 'Tis such a bountie, and the charge so deepe,
> That nothing can afford the like, but *Sheepe*.
> For should the world want *Sheepe*, but five whole yeare,
> Ten thousand millions would want cloaths to weare:
> And were't not for the flesh of this kinde beast,
> The world might fast, when it doth often feast.
> There's nothing doth unto a *Sheepe* pertaine,
> But 'tis for mans commoditie and gaine. (C3r)

Godlike in its ability to generously clothe all nations "good and bad" of the world, and Christlike in its "kinde" willingness to offer its flesh and "die, so that we may live," Taylor's representation of the sheep reaches new heights of idealization. The world's population, baldly put, would become extinct except for the gifts of this wondrous animal. Taylor's emphasis on the benefits that the material bodies of the sheep provide, however, compels us to to appreciate them as much for providing "*mans* commoditie and gain," as for containing any inherent symbolic properties.[17]

If, like the lovelorn shepherd, I have strayed too long in the pastures of England, discussing the pervasive and prominent position of sheep in several types of texts, it is primarily to underscore what so many have ignored: that sheep mattered deeply in the early modern mind. It is not simply happenstance that the rise of the wool broadcloth industry coincided with the tremendous textual output concerning sheep. Rather, it is the very understanding that sheep were the source of England's most prominent product that authors of the period took such pains to write of the pleasures derived from sheep.

---

16 The text, a hyperbolic celebration of the ovine and his caretaker, throughout aligns the sheep and shepherd with the sacred. He begins his poem with an invocation to Apollo and Pan, but then asks for God's grace in helping write the poem. Taylor catalogs the shepherds found in both the Old Testament as well as those of antiquity, leading up to Jesus who "did the harmlesse name of *Shepheard* take / For our protection, and his mercies sake" (B3r). Fond of anagrams, Taylor finds that the only words that are made up solely of the five vowels are IEOVA (Jehova) and OVEIA (sheep), "which doth admonish us in the feare and reverence of the Almightie" (B4r). Taylor also demonstrates that two anagrams for LAMBE are BLAME and BALME: "and *Christ*, the *Lambe*, upon him tooke our *Blame*, / His precious *Blood*, (Gods heavy wrath did *calme*) / 'Twas th'onlely *Balme* for *Sinne* to cure the same" (C2r).

17 In another echo of Mascall's text, Taylor also delineates the variant uses of the sheep's body. See C4r.

Undoing the Land: Greedy Sheep, Anti-Enclosure Literature, and Rebellion

Although the portraits of shepherds and their sheep in these literatures are both highly idealized and rendered real through the descriptions of their sufferings, the shepherds are nevertheless primarily lauded as agrarian heroes and their charges are to be protected as if they were the Golden Fleece in the sacred grove of Colchos. Whereas in the literature celebrating their existence, sheep contribute to an idyllic landscape and indeed to England's well-being, in the texts that engage with the social and economic effects of enclosure, sheep become ravenous beasts, the source of all of England's woes.[18] Sabie's *Pan's Pipe*, for example, shows us that sheep are not animals that can subsist on their shepherd's musical talents, but instead require real food:

> Hasting sheep from fouldes to let,
> Sheepe which bleated for their meate.
> Sheepe let out from place to place,
> Greedilie did plucke up grasse. (A3v)

The sheep here begin to lose their bucolic essence as they are "hasting," "bleating," and devouring the grass "greedilie." While the sheep hardly seem sinister, when we look at the description in the context of anti-enclosure literature of the sixteenth century, the image of the avaricious sheep takes shape. Much of the biting invective against enclosures was written in the first half of the sixteenth century when the practice was relatively new and was perceived to be widespread due to the booming wool industry. In the first decades of the sixteenth century, anti-enclosure literature "became something of a subgenre of agrarian complaint" (McRae, *God Speed*, 43). Montrose claims that it is only when this strain of literature subsides that we find an increase in the popularity of imaginative pastorals: "English literary pastoralism began to flourish in the last quarter of the sixteenth century ... that is, only after the diminution of the bitterly controversial agrarian literature whose subject was precisely those material practices and relations that provided a social matrix for Elizabethan pastoral conventions" (427). I would argue, however, that while anti-enclosure literature was most pervasive in the earlier decades of the sixteenth century, the sentiments that it engendered reached into the late sixteenth and early seventeenth century. The complaints against enclosing landlords and their greedy sheep gained perhaps even greater popular currency—even with those unaffected by such changes—as the century wore on, as they were found not only in agrarian literature but also in popular verse and, most significantly, parliamentary statutes

---

18 Assessing exactly which sector of the population, aside from dispossessed farmers, opposed enclosure practices is difficult. Some anti-enclosure texts are economic in nature, written by authors invested in tax reform; some were generated by government officials to quell discontent; but most were at least to a certain extent literary. One might conclude from this fact that the anti-enclosure movement was largely a liberal one, stemming from the observations of London writers who witnessed the adverse aftereffects of depopulation, whereby displaced farm laborers migrated to the city.

and royal proclamations.[19] The pervasiveness of such complaints throughout the period shows that pastoral literature must, however uncomfortably, share the textual landscape with anti-enclosure polemic.

In the last century, early modern enclosure practices have been the subject of great debate among historians.[20] The extent to which arable land was actually enclosed and the economic damage that such practices wrought may never be clear and thus is the subject of much contention. Still, the phenomenon was perceived in the period as a dire problem and thus a brief overview is necessary in understanding the issue. Most agricultural land in England consisted of open fields divided up by strips of unplowed land. Although the fields were owned by landlords, they were considered common because after harvest the land was plowed and left fallow, forming a common pasture on which poor farmers gleaned or on which agrarian laborers let their animals graze. In enclosure practices, land that was previously considered common was divided by the landlords into distinct plots and enclosed by hedges, fences, or ditches. Often, but not always, open fields were converted to sheep pastures; the only way to keep a substantial number of sheep was to enclose land so that the sheep could graze and produce manure and so that they could be kept separate from those of other farmers.[21] Additionally, separate landholdings were combined, or engrossed, to create larger pastures for the sheep. The conventional explanation for the spike in enclosures was a supposed advance in the price of wool, a result of an increase in the trade of the raw staple in the fifteenth and sixteenth centuries. Selling wool was more profitable than farming so landlords were willing to evict tenants to promote sheep farming.[22] Far fewer laborers were needed to tend sheep and in general shepherds were the lowest paid of agricultural workers (Cheney, 24).[23] Enclosed lands resulted in a depopulation of farm houses and were perceived to turn the working poor into unemployed vagrants,

----

19 Between 1489 and 1587 Parliament passed 11 Acts attempting to prevent depopulation due to enclosures (Bowden, 110).

20 See Allen, *Enclosure and the Yeoman*; Bradley, *The Enclosures in England*; Carroll, "The 'Nursery of Beggary'"; Cheney, *Social Change in England*; McRae, *God Speed the Plough*; Neeson, *Commoners: Common Rights, Enclosure and Social Change in England, 1700–1820*; Siemon, "Landlord Not King"; Thirsk, "Tudor Enclosures"; and Wrightson, *Earthly Necessities*. The primary period in which land was enclosed on a wide scale was between 1440 and 1520. By mid-century the practice had slowed although the angry rhetoric against it was just heating up (Land, 10).

21 Common pastures were often enclosed by general agreement between landowners and tenants and remained farmland for tillage. These kinds of enclosures generally signaled greater productivity and, for the farmer, more wealth (Land, 7). Occasionally land was enclosed to allow ground that had been consistently under the plow to regain its fertility. See Carroll, p. 35.

22 Tenant farmers, however, often agreed to enclosure and enclosure was not the only means by which farmers were dispossessed of their lands (Carroll, 35). According to W. Jones, "sometimes a lease ran out; sometimes the death of a tenant allowed a revision of rent so exorbitant as to justify the expressive contemporary term 'rack-renting'; sometimes a prohibitively high entry-fine was demanded of the heir to a tenancy" (118).

23 According to Cheney, "a stretch of country which had required perhaps one hundred and fifty persons to cultivate it in grain crops, when transformed into sheep farms could be looked after by less than a dozen" (33).

beggars, and thieves. While enclosure polices did not always have deleterious effects, and may have even been beneficial to the communities in some instances, they were nevertheless regarded as a scourge on the sixteenth-century rural laborer. Shepherds and their sheep were in turn cast as the villains in this agrarian drama.

One of the earliest and most famous portraits of ravenous sheep in the context of anti-enclosure sentiment is in Thomas More's *Utopia* (1516). While much attention has been given to this section of the text, the issues that it brings up and the rhetoric with which it does so are worth repeating here because it influenced so much writing in the ensuing decades. The context of Book I involves a character by the name of Thomas More, who visits Flanders in 1515 to act as an emissary for Henry the Eighth, "in controversy with Charles" (13), the Dutch King, who had made an alliance with the French.[24] During a lull in the negotiations, while the Netherlandish commissioners travel to Brussels for further instruction on how to proceed, More goes to Antwerp and visits with Peter Gillis.[25] While in Antwerp, More encounters Raphael Hythloday, a world traveler who finds many faults with the policies of European nations. Hytholoday tells More that "many times have I chanced upon such proud, lewd, overthwart, and wayward judgements, yea, and once in England" (21). The main problem in England that Hythloday sees is the inextricable relationship between criminal behavior and poverty. The extreme punishment for theft—execution—"passeth the limits of justice" (22) and does not account for the commonwealth's own role in creating the penury of their subjects. Thievery, Hythloday claims, is a result of the fact that impoverished men "have no other craft to get their living" (23). A primary cause of the "stealing" (26), which is the result of poverty, idleness, and vagrancy, is that which "is proper and peculiar to you Englishmen alone"—enclosure policies (26). Landowners, who could turn a greater profit in the wool trade than through agricultural tillage, had enclosed the land for sheep pastures. The blame, however, is initially put upon the sheep who in the past "were wont to be so meek and tame and so small eaters" (26). A result of the enclosures is that the sheep have "become so great devourers and so wild, that they eat up and swallow down the very men themselves. They consume, destroy, and devour whole fields, houses, and cities" (26). More's emphasis on the literally insatiable and figuratively man-eating sheep suggests that they are at least as responsible for the deleterious effects of enclosures as the greedy men who "leave no ground for tillage" (26). The "covetous and insatiable cormorant and very plague of its native country," however, is not the sheep, but the man who "may compass about and enclose many thousand acres of ground together within one pale or hedge" (26). The language used to describe the "noblemen and gentlemen, yea and certain abbots" (26) who have

---

24 The historical Thomas More had also gone to Flanders on a similar mission, one which had as its focus negotiations surrounding the cloth trade. In 1515, at the request of the King's Council and the Merchant Adventurers, More was sent to Flanders "to renegotiate commercial and diplomatic treaties" and to resolve disagreements over levies and shipping ports (Ackroyd, 165).

25 More had previously been to Antwerp, one of Europe's key port and the primary site for importing English wool, where he had engaged in discussions surrounding the English Merchant Adventurers vis-à-vis the Antwerp market (Ackroyd, 168).

enclosed the lands and evicted their tenant farmers overlaps so closely with that used to blast the sheep that ovine and man have become fully merged—money-hungry animals who are directly responsible for England's poverty.

The irony of the proliferation of enclosures is that, despite the increase in production, the cost of wool had spiked: "the price of wool is so risen, that poor folks, which were wont to work it and make cloth thereof, be now able to buy none at all" (27).[26] The reason for this conflict is that there were only a small number of sellers of wool, "a few rich men's," who only buy or sell at their own pleasure (27).[27] More moralizes enclosure practices by suggesting that God has been watching. He refers to the "infinite multitude" of enclosed sheep that have "died of the rot" (27). God, he claims, took vengeance "of their inordinate and insatiable covetousness, sending among the sheep that pestiferous murrain which much more justly should have fallen on the sheepmaster's own heads" (27). Just as sheep become stand-ins for their masters and incorporate the physical afflictions that the lovesick shepherds suffer in pastoral literature, in More's text the "covetous" sheep are aligned with their greedy owners, taking on the diseases as punishment for the landlords' sins.

While the insatiable sheep must bear the blame for the increasing problems of poverty, vagrancy, and roguish behavior, they are at fault for something far worse: the decay of the nation. Again and again in the sixteenth century we see that enclosure policies detract from the nation's vigor. As the author of the tract "Vox Populi Vox Dei," a complaint against taxes by commoners (1547), puts it, transforming land for tillage into sheep-grazing land will lead to England's ultimate demise:

---

26 The collocation of enclosure and poverty took hold with More's text and remained a cornerstone of the anti-enclosure debate for decades to come. In an early English ballad, called "Now A Days" (1520?), the speaker laments the unfortunate changes wrought by enclosures of arable land: With the increasing of "commons," towns are "pulled downe to pastur shepe," causing the "Poor folk for bred [to] cry & wepe" (97).

27 The high price of wool was often a complaint that attended enclosure policies; both were usually directed at the landlords: In 1533 Henry VIII supported a statute limiting the number of sheep that a landlord could own to 2,000. The act states that the reasons that "provoketh those greedy and covetous people" to convert tillage to pasture is "the great profit that cometh of sheep" ("An Act for the Maintenance of Husbandry and Tillage," 265). Because wealthy sheep farmers often set the sale price of wool, the costs were seen as inordinately high and ushered in a host of problems, both sacred and secular. Rising wool prices led "to the high displeasure of Almighty God, to the decay of the hospitality of this realm, to the diminishing of the King's people, and to the hindrance of the clothmaking" (265). In "The Decaye of England Only By the Great Multitude of Shepe" (c. 1550), the author charges that "they that have great umberment of shepe muste nedes have greate store of woll, and we cannot thynke who shuld make the pryse of woll, but those that have great plentye of shepe" (96). Similarly, in 1564 Thomas Becon wonders why the rich landlords, "the caterpyllers of the commune weale," are so covetous: "And yet when was wool ever so dere, or mutton of so great price? If these shepemongers go for as they begyn, the people shall both miserablye dye for colde, and wretchedly peryshe for honger. For these gredy woulves and comberous cormerauntes, wyll eyther sell theyr woll and theyr shepe at theyr owne pryce or els they wyll sell none." (Fol., 15r–v).

With soe many shepe maisters
That of erabell grounde make pasters
Are they that be thes wasters
That wyll undoe this land. (4)

In literature that celebrates the sheep as the glory of England and emblem for its economic success, the superabundance of sheep seems a sign of England's welfare. Conversely, in anti-enclosure literature, the multitude of sheep is a canker on the landscape. "Vox Populi" continues:

And whye the powre men wepe
For stawryng of such shepe
For that soo many kype
Suche number and suche stowre
As never was sene before
What wolde ye any more
The ingresse was never more
Thus gothe the woyse and rower. (5)

According to the "woyse and rower," or the "voice and roar" of the *vox populi*, those who "keep" large "numbers" of "sheep" bring about the "weeping" of "poor men," or perhaps the creation of men who are "poor." Inflated rhetoric surrounding economic crises is, of course, not confined to land use. However, in anti-enclosure literature, we have a convenient scapegoat for the problems brought on by land conversion. In Epigram 20 of *Chrestoleros* (1598), by the unfortunately named Thomas Bastard, we see that sheep contribute to the breakdown of the social order as well as law and order:

Sheepe have eate up our medows & our downes,
Our corne, our wood, whole villages & townes,
Yea, they have eate up many wealthy men.
Besdies widowes and orphan childeren.
Besides our statutes and our iron lawes,
Which they have swallowed down into their maws. (90)

Thus, in much anti-enclosure literature, sheep—the erstwhile source of national pride—become the source of shame of England and its eventual undoing.[28] In addition to grazing on their proper pasture, these sheep eat what men eat, "corn," eat up where men live, "the villages and towns," before turning, like the sheep of *Utopia*, into man-eating ovine. Philip Stubbes even chimes in on the debate in his *Anatomie of Abuses* (1583): rich landowners and sheep "are Caterpillars and devouring Locustes that massacre the poor, and eate up the whole Realme, to the destruction of the same" (170). And worst of all, the nation decaying just as fast as the sheep eat up pasture is no longer in the favor with God himself. As we see in a religious pamphlet of 1604,

---

28 While land enclosure was clearly decried by many authors, it was embraced by some farmers. In Thomas Tusser's popular *Five Hundred Points of Good Husbandry* (1573), Tusser lauds enclosure as a way to promote thrift and personal wealth, a theme running throughout the text. See p. 96. As McRae notes, the enclosure movement was perpetuated by such calls for financial freedom (*God Speed the Plough*, 151).

Tillage was the first worke, that was imposed upon man, after that he was banished out of
Paradise ... But if all men should follow Inclosers steps, why then in all townes we should
have no tillage (or very little) but all sheepe. Is this not to contradict the ordinance of God?
(Trigge, B3r).[29]

Rather than focusing on specific locales or particular effects of changes in land use,
the rhetoric of anti-enclosure texts becomes highly symbolic and heavily moralized,
focusing specifically on the ill brought on by ravenous sheep as well as the harm that
is done to England through the apparent enclosure of arable land for pasture.[30]

While those arguing against enclosure took a morally superior tone, the authors
often had the writings of economic thinkers and the state to back up their complaints,
tracts that were at times no less inflammatory. The popular debates surrounding
enclosure were reflected in Tudor legislation throughout the sixteenth century. As
early as 1489, parliament approved an "Act Against Pullyng Doun of Tounes,"
which blamed "leyeng to pasture londes which custumeably have been used in tilthe,
wherby ydilnes grounde and begynnyng of all myschefes daily doo encrease" (4). The
complaint that enclosure engendered idleness and other catch-all "mischiefs" was to
be the standard rhetoric throughout the sixteenth century.[31] In his *Anglica Historia*
(1534), Polydore Vergil, an Italian diplomat who lived much of his life in England,
wrote about the problem facing Henry VIII in the early 1520s.[32] The lengthy passage
is significant because it outlines the primary arguments against enclosure policies
that would recur throughout the century. After being named Defender of the Faith,

the king turned his attention to the material well-being of his state. For half a century
or more previously, the sheep-farming nobles had tried to find devices whereby they
might increase the annual income of their lands. As a result the yeoman had incurred
very considerable losses. The sheep farmers, cultivating pasturage (after the manners of
Arabs) rather than arable, began everywhere to employ far fewer agricultural labourers,
to destroy rural dwelling-houses, to create vast deserts, to allow the land to waste while

---

29 In an earlier sermon (1549), Hugh Latimer expresses similar concerns: "these grasiers,
inclosers, and renterearers, are hinderers of the kings honour. For wher as have bene a great
meany of housholders and inhabitauntes, there is nowe but a shepherd and his dogge, so thei
hynder the kinges honour most of al" (40). In Stubbes's polemical *The Second Part of the
Anatomie of Abuses*, the author echoes the tone and content of Latimer's sermon: "wheras
before time there hath bin a whole parish or towne maintained upon the same, now is there
no bodie there dwelling, but a shepheard and a dogge lolling under a bush. Thus are whole
parishes and townes made praise to rich grasiers" (E3v). According to Maclure, there were
surprisingly few sermons against enclosure during the early modern period. This may have
been either because the sermonists generally spoke to urban audiences or that enclosure
policies were less deleterious or prolific than scholars have believed (128).

30 McRae finds that invective against agrarian abuses "tend to be raised merely as
particular illustrations of moral decay, rather than as fundamental causes of corruption in the
body politic" (*God Speed*, 67–8).

31 Other official documents pertaining to enclosure in the sixteenth century include
a proclamation "Prohibiting Enclosure and Engrossing of Farms" (1514?), two "Ordering
Enclosures Destroyed and Tillage Restored" (1526 and 1529), and another "Enforcing Statutes
Against Enclosures" (1549).

32 Vergil began this text at Henry VII's request. DLB. V. 132, p. 319.

filling it up with herds, flocks, and a multitude of beasts; in like fashion they fenced off all these pastures to keep them private, thus establishing in their own right a monopoly of wool, sheep and cattle. From this three evil consequences ensued for the state. First, the number of peasants, upon whom the prince chiefly relies for waging war, was reduced. Second, a larger number of villages and towns, many stripped of inhabitants, were ruined. Third, the wool and cloth which was thus produced, as well as the flesh of kinds of animals which is fit for human consumption, began to sell much more dearly than it used to do, so that the price has not really dropped even to this day. Since in the past these abuses were not checked early in their development, they were afterwards hardened and became much more durable, so that later they could not be easily remedied. (277)

The complaints facing Henry VIII did not subside in the ensuing decades and in 1548 an enclosure commission was set up to review agrarian policy and ascertain to what extent agricultural practices had suffered, how many towns had fallen to ruin, and which landlords owned more than the set limit of heads of sheep.[33] One of the primary anti-enclosure writers, Thomas Smith, used the inflated rhetoric of More or Bastard, or indeed earlier parliamentary tracts, to express his stance: "those sheep are the cause of all these mischiefs, for they have driven husbandry out of the country, by the which was increased before all kind of victuals, and now altogether sheep, sheep, sheep" (222). Agricultural farming was perceived as having been erased from the landscape and replaced by a canvas full of "shepe, shepe." Smith also explores the plight of husbandman by acknowledging the extent to which sheep pastures had disrupted their agricultural economies.[34] Written as a series of discussions amongst men of various professions just after the hearings of the enclosure commission, *A Discourse of the Commonweal* (c. 1549) expresses the populist point of view, even as it constantly complicates it.[35] The husbandman, for instance, complains that "these enclosures do undo us all; for they make us to pay dearer for our land that we occupy, and causes that we can have no land in manner for our money to put to tillage.

---

33 The commission worked with the following definition of enclosure: "it is meant therby, when any man hath taken away and enclosed any other mens common, or hath pulled down houses of husbandry, and converted the lands from tillage to pasture. This is the meaning of this word, and so we pray you remember it" ("Instructions to the Enclosure Commissioners," 41). The commissioners found numerous offenders in their investigation. Of particular note was one Mr Hynde who "unlawfully dothe bringe into Cambridge felde a flock of shepe to the number of vi or vii Cth to the undoinge of the fermors and great hyndraunce of all the inhabitauntes of Cambrydge" ("Presentments," 45). After the commission had reported their results, Edward VI's uncle and Lord Protector, the Duke of Somerset, issued yet another proclamation "Enforcing Statutes Against Enclosures."

34 In 1547 Smith had become a servant to Somerset. He wrote the *Discourse* in 1548, while temporarily out of Somerset's favor, although it was not published until 1581. (*DLB* v. 132, p. 265).

35 The conceit of the dialogue allows Smith—like More—to offer rebuttals and alternative opinions, so it is never entirely clear on which side his own thinking settles. For a discussion of Smith's text and the "limitations of complaint," see McRae, *God Speed the Plough*, pp. 52–7, where McRae finds that "while Smith is acutely aware of the dangers of enclosure, he wants to consider the phenomenon as a symptom of change, rather than the evil denounced by the gospellers" (54). Smith was the son of a sheepfarmer, so his sympathy with the landlords seems to have some basis.

All is taken up for pasture, either for sheep or for grazing of cattle" (17). Smith's main topic in the text is how to solve the problems of increasing poverty and hunger in the realm. The changing landscape, enclosed for sheep pasture, was widely seen as the root. The proliferation of sheep farms, and the superabundance of sheep were the visual signifier of the more abstract problem of lack.

We only have to look to the title of a mid-century economic tract to understand how damaging the sheep were perceived to be to the well-being of England. "The Decaye of England Only By the Great Multitude of Shepe" (1550–1553), a document arguing that the proliferation of sheep would create a scarcity of grain, also claims that too many sheep would drive up wool and mutton prices, as wealthy sheep farmers often set these prices. Sheep and their shepherds are blamed for everything from the dearth of grain in England, to the high price of the staple, to the utter decay of the commonwealth. The reason that "there is not corne ynough" in England is the clear result of sheep: "We saye, as reason doeth lead us, that shepe & shepemasters doeth cause skantyte of corne" (51). Of course, these sheep are not actually *eating* the grain, but rather their eating habits lead to the utter demise of the established order of things. Interestingly, the landlord, who presumably employs the shepherd and owns the sheep is absent from blame. The representation of the ovine as omnivorous is so troubling because, as McRae suggests, it "reinforces the image of an agrarian world turned upside down" (*God Speed*, 10). This topsy-turvy state of affairs is especially well-illustrated in John Hales's charge to the Enclosure commission: "Sheep and cattle that were ordeined to be eaten of men, hath eaten up the men; not of their own nature, but by the help of men" (Hales, 359).

Despite the laws limiting enclosures as well as the number of sheep farmers could have, there was apparently a laxity in their enforcement. By the early years of Elizabeth's reign, this had become enough of a problem to warrant yet another royal proclamation. In 1569, the proclamation "Enforcing Statutes on Tillage and Enclosures," decried the landlords who flouted anti-enclosure laws. These landlords, the proclamation complained,

> do daily decay towns and houses of husbandry, and inclose their grounds, and convert the same from tillage into pasture, and keep not such hospitality as by the said laws they ought to do, to the great displeasure of Almighty God, the provocation of idleness, and destruction of her majesty's people; whereby her realm is in some part weakened, and more is like, if speedy reformation be not had therein. (311)

By Elizabeth's reign, there already certainly had been a number of proclamations asserting that enclosures engendered a "decay" of villages and an increase in idleness. Indeed, this rhetoric was commonplace as was the expression that enclosures were unchristian and displeased God. However, with Elizabeth's reign we see an increasing articulation of the notion that the health of England as a whole was at stake. Perhaps the most significant piece of legislation surrounding enclosure in the second half of the sixteenth century, and proof that the debate over land use was not on the wane, was the "Act for the Maintenance of Husbandry and Tillage" of 1597.[36] The

---

36 The bill that precipitated this Act was written by Francis Bacon and argued that entire towns had disappeared as a result of enclosure and there is "nought but Greenfieldes a Shepheard and his dogg" (Townshend, 10). The legislation over enclosing did not always side

statute enacted that land, which had been devoted to tillage for twelve years prior to being converted to pasture, be restored to tillage. The offending individual would be charged twenty shillings for each acre not restored. While the Act had a clear and focused intent, it was nevertheless peppered with the same nationalistic rhetoric of Elizabeth's earlier proclamation. The Act begins by asserting that the "Strength and florishinge Estate of this Kingdome hath bene allwayes and is greately upheld and advaunced by the maintenaunce of the Plough & Tillage," continues to express that "the Wealthe of the Realme is kept dispersed and distributed in manie hands," and further explains that England's agricultural vibrancy "is a cause that the Realme doth more stande upon it selfe." Enclosures not only promoted the covetousness of landlords and the degeneration of farmers; *all* of England's subjects suffer because enclosures "weaken" the nation. By demonstrating that enclosed lands were a problem for the entire realm and that the increase of tillage directly resulted in a stronger and more independent England, Parliament ensured that the interest in the subject would stay current in the cultural milieu.

It is no wonder, then, that the resistance to enclosures and rebellion against those who instigated them became a moral imperative of those most deeply affected—the agricultural laborers. Anti-enclosure literature, like the husbandry manuals that also take up the subject of sheep, becomes a type of didacticism. While it may not have directly incited people to riot against enclosers, the constant and repeated invective throughout most of the sixteenth century, as well as the persistent legislation in the same period, might be seen as that which encouraged those adversely affected by enclosed land and sheep farming to take up arms against the landlords. Thus, one of the most common forms of social protest in the sixteenth century was the enclosure riot.[37] Up until the mid-sixteenth century, the riots were mostly aimed at new landowners who disregarded the traditional land use rights of farmers, and whose livelihood depended on the ability to use common land for tillage and grazing of livestock (Manning, "Violence and Social Conflict," 24). These complaints, if not the riots, were initially supported by the crown. But in 1548–49, when rumors emerged that a conspiracy of landowners had tried to obstruct Edward VI's laws maintaining tillage and restricting enclosures, grievances against enclosures became grievances against greedy landlords and their sheep, thus ushering in a period of riots that began to look like class warfare.

---

against the sheepmaster. As Joan Thirsk points out, "in 1593 the abundance and cheapness of corn caused Elizabethan legislators at last to shed their fear of enclosure and pasture farming and to repeal their acts to maintain tillage, but this opened the flood-gates to fresh enclosures, and, following the bad harvest of 1595, panic caused them to be revived" ("Tudor Enclosures," 14).

37 As Manning puts forth, the enclosure riots that occurred before those of 1548–49 were not necessarily targeted at the rich landowners as much as they were directed against agricultural "innovations" that "threatened the traditional agrarian routine within the manorial or village economy" ("Violence and Social Conflict," 18). The riots were "more frequently directed against new owners and farmers of leases than against the older gentry. Indeed, the latter frequently procured these enclosure riots" ("Violence and Social Conflict," 24). In *2 Henry VI*, Shakespeare anachronistically suggests that one of Jack Cade's complaints is against enclosure, as he declares "[a]ll the realm shall be [held] in common" (IV, ii, 60–61).

While there were several minor skirmishes involving commoners tearing down hedges in protest of the enclosures, indicating the extent to which anti-enclosure sentiment had aggravated the populace, only a few resulted in large scale violence.[38] The most famous among these riots was Kett's Rebellion, named for a landlord who, sympathetic with the plight of the displaced and impoverished commoners, in 1549 led an army to Norwich to air grievances in order to regain the common right to land use.[39] The rebellion began rather benignly: During a customary festival in central Norfolk celebrating Thomas à Becket, several villagers discussed the lack of action taken after the investigation of enclosures had been ordered by the commission (Cornwall, 137). Aggravated by their situation, and perhaps drunk with feasting, some of the villagers took it upon themselves to root up nearby enclosing hedges. One of the landlords who had his hedges destroyed was Sir John Flowerdew, who tried to redirect the villagers' aggression against Robert Kett, member of a rival family and another landowner who also had enclosed common land. However, Kett agreed to restore his land as commons, sided with the villagers, agreed to help them obtain their rights, and became their de facto leader. On 10 July, Kett and his followers marched just outside of Norwich, then England's second largest city, and set up camp at Mousehold Heath, where they soon gathered a force of 16,000 men (Fletcher, 65), some of whom were from "at least two other spontaneously insurgent groups" (W. Jones, 49).[40] While Kett's demands had commoners' general rights at

---

38 Most of the mid-century uprisings occurred in Southern England. The Western Rebellion, also of 1549, resulted in the loss of at least four to five thousand rebels and was finally squelched by William Herbert, Earl of Pembroke, who arrived with over one thousand, men (W. Jones, 48). This rebellion was primarily against governmental religious policy, specifically aimed at church reforms imposed on the parishes. Although the resistance was not primarily against enclosure, there is some evidence to suggest that this may have been one of the grievances. In addition to religious grievances, the rebels disputed rumors about the Act of Relief, a sheep and cloth tax, which they thought would harm them in an already bad financial year (Barrett L. Beer, 71–2). John Cheke's *The Hurt of Sedition* (1549) was one contemporary text that addressed the general climate of rebellion in 1549. Cheke's text was reprinted in 1569, the year of the Northern Rebellion, and again in 1576.

39 Kett took advantage of a pre-existing climate of disgruntlement on the part of the commoners. In June 1549, there were two separate instances of commoners tearing down hedges of enclosed lands. The rebellion in all lasted several weeks and is thus very complicated and filled with intrigue, to which I cannot do justice here. For thorough narratives and analyses of Kett's Rebellion, see Beer, *Rebellion and Riot*; Bindoff, *Ket's Rebellion;* Cornwall, *Revolt of the Peasantry*; Fletcher, *Tudor Rebellions*; Land, *Kett's Rebellion*; and Jones, *The Mid-Tudor Crisis*. Bindoff's pithy summation of the events is helpful here: "What we name, or misname, Ket's Rebellion began as a local riot, developed into a great popular demonstration, and ended in the violence and bloodshed of rebellion ... . The first is an episode in the long drawn-out conflict between landlords and tenants; the second turns on the relations between governors and governed, and its framework is the county; while in the third these local strands become interwoven with the thread of national politics" (7).

40 Neville puts the number of rebels at 20,000 while the loyalists were numbered at 1,500 (G4r).

their core, nearly half of his demands were related to land use issues.[41] Indeed, the first article on the list of grievances demanded that "noman shall enclose any more" grounds in Norfolk ("Kett's Demands," 142).

The royal proclamation of April 1549 protecting land "against the unreasonable multitude of sheep, decay of farms and of houses of husbandry, by enclosing them into a few men's hands" ("Enforcing Statutes," 451) had initially encouraged farmers who had been victims of enclosure. The rebels believed the law was on their side; Kett and his followers in fact insisted that they were the King's representatives at Mousehold.[42] Throughout July, Kett's men remained encamped at Mousehold Heath, where they discussed strategy and awaited orders. Matthew Parker of Norwich, who was later to become Archbishop of Canterbury, visited the camp. He found the common men among Kett's rebels "over-charged with meat and drinke" and later returned to deliver a sermon on temperance (Neville, C4r). The rebels tried to establish a truce with Norwich officials on 23 July, but the aldermen of Norwich refused, resulting in a storming of the gates where the rebels "made a full assault armed with spears, swords, and pitchforks" (Fletcher, 66). Although Kett himself was a member of the gentry (and a tanner by trade), the rebellion against enclosure was waged as a class war, with the landlords seen as the enemy.[43] Writing about the causes of Kett's Rebellion, Robert Crowley in 1550 claimed that the enclosing landlords were the "cormerauntes" that "are the causes of Sedition!" (132)" and these "gredye gulles" "take our houses over our headdes, they bye our growndes out of our handes, they reyse our rentes, they leavie great (yea unreasonable) fines, they enclose oure commens!" (132–3).[44] While enclosed land was only one among several complaints of the rebels, it continued to stand as the primary source of agrarian discontent and a symbol of the landlord's wealth and power. During the trials that resulted from the uprising, a Norwich innkeeper testified that one William Cowper said, "[t]hat as shepe or lambes are a praye to the woulfs or lyon so are the poore men to the Riche men or gentylmen" ("Aftermath," 51). The urban rich were not spared in the melee. Bands of rebels set fire to some parts of the city and looted shops and homes. And although the hatred towards sheep might have been symbolic in anti-enclosure literature, the ovine became a literal victim of the rebellion as well. Kett and his multitude of followers dealt with problems of supply by participating in "large-scale feasting upon the hated sheep" (W. Jones, 50). Ironically, Thomas Woodhouse, a landlord who had sympathized with the anti-enclosure camp, lost

---

41 None of the demands named sheepfarming as a point of contention, although it was certainly implied by the emphasis on enclosures. Beer suggests that this was because there were likely wool-producing yeoman who were in support of the rebellion (*Rebellion and Riot*, 111).

42 Kett and his band also took possession of Mount Surrey, the household of Henry Howard, Earl of Surrey, which they used as a prison for the gentleman and other loyalists that they captured (S.T. Bindoff, 4).

43 Although many of the rebels were poor farmers, the insurgency was fueled by support from urban artisans from Norwich (W. Jones, 49–50).

44 By and large, Crowley's text is a discussion of the intractable animosity between rich and poor. Although he decries the landlord's greediness, he nevertheless does not condone the uprising of the peasants.

2,000 of his sheep to the rebels' feast (Barrett Beer, 139).[45] Even the most vigilant of shepherds could not have protected these sheep from the hungry and incensed rebels.

Once Kett advanced a siege of Norwich, the government stepped in to squelch the rebellion, effectively reneging on its prior anti-enclosure stance.[46] Although the Lord Protector himself was supposed to be in charge of suppressing the rebels, Somerset called upon John Dudley, Earl of Warwick to take command of the forces sent to combat the insurgents (S.T. Bindoff, 5).[47] Initially Warwick tried to negotiate a truce, which was again refused by Kett and his followers. On 24 August, Warwick and his soldiers, "now numbering over seven thousand, including many foreign mercenaries," recaptured Norwich, hanging many prisoners in the process (W. Jones, 50). Kett's troops abandoned their camp at Mousehold Heath and waged a battle against Warwick's troops in a field at Dussindale, where the rebels were ultimately soundly defeated. In the end, upwards of 3,000 rebels were killed, and Kett—after facing trial in London—was eventually hanged.[48]

The poor farmers, whom Somerset had originally desired to protect with his policies, were criminalized and discursively constructed as mindless and violent rabble in the contemporary accounts of the riot. Kett and his followers were accused in one account of "robbinge" and "spoylinge" and possessing "evil demeanors" (Sotherton, 145); rather than seeking a redress of grievances, the peasants were portrayed as looking "for utter destruction both of lyfe and goods" (146).[49] According to Sotherton, after taking a gentleman into their custody, the rebels "cryed hang him and some kill him and some that heard noe word criyd even as the rest when themselvs being

---

45 Cornwall claims that 20,000 sheep were "driven and consumed ... in a few days" (147).

46 Throughout the conflict, the rebels were repeatedly offered pardons for their actions. On 16 July, the King offered a proclamation "pardoning enclosure rioters," while "ordering martial law against future rioters" (475). Kett and his followers dismissed the offer as they felt they had not committed any pardonable offense.

47 It is not known why Somerset neglected to take command; possibly his earlier sympathy to the peasants' plight rendered him an unconvincing leader.

48 The combined loss of life of rebels and loyalists during the seven or so weeks of the conflict was probably around 4,000 (W. Jones, 51). Kett's Rebellion and other rebellions of the mid-sixteenth century resulted in anti-riot legislation and made it a treasonable offense for a group to gather to tear down enclosures. In the 1590s it was deemed treason for rioters to even "advocat[e] the general destruction of enclosures" (Manning, *Village Revolts*, 56). Revolts in 1596 and 1607 were directly linked to grievances over enclosed lands for sheep farming. In the fall of 1596 at least forty men petitioned Lord Norris to "throw down" illegal enclosures. His unresponsiveness to the pleas caused one of his own servants to plan a rebellion (Manning, *Village Revolts*, 221). The Midlands Revolt of 1607 involved 5,000 rioters who leveled hedges in southern Leicestershire and was at least in part directed at Thomas Trasham, an engrossing and enclosing landlord who had almost 7,000 head of sheep (Manning, *Village Revolts*, 238). In general, the enclosure riots of the early modern period were deliberate in purpose with specific grievance to be aired and particular goals in mind. Despite the spectacularly bloody outcome of Kett's rebellion, most were relatively tame. See Wrightson, p. 152.

49 Son of a Mayor of Norwich and a city alderman, Sotherton was the only chronicler who was a firsthand witness to the events (Land, viii).

demanded why they criyd answerd for that thyr fellows afore did the like" (146). Thus, the poor working farmer, once portrayed sympathetically, had become a kind of rustic marauder, blindly following the mob. The late sixteenth-century chronicles of the rebellion are no more sympathetic to the plight of the peasant farmers. Indeed the two primary accounts of the two month ordeal construct the rioters as monstrous and threatening figures. Published in 1575 and 1578 respectively, Alexander Neville and Raphael Holinshed's accounts of the rebellion, despite the fact that they were published almost three decades after the event, solidified the historical understanding of the peasants in Norfolk. They are represented as an ignorant and rude mob. The texts, then, served as a warning to those who would dare launch a rebellion in the latter part of the century and, as I will argue, were an important source for Sidney's *Arcadia*.

Neville's account of the events of July and August 1549 has served as the primary source for future historians.[50] However, his obvious bias against Kett and his followers places Neville's chronicle securely in the gallery of texts that question the historical validity of the rebels' complaints. Although Neville acknowledges the rebels' discontent against enclosures in Norfolk, he begins his tract by stating the resulting events were brought on "by the villany, and the treachery of beastly men" (B1r), who "bound themselves" to their cause "with bruitish rage" (B1v). Their camps were replete with men prone to "ryot and excesse" (B3v), gluttonously devouring their provisions. Just as they are described by Sotherton as rustic and stupid clowns, Neville also claims that they act as an "ignorant and rude multitude" (D3r), almost purposeless in their violence: "through rage and fury, nothing left any where untouched, but by a popular frenzie all things consumed" (E1r). Warwick's violent recapture of Norwich and undoubtedly brutal slaughter of the rebels is not described in detail. Kett's men, though, are surely dispensible as they are equated with a disorganized pack of wild animals: the men "came running from their dens with confused cries, and beastly howlings" (G1v). Dehumanized by their pervasive representation as subhuman, they are also deprived of God's gift of rational thought; they are "not led by judgement or reason ... but led by a certayne blind and headlong rage of the minde" (F3r).

Drawing heavily from Neville's history, Holinshed's account of the two-month standoff and battle seems more a series of name calling than an historical account of the events. Although Holinshed does give some background of the peasants' complaints over enclosure practices, their grievances are completely obfuscated by the depiction of their behavior as immoral. Holinshed calls the rebels "ungracious unthrifts" (966), "greedie vagabonds (967)" and part of an "outrageous multitude" (967). He describes how the rebels from the Norfolk countryside were joined by "a great multitude of lewd disposed persons" from Suffolk and "a number of rascals & naughtie lewd persons" from Norwich (965). The peasants' actions are as uncouth as their demeanor. When encountering an enemy, they despoil him of his armor and then kill him. This action is that of "vile wretches" who kill their captive with

---

50 Neville's text was published first in Latin and then translated by Richard Woods and printed in 1615. Neville was close to Matthew Parker and received information regarding the rebellion from the Norwich resident and future Archbishop (Bindoff, *Ket's Rebellion*, 24).

"beastlie crueltie" (72). And although by all accounts the rebels were summarily slaughtered at Dussindale (Holinshed claims 3,500 rebels were killed), the actions of the loyalists/aristocracy are never questioned: Warwick is "of a noble and invincible courage, valiant, hardie, and not able to abide anie spot of reproach" (981), while Kett is rendered a "wicked caitife" (969). Both Neville and Holinshed's accounts of Kett's rebellion cast the opposition is such an unforgiving light that their original, highly articulate demands are occluded and the men themselves are bestialized. The depiction of the rebellion as the belligerent actions of an ignorant mob rather than the deliberate actions of a group of men with legitimate concerns shaped the ways that riots and rebellions would be viewed for some time to come.

"Under Pretty Tales of Wolves and Sheep": The Mad Multitude of *Arcadia*

I would like now to turn to Philip Sidney's *The Countess of Pembroke's Arcadia*. By investigating Raymond Williams's remark in *The Country and the City*—that this most representative of early modern pastorals "was written in a park which had been made by enclosing a whole village and evicting the tenants" (22)—we may be able to see how the everyday realities of land use show us the discontents of Arcadia. The site where Sidney retreated to write the prose romance, Wilton House in Wiltshire, a major wool region, was the estate of William Herbert, the first Earl of Pembroke.[51] After confiscating monastic lands, King Henry VIII granted the manors of the parish to Herbert in 1540. His son, Henry Herbert, was Sidney's brother in law, husband to Mary Sidney, Countess of Pembroke, for whom the *Arcadia* is named and to whom it is dedicated. Certainly not on the scale of Kett's rebellion, there was nevertheless an uprising at Wilton in 1548–49 as a result of arbitrary enclosure that apparently depopulated the land, turning farmers out (Kerridge, "Agriculture," 48–9; Tawney, 326). Sidney would no doubt have known about these events as they were part of the spate of uprisings of the same year. Further, Sidney would have known of William Herbert's key role in putting down the Western Rebellion of 1549 with the help of Sidney's great uncle, John Dudley, Earl of Warwick. Dudley, himself a "notoriously unpopular landlord" (Tawney, 325) was, of course, in command in the suppression of Kett's rebellion. And Sidney's uncles, Robert and Ambrose Dudley, served in the army of their father in Norfolk. While Sidney would have been surrounded by first or secondhand tales of Kett's rebellion, he also would have been able to read about them. The two major chronicles of Kett's Rebellion, Neville's and Holinshed's, both came out in the 1570s, only a few years before Sidney wrote *The Arcadia*.[52]

Sidney's association with the anti-enclosure riots is not merely an interesting anecdote. I would argue that we cannot fully understand the scene in which the

---

51 Sidney's stay at Wilton House is commonly seen as a retreat from court where Sidney recently had fallen out of favor due to his opposition to Elizabeth's match to the Duke of Anjou. See in particular Worden, *The Sound of Virtue: Philip Sidney's Arcadia and Elizabethan Politics*.

52 For recent discussions of Sidney's sentiments about historiography see Sussman, "Histor, History, and Narrative Memory," and Kinney, "Sir Philip Sidney and the Uses of History."

Phagonians rebel without also looking carefully at the culture of anti-enclosure protest in the period before the composition of *Arcadia*. In Book Two of the *Old Arcadia* there is a rather alarming scene in which a group of rustics, angered with their Duke, seek him out with the intention of killing him.[53] Sidney includes the rebellion of the rustics to show not only the potential harm that may come from poor governance, as several critics have argued. It is my contention that the uprising of the rustics may also be read as Sidney's comment on the enclosure riots that had occurred several decades prior and were still a threat to the aristocratic landowner. The uncharitable portrayal of the rebels as a mad mob, their association with agricultural workers, and their decisive defeat by their social betters all indicate Sidney's knowledge of the events of 1549. Kett's rebellion, however, is not merely a source for Sidney. Sidney himself knew very well the potential to read pastoral literature as allegory. In *The Defence of Poesy*, Sidney demonstrates the gravity that pastoral poetry may reveal:

> Is it then the Pastoral poem which is misliked? (For perchance where the hedge is lowest they will soonest leap over.) Is the poor pipe disdained, which sometime out of Meliboeus' mouth can show the misery of people under hard lords or ravening soldiers, and again, by Tityrus, what blessedness is derived to them that lie lowest from the goodness of them that sit highest[54]; sometimes, under the pretty tales of wolves and sheep, can include the whole considerations of wrong-doing and patience; sometimes show that contentions for trifles can get but a trifling victory. (693–701)

While we know that Sidney wrote contemporaneous (and sometimes personal) contexts into his work, it is difficult to read this passage and not imagine that Sidney understood it on a more literal level: that low hedges may be leapt over or torn down; that rural laborers suffer under the yoke of "hard lords;" that those who suffer are often disregarded by those who have the power to help them; and that discord with "sheep" as its source and the "patience" to bear it is often what is found "under the pretty tales" of pastoral literature. I am not suggesting here that Sidney was necessarily sympathetic with the plight of the agrarian worker. I am arguing, though, that he recognized that even the lowest members of society were subject to the proclivities of their social betters and that poetry could give a voice to this underclass which, although noisy in its rioting, was often ignored. As an observation of class dynamics, Sidney's text is characteristically complex. We see that his sympathies lie with the aristocratic privilege of Arcadia, even as he brings to light some of the morally questionable actions of the higher orders. And importantly, the shepherds of Arcadia are clearly distinct from the other agrarians, so that those who tend the flock may remain in the camp of the landowning wealthy.

---

53 Sutton first introduced Kett's rebellion as a possible source for *The New Arcadia*, but not the *Old Arcadia*. His brief essay is important in that it offers a correlation between the events of 1549 and Sidney's text. Here, I intend to deepen this analysis and also argue that Kett's rebellion bears strongly on the original version of the text as well.

54 Meliboeus and Tityrus are both shepherds in Virgil's *Eclogues* and give their names to countless early modern British shepherds as well. In the *Eclogues*, Meliboeus laments the loss of his land and cattle that had been confiscated, which had actually happened to Virgil himself.

The "tumult" in Arcadia begins just as that of Kett's rebellion had, with a celebratory feast that gave occasion for men to air grievances. Gathered together to "solemnize" the nativity of their Duke Basilius, the men of Phagona grow drunk and increasingly incensed with what they see as the poor governance of Arcadia:[55]

> There being chafed with wine and emboldened with the duke's absented manner of living, there was no matter their ears had ever heard of that grew not to be a subject of their winy conference. Public affairs were mingled with private grudge; neither was any man thought of wit that did not pretend some cause of mislike. Railing was counted the fruit of freedom, and saying nothing had his uttermost praise in ignorance. (111)

The Phagonians' festival descends into chaos as the narrator describes them becoming increasingly irrational and mob-like: A "furious storm presently took hold of their well inclined brains;" the cacophony of the voices "was the only token of their unmeet agreement" (112). And just as the historical accounts of Kett's rebellion depicted the peasants as an undisciplined and unorganized band of rebels, an "outrageous multitude" (Holinshed, 967), Sidney describes the Phagonians as unable to decide how to arm themselves or even if they should proceed with their assault, a "many-headed multitude" (105).[56]

On their way to the Duke, the Phagonians interrupt another troubling scene: Gynecia's attempted seduction of Pyrocles, disguised as the beautiful Amazon, Cleophila. Basilius's wife, Gynecia, begins to "display to Cleophila the storehouse of her deadly desires," setting a scene of danger and illicit sexuality and calling into question the moral grounding of the aristocrats. Just as this occurs, "a confused rumor of a mutinous multitude" interrupts them and Gynecia and Cleophila attempt to flee (108).[57] These "unruly sort of clowns" share many characteristics with the members of Kett's rebellion both in demeanor and action. They are likened to "enraged beasts" and take pleasure in violently assaulting the "fair ladies" (108). Mirroring almost exactly the language used by Sotherton to describe Kett's rioters, Sidney presents them as distracted, ignorant rebels: "Yet so many as they were, so many almost were the minds all knit together only in madness. Some cried 'take!,' some 'kill,' some 'save!'; but even they that cried 'save!' ran for company with them that meant to kill" (109).[58] On the one hand, the frenetic scene mirrors the sexual chaos wrought by Pyrocles's disguise and Gynecia's unnatural desires; the Phagonians'

---

55 Phagona is derived from the Greek "glutton" and suggests the town's character (n. 374.).

56 According to Christopher Hill, the term "many-headed multitude" relates to the structure of the feudal household: The "many-headed monster was composed of masterless men, those for whom nobody responsible answered" (298). See Hill for a discussion of the contemptuous attitude toward the masses in the early modern period.

57 In Book Three of *The Arcadia*, Musidorus's intended ravishment of Pamela is thwarted by a group of "clownish villains" (177), the "scummy remnant" (265) of the first rebellion who wake Pamela with their cries. See McCoy, p. 193, for a discussion of this scene of seduction/rebellion.

58 Shakespeare may have been influenced by Sidney's text when writing the scenes of Jack Cade's rebellion in *2 Henry VI*. Cade's followers are portrayed as a confused multitude who one moment cry, "God save the King!", the next claim "We'll follow Cade!", and then immediately claim they will "follow the King and Clifford!" (IV, vii, 162, 175, 195–6).

threats to "kill" the two "ladies" seem to suggest a literal manifestation of Gynecia's "deadly desires." However, given that the language is extraordinarily close to that of Sotherton's, and I would suggest is borrowed from his account of Kett's Rebellion, this dramatic scene is at least in part about the results of rustic misrule. Bordering on the burlesque, the scene shows just what happens when uncouth men are incited to action and forget their position: "Everyone commanded, none obeyed" (109). The literal interruption of Gynecia's seduction is indicative of a more symbolic notion: no matter how ill-behaved aristocrats are, what is more troubling is the rejection of a hierarchical system of rule.

This rebellion is put down after some effort on the part of the nobles. Basilius, "having put on an armour long before untried, came to prove his authority among his subjects" (109). Like the troops initially organized to fight against Kett's rebels, Basilius also needs to show puissance in Arcadia to maintain control.[59] He cannot, however, do this alone. Cleophila's involvement in the fray demonstrates that this is a battle between high and low as she "did quickly make them perceive that one eagle is worth a great number of kites" (109). Her nobility above all (as both an Amazon and a disguised Prince) is that which metes out justice: "no blow she strake that did not suffice for a full reward of him that received it" (109). The combined forces of Basilius and Cleophila are still not enough to suppress the rioters completely. Like the Earl of Warwick, Sidney's great uncle, who stepped in to put a decisive end to Kett's rebellion, "the noble shepherd Dorus" hears the tumult and comes to the aid of Basilius and Cleophila (109). Musidorus, disguised as a protector of sheep, participates in putting down the madness of the multitude.[60] Importantly, like the members of the rebellions of 1549, the marauders are associated with ploughmen: to launch their attack, they took up "bills," "pitchforks and rakes," thus "converting husbandry to soldiery" (112).[61] As Montrose asserts, in accounts about enclosing, "the fundamentally opposed interests of Commons and Gentles were metaphorized in the opposition of Ploughman and Shepherd" (425) and nowhere is this more obvious than in the suppression of the rebels of Arcadia: Dorus "felled one of them with his sheephook ... taking his bill from him, valiantly seconded by Philisides and the other honest shepherds" (110–11). The weapons used in this skirmish are symbolic of the triumph of the shepherd/landlord over the agricultural laborer/enclosure rioter. The sheephook prevails over the "bill" in this melee and Dorus is able to put down the rebels with the help of other shepherds. Significantly, the shepherd Philisides, who is primarily found in the text's Eclogues and is widely regarded as Philip Sidney's shepherd alter-ego, participates in the quashing of the Phagonians. Thus Sidney himself is aligned with the exultant actions of his kinsmen who fought against Kett's rebels.

---

59 This display of power is somewhat undermined by the narrator's suggestion that Basilius's motive in fighting the rebels is "to adventure his life with his dear mistress," Cleophila (109).

60 Before hearing the "horrible cries of the mad multitude" (110), Dorus is playing the part of the noble shepherd-poet perfectly: he stands in the "shade of a few pleasant myrtle trees, feeding his master's sheep, practicing his new-learned shepherd's pipe, and singing with great joy for the long-pursued victory he had lately gotten of the gracious Pamela's favour" (109).

61 A "bill" is a pruning implement.

But finally it is Cleophila who performs the role of the diplomat, "with a sweet magnanimity and stately mildness" (115). She is able to show the Phagonians that they are wrong in their attempt to "defac[e] such an excellent monarchy, which they with much labour and blood so widely established" (114). Cleophila's success in quelling the masses stands in stark contrast to the multiple attempts on the part of the government envoys to appease Kett and his men. In Neville's account, the King "hath commanded once againe to bee offered vnto them peace; and pardon (notwithstanding al that they had committed) yea, to euery of them (one or two excepted) so as they would turne to dutie now at the last (being ledde with repentance) from this course of malice and wickednesse" (K2r). The rebels have two options: stay the course of "malice and wickedness" or "turn to dutie." Rejection of the King's pardon, then, necessarily indicates not only a refusal of the King's graces, but also a clear indication that duty will be subordinated to wicked hatred. Kett's men refused, defying the King who for so long was sympathetic to their plight and "stoutly made one answere: *That they would not*" (K2r). In *The Arcadia*, on the other hand, we have Sidney's fantasy of aristocratic suppression. The ease with which Cleophila is able to convince the Phagonians of their missteps and their immediate acceptance of Basilius's "general pardon" (116) demonstrates that they know their place and have learned a lesson: "that to be leaders in disobedience teacheth ever disobedience to the same leaders" (115–16). While Sidney may likely have read Sotherton, Neville, or Holinshed's accounts of Kett's rebellions, he does not seem to be satisfied with the outcome of their chronicles. In the historical accounts, the rebels remained loyal to their leader and their cause and thousands died defending it. *The Arcadia* offers a corrective to this version. The rebels are able to listen to reason coming from the mouth of an aristocratic prince disguised as an Amazon. Despite their bestial nature, they are able to accept the magnanimous gift of a pardon and once again become loyal subjects. Indeed, they grow so ashamed that they become "their own punishers" (116). The answer that Kett's rebels gave to Warwick, "that they would not" accept the King's offer is revised in *The Arcadia* as a cry of "'God save the duke!'" (115).

In *The New Arcadia* the scenes are revised to include that which specifically incited the rebels.[62] After several rebels are dispatched, Zelmane (Cleophila of *OA*) asks the rioters to "relate your griefs or demands" (284). Mirroring the incidents

---

62 Critics have debated the significance of this revision, although most insist that Sidney is commenting on his tenuous relationship at court. In "The Uprising of the Commons," Zeeveld views the rebellion as Sidney's involvement in courtly politics, arguing that the inclusion of the list of grievances in the *NA* renders it less politically charged. Whereas he believes the *Old Arcadia* relates directly to Sidney's troubles at court for opposing the Alençon marriage, in the *NA*, the uprising of the commons coincides "significantly with Sidney's withdrawal in 1580 from active opposition to the French marriage" (213). Sutton argues that Zeeveld ignores the list of grievances, thus discounting Kett's rebellion as a source. Still Sutton also believes that the scene in the *OA* represents a "criticism of Queen Elizabeth's projected marriage" (11). Wodern also reads the uprising of the Phagonians as representative of Sidney's complaints against the Anjou match. However, even if there were not such strong resemblances between this scene and the events of 1549, it seems unlikely that Sidney would align himself with the rebels of Arcadia given their highly unsympathetic portrayal.

of Kett's rebellion even more closely than the previous version of the text, Sidney shows that the rebels have multiple, and sometimes conflicting demands due to the diversity of their group. However, the chief complaint of "the country fellows" is the "laying out of commons" (284), a complaint not found in *The Old Arcadia*. In an attempt to supress their anger, Zelmane retorts that their rage is misdirected: "here be neither hard lords nor biting usurers" (285). Although Basilius may make poor decisions regarding the way he governs, and may—as the text suggests—allow for enclosures, Zelmane attempts to appease the rebels by insisting he is not a cruel landlord. However legitimate their complaint of enclosures may be, it is utterly subordinated in the text to the fact that the rebels do not speak with one voice. Zelmane's dismissal of their grievance effectively makes it ridiculous. The anti-enclosure stance is made to look as mad as the men who take it.

The physical suppression of the rebels in *The New Arcadia* is also significantly more violent than the original text, adding scenes of dismemberment and grotesque farce. Dorus's victory with the sheephook is extrapolated: Dorus, "lifting up his brave head, and flashing terror into their face, he made arms and legs go complain to the earth how evil their masters kept them" (281). Another rebel attacks Dorus with a pitchfork and, as the rebel falls at the gentle shepherd's feet, Dorus "thrust his sword quite through [his neck] from one ear to the other" (282). The violent resolution to the uprising is another sort of fantasy of the aristocratic classes over the threat of the riotous peasant. As Stephen Greenblatt has argued, "instead of depicting the ordinary operation of the law, functioning to defend property, English artists most often narrate events at once more menacing and more socially prestigious ... instead of the assizes and a hempen rope, we have tales of mass rebellion and knightly victories" ("Murdering Peasants," 15). In *The New Arcadia*, the decisive victories are over those who, among other things, complain about enclosure policies. If for Sidney poesy had a decidedly didactic purpose, here we clearly see the lesson.

The plowmen who create havoc in Arcadia are positioned both against the shepherds and the royal family; they are representative of the rioting mob that so threatened aristocratic privilege to enclose land and have "altogether shepe, shepe." It is no surprise, then, that the rioting in Arcadia is subordinated to song: In the Second Eclogues, "the rude tumult of the Phagonians gave occasion to the honest shepherds to begin their pastorals." The Eclogues of the *Arcadia*, like those of Virgil, are the sites in the text where we see the shepherds convene. However, they have little to do with actual pastoral labor, but rather are a reification of the traditional pastoral fantasy of *otium*. The Second Eclogue is partially comprised of "a dance which they called the skirmish between Reason and Passion," the song a debate between the two sides and ending with Passion and Reason embracing and agreeing to "give place" to "heav'nly rules" (120). For Sidney, the passion of commoners is what Greenblatt would call "the great ruling class nightmare of the Renaissance: the marauding horde, the many-headed multitude, the insatiate, giddy, and murderous crowd" ("Murdering Peasants," 5). Those who would be "appassionate" are significantly figured as "rebels vile," the "mutinous" mob. Despite the fact that the shepherds are able to remain in Arcadia playing their pipes and serving their landlords, they make way for the true heroes of the text, the nobles. When we move from the populist agrarianism of anti-enclosure literature to the elite, highly formalized pastoral literature of the country house nobility, the symbol of agrarian discontent drops out. The sheep are figuratively led to the slaughterhouse in the interest of reinserting the dominance of the noble landlord. However, despite the highly traditional structure of the text's Eclogues, we are necessarily reminded that there *needs* to be a debate about a "skirmish," that the text calls attention to the material realities that exist "under the pretty tales of wolves and sheep."

While the anti-enclosure riots and the printed propaganda against turning tillable land into grazing pasture took aim against sheep and the landlords who kept them, it is important to recognize the corollary source of derision: the cloth industry. Indeed, if we believe that Sidney's text exists in the context of these debates, we must also acknowledge its engagement with England's cloth trade. The mid-century shift in the industry from the export of raw wool to that of wool broadcloth expanded the demand for wool in ways that could not have been anticipated. The landlords who enclosed their lands, whether to contain more sheep or for other reasons, found themselves ineluctably aligned with the interests of the wealthy merchants of the cloth trade and against those of farmers who struggled to stay solvent. The riots against them, in reality or in fictional representations, must be considered as part of the larger conversation concerning England's wool trade. Indeed, in a period where the cloth trade faced unprecedented challenges, we must count anti-enclosure sentiment among them.

Chapter 2

Clothworkers and Social Protest: The Case of Thomas Deloney[1]

As I have argued in Chapter 1, sheep and landlords were targets of protest in the mid-sixteenth century among agrarian workers. The enclosure of tillable land for sheep farming, perceived as the result of increased domestic wool production, evoked derision and incited rebellion among those who felt that the nation would become undone by such emphasis on wool cloth. When we look to the end of the sixteenth century, we find that the cloth industry is still tied to an understanding of England's nationhood, but with an important difference. Rather than asserting that the wool industry was detracting from the nation's vigor, popular authors instead offered the opposite argument. In the 1590s, a time when the industry faced important challenges, wool cloth becomes the focal point for organizing sentiments of nationalism. Those involved with its manufacture emerge as key figures in promoting England's well-being, while those who are seen as obstructing its production, however indirectly, become the new objects of protest. This chapter focuses on one author in particular, Thomas Deloney, who combined his two careers—writing and weaving—to emphasize that clothmaking was crucial to the makeup of England and should be recognized as such by the government.

Deloney, a prolific balladeer and impoverished silkweaver, was twice wanted for arrest by the London authorities in as many years for writing documents that criticized government policy. The two publications—one, a letter regarding the nuisance of immigrant weavers, and the other, a ballad complaining about the scarcity of grain—were both written at the height of Deloney's balladeering in 1595 and 1596. Both publications respond directly to what Deloney saw as challenges to his weaving profession: immigrant weavers infringed upon the rights of the native workers, while grain shortages detracted from the health of the cloth industry. Crop failures of the late sixteenth and early seventeenth centuries and particularly those of the years 1595–97, which also coincided with depressions in the cloth trade in overseas markets due to the conflict with Spain, had a deleterious effect on the clothworkers who relied on the grain market for provisions (Sharp, 3).[2] By looking to his writing of the mid-1590s as the immediate context for his next literary effort, *Jack of Newbury* (1597), we begin to understand the crucial contribution that Deloney's work made to the culture of protest in the difficult decade of the 1590s and importantly to early modern nation formation.

---

1 An earlier version of this chapter appears in *Comitatus*.
2 See Sharp, p. 18, for the trajectory from clothworker to social misfit in the late 1590s.

A fictionalized tale of the improbable rise to fame of an actual early sixteenth century broadcloth weaver named John Winchcombe, Deloney's best known and most popular prose work, *Jack of Newbury*, is sentimental in its account of the life of an artisan turned citizen.[3] Indeed, Jack's advancement from weaver-servant to the premiere master-clothmaker in all of Berkshire, if not England, is so celebrated that even the king, Henry VIII, recognizes Jack as a national treasure. Given the sympathetic portrayal of Jack's fame as the reward for a life of hard work, it is no wonder that critics have for decades regarded Deloney as a benevolent proponent of the interests of the citizen classes whose writing confirms social hierarchies and stratifications. Noticing how Deloney's characters coexist peacefully with their social betters, R.G. Howarth claims that "Deloney evinces no jealousy, no hostility, toward nobles and gentlemen" (42). Bernard Capp suggests that in Elizabethan prose narratives including Deloney's, where distinct economic groups come into contact with one another, no social tension exists: "There is no direct challenge to the political or social order in these tales, and their message is primarily conservative" (210). Further, E.D. Mackerness argues that, while Deloney "is anxious to glorify the smaller trades and make out a case for the dignity of work," he also teaches "a doctrine of acquiescence and passivity so as to avoid the fear of social disturbance" (47). More recent critics have offered a corrective to this version of Deloney's story, both by taking into account Deloney's own biographical details and by attending closely to the culture of protest that he invokes in his fiction.[4] To be sure, Deloney idealizes the gracious nature of many of his laborers. However, if *Jack of Newbury* celebrates the wonders of the weaver, it is to emphasize the importance of the labor of the cloth industry and, in turn, to protest the treatment of clothworkers at the hands of the government at a time when the cloth industry was facing a major depression. By glorifying the clothworkers above all trades at a time when they were beleaguered by a dearth of grain at home, the closure of markets abroad, and a government unsympathetic to these problems, Deloney authors a radical narrative of national history in which social and economic prosperity and political security lie in the hands of the clothworkers rather than the crown.

The Silence of the Looms: Deloney's Plight and the Clothworkers' Peril

Before turning to *Jack of Newbury*, I would like to look more closely at the episodes that helped to shape Deloney's later career to show the logic of protest that defined Deloney's writing in the 1590s. The first incident, in June of 1595, was the result of

3   As Merritt Lawlis explains, Jack of Newbury is most likely a composite of two John Winchcombes, a father and son who "were pioneers in the manufacture of clothing in Newbury, Berkshire" (*Novels*, n. 350).

4   For recent work on Deloney's role as protester, see Burnett, *Masters and Servants*, especially Chapter 2; Kinney, "Rewriting History"; Suzuki, *Subordinate Subjects*, Chapter 1; and Tribble, "'We Will Do No Harm With Our Swords'." Ladd's recent essay, "Thomas Deloney and the London Weavers' Company," is especially helpful in its discussion of *Jack of Newberry* and *Thomas of Reading* in the context of Deloney's role as a member of the London Weavers' guild.

his collaboration with 14 other silkweavers in writing a letter to the pastors of the French and Dutch churches in London.[5] Frustrated with the perceived threat to their profession by the immigrant silkweavers, the members of the Weavers' Company drafted a complaint against Dutch and French clothworkers who had come to England in the 1560s and 70s "for the Gospell's sake," that is, to escape religious persecution by the Spanish Catholics in their own countries ("Complaint," 312).[6] Although the immigrant weavers came to England to seek asylum for their Protestant beliefs, by the late sixteenth century, the London weavers began to question their motives and decry their methods:

> they onely seeke their own private Lucre without any Christian regard of the native borne of our Country and without respect of the liberties and priviledges graunted to the Freemen of this honorable Cittye, to the great and amazing endamaginge of the Comon wealth and to the utter spoile and begerrie of the Queenes liege people of this facultye. ("Complaint," 312–13)

The weavers charge the Protestant immigrants with several transgressions: the immigrants "kepe Apprentices and Loomes twyce or thryce as many as they ought," thereby increasing productivity through illegal means.[7] The strangers teach their fellow unapprenticed countrymen "the Arte of Silke weaveinge" and further teach the women in their community how to weave, women who then marry men to whom they teach the trade. Finally—and perhaps most disturbing to Deloney and the London silkweavers—the immigrants "have opened and discovered the secrete of our Occupacon to their worke Maisters." By revealing the trade's "secrets," the immigrant population has "growne as Cunning in any worke," thereby threatening the Londoner's pride and livelihood (314). The immigrants had become too proficient in silkweaving; art in weaving skills, while desirable in Englishmen, becomes deplorable in the foreigners.

---

5   My narrative here draws from Merritt Lawlis's introduction to *The Novels of Thomas Deloney*, pp. xxvii–xxviii. Housed in the London Weaver's Company record office, the "Complaint of the Yeomen Weavers Against the Immigrant Weavers" is found in Appendix 22 in Frances Consitt, *The London Weavers' Company*. The authors sent forty copies of the letter: eleven to the pastors of the French church, the same number to the pastors of the Dutch church, and one copy each for the Lord Mayor and the City's aldermen (Lawlis, xxviii). The letter was signed by "William Muggins, Thomas Delonye and others, June Anno domini 1595" ("Complaint," 316).

6   There is also evidence to suggest that the craftsmen were encouraged to move to England, "with the object of improving and extending worsted manufacture" (Priestly, 7). Indeed, in November of 1565 the Queen issued a Letter Patent providing for the "settlement of thirty specialist craftsmen and their families" "for the benefit of Norwich" (Priestly, 9). For further discussion of the immigrant weavers, see Kerridge, *Textile Manufactures*.

7   The ordinance of the Weavers' Company of 1589 and 1594 asserts "1. That noe person of our Guild shall kepe above twoe Forreine Jorneymen, English or Stranger, at one time, for that no Forreine Jorneyman shalbe admitted a Master before they have wrought as a Servant the space of seaven yeares. 2. That noe Stranger not beinge denizon shall keepe above the number of Four Loomes in his house" ("Ordinance," 311).

Central to the English workers' list of grievances is that the city government actually privileges foreigners *over* the London weavers: "In all well-governed Commonwealthes the natyve borne are preferred before the Straunger" (315). By not taking action against the encroaching immigrants, according to Deloney, the government unforgivably aligns itself with the foreign silkweavers. Deloney complains that while the strangers are the cause of the weavers' "great decaye and ympoverishinge," the city leaders and clergy ignore that debasement (316). In addressing the letter to the Dutch and French pastors, Deloney and his fellow yeomen hoped that the churchmen would remedy the situation by influencing their parishioners to obey English laws and respect the native weavers in order to enable the Londoners to prosper again. The letter backfired, however, and the city government returned the insult: the Lord Mayor called for the confiscation of all copies of the letter and threw the freemen in Newgate prison.[8] Reiterating their grievances and complaining that they had been "restrayned from their occupacions and their families [were in] in great distresse," Deloney and his fellow weavers successfully petitioned the Lord Chief Justice and were released soon after (317).

Just a year later, in July of 1596, Deloney's writing again caused trouble with the London authorities. He was charged with composing a "scurrilous" ballad on the shortage of grain (Stow, 333). While the actual ballad has not survived, evidence of its offensive subject matter is found in a letter from the Lord Mayor, Stephen Slany, to William Cecil, Lord Burghley. In the letter, Slany describes the ballad's scandalous contents and its culpable author:

> Thear was brought to my hands a certain ballad contaynyng a Complaint of the great want and scarcity of corn within the Realm wich forasmuch as it contayneth in it certain vaine & presumptuous matters bringing in her highness to speak with her people in dialogue wise in very fond and indecent sort & prescribeth orders for the remedyng of the dearth of Corn & extracted (as it seemeth) out of the book published by your lords the last year butt in that vain & indiscreet manner as that thearby the poor may aggravate their grief & take occassion of soom discontentment, I thought it good to call before me the printer & the partie by whom it was putt to print, who pretended a lycence ... The maker himself who is one Delonie (an idle fellow and one noted with the like beefore in printing a Book for the Silkweavers wherein was found some like foolish & disordered matter) I cannot yet find.[9]

Although we may never know the ballad's exact content, we are able to speculate on why Slany deems it so "vaine," "indiscreet," and "presumptuous" that it prompted the Lord Mayor to attempt to arrest the author. Traditionally, the ballad's content has been considered licentious because it so offended the Queen, who in the ballad— according to Slany—speaks in a familiar manner with her working-class subjects.[10] To be sure, written discourse about the queen was carefully monitored and court officials may have considered representations of Elizabeth in conversation with the

---

8   See "Report of the Lord Mayor on the Weavers' Pamphlet" in Consitt, pp. 317–18.

9   The letter is in the Landsdowne ms. 81.30. in the British Library, London. Deloney's "Book for the Silkweavers" that Slany mentions is lost.

10 See Wright, *Thomas Deloney*, p. 37; Lawlis, *Novels*, p. xxviii; Tribble, p. 148.

commoners seditious.[11] Indeed, according to Strype in Stow's *Survey of London*, "[t]he Magistrates of the City would by no means allow in those Days any unworthy Reflections or Speeches against" the sovereign (333).

Neither the queen's presence nor her "dialogue" in the ballad, however, were most likely the principal cause of the Lord Mayor's distress. Slany's alarm may quite possibly have lain in the resemblance between a 1595 royal proclamation and Deloney's "vain and indiscreet" ballad. Slany seems to recognize that the ballad was "extracted" from a royal pamphlet that called for restrictions on the sale of corn and promised "that the markets will be well served and the poor relieved in their provisions during this time of dearth" (qtd. in Steele, 11).[12] Although using the language of the proclamation to propose a new solution to the problem of grain shortage does not break any laws, doing so implicitly underscores the impotence of the government's proclamation. Therein lies Deloney's "presumptuousness." Deloney's document indicates his distrust of official inaction: while the royal pamphlet claims the "poor" will be "relieved," it does not say exactly *how* the projected changes will directly help the poor. Deloney's text, on the other hand, "prescribeth orders for the remedyng of the dearth of Corn" in a way that "the poor may aggravate their grief & take occasion of soom discontentment." In other words, Deloney calls the poor workers to action in specific ways and thus undermines the authority of the royal document.[13]

Detecting Deloney's distrust of ineffective legislation and recognizing his position as a popular ballad writer, Slany may have predicted and feared the widespread appeal the ballad would have for the laborers of London. The primary cause for the Lord Mayor's alarm would have been the civic disruption the ballad could potentially cause. Events of the recent past—two social uprisings in London on the part of the workers in June 1595 in response to grain shortages—could not have been far from Slany's memory (Manning, *Village Revolts*, 204). In one instance, a silkweaver went to the home of John Spencer, then Lord Mayor, to rail against the government. The Lord Mayor, presuming the weaver mad, had him thrown into Bethlehem Hospital, when on the weaver's way there he was "rescued by a crowd of two or three hundred apprentices" (Penry Williams, 329). Slany surely did not want a repetition of these past incidents and perhaps, in an attempt to prevent any deranged weavers from coming to *his* door, he ordered Deloney's arrest before violence erupted in the city. From Slany's perspective, the weaver's complaint against the government could usher in

---

11 For reactions to writings about Queen Elizabeth in the early modern period, see Patterson, *Censorship and Interpretation* and Levin, *The Heart and Stomach of a King*, especially pp. 116–18.

12 The pamphlet is titled *A New Charge Given By the Queen's Commandment, to All Justices of Peace, and all Mayors, Sheriffs, and All Principal Officers of Cities, Boroughs, and Towns Corporate, for Execution of Sundry Orders Published the Last Year for Stay of Dearth of Grain*. The pamphlet orders town officials to investigate any who might be hoarding grain, keep track of middlemen between producer and consumer, and be present at market to survey the dealings.

13 As Manning notes, protests about grain shortages "suggest a decline of popular confidence in the ability of the city magistrates to dispense justice in an even-handed manner" (*Village Revolts*, 206).

more widespread social protest. As Mihoko Suzuki has argued, what is remarkable about this episode, as well as other contemporaneous instances of insubordination, "is the apparent recognition by the apprentices themselves that they held common political interests as a collective" (29). While the printer and publisher were both jailed for their part in the production of the ballad, officials never apprehended Deloney. He apparently disappeared from London and may never have published another ballad, "scurrilous" or otherwise (Atkins, 367).

While the explicit subjects of Deloney's two publications were the silkweaving immigrants and the perilous grain shortage, they are implicitly concerned with the victims of those vexations, the English clothworkers. In both documents, Deloney suggests that the producers of England's most famous product suffered a grievous loss as a result of unwanted immigrants, grain shortages, and, most disturbingly, a government that should control those problems.[14] Threatened by laborers who would work for less money, the clothworkers found themselves using language which pitted "stranger" against "native" to defend what they saw as their rightful occupation. Deloney's complaints against the population of immigrant weavers indicate that native silkweavers felt that they were becoming replaceable by foreign immigrants who neither knew nor cared about the long and glorious tradition of English clothmaking. Deloney's plea to the immigrant churchmen was part of a general disgruntlement with foreign clothworkers who earlier in the century had been enthusiastically welcomed into England to help increase the production of cloth.[15] But while the English clothworkers embraced the commercial expansion of the trade, they also felt an increasing hostility toward the immigrants. Native clothworkers charged the immigrants with a multitude of transgressions including "producing inferior goods ... trading secretly with each other, sending their profits home ... and even conspiring against the state. It was also complained that they held themselves too much apart, and failed to share the secrets of their trade with the native population" (Goose, 271). The inflated accusations of the immigrants point to a growing anxiety regarding the foreign clothworker in England. The English clothworkers, first deeming the foreign clothworkers' presence as beneficial, came to see it as an usurpation of the national product and by extension a violation of the nation.

Similarly, Deloney's pamphlet on the grain shortages participated in a growing distress among clothworkers over poor harvests. Although grain shortages affected the nation's economy at large, communities of clothworkers were particularly devastated. Harvest fluctuations affected the demand for material goods, particularly textiles (Supple, 16). Beginning in 1594 torrential summer rains ruined crops. Clothworkers were hit from both ends: if they could not sell their cloth, neither

---

14 Like Deloney, I use the term "clothworker" loosely to describe anyone who is involved in the manufacture of cloth (including wool, kersies, and silk), from the carder to the dyer. "Clothworker" also more specifically refers to those workers particularly associated with the finishing of the wool production process such as fullers, dyers, and shearmen.

15 The English government and indeed the native clothworkers initially perceived the textile skills of immigrants from Flanders and the Netherlands as well as those of the Walloons as a fortunate expansion of the English broadcloth industry. See Goose, "The 'Dutch' in Colchester," p. 266.

could they buy their food. Although most riots were first preceded by an official appeal in writing, laborers who existed at a subsistence level resorted to sometimes violent disturbances to make their plight known to an uncaring government (Walter and Wrightson, 41). The majority of food riots in the 1590s occurred in large cloth-producing centers and the participants were mainly clothworkers (Sharp, 13). In the late 1590s, harvest failure, the throttling of the cloth trade abroad due to market closure as a result of conflict with Spain, and an absence of expendable income at home led clothworkers into what was regarded as a national crisis.

As a result of his ballad on the grain shortage and pamphlet against the foreign silkweavers, Deloney earned notoriety amongst a readership he had never targeted—government officials. Strype posits that certain "ballads" and "libels" written during the late sixteenth century reflected "boldly and seditiously upon the Government, particularly in the case of a Dearth: often against the Strangers that came and settled here, and followed their trades: which the Apprentices and others took grievously" (Stow, 333). In his focus on complaints against "dearth" and "strangers," Strype may certainly refer to Deloney's two illicit publications. While Deloney's "libels" might have earned him a place in the *Survey of London*, his discontent was indicative of the frustrations among clothworkers at large. Like many other silkweavers, Deloney's profession was disrupted, if not altogether halted, by the growing crisis of the 1590s. According to Thomas Nashe, Deloney was driven to poverty by the "silencing of his looms" in 1596 (84).[16] However, Nashe indicates that Deloney would suvive the times of difficulty because he "hath rime inough for all myracles." While Deloney was weaving silk in the 1590s, he was also writing ballads; he was, after all, not just a silkweaver, but a "Balletting Silke-weaver" (Nashe, 84). The conjunction of these two types of work underscores Deloney's unique position as a writer of imaginative texts who attempts to transform, even as he questions, the state of the cloth industry.

"A Faithful Unity": The House that Jack Built

That Deloney most likely never published another ballad after 1596 suggests that the depression in the industry as well as his two recent scrapes with the London authorities might well have changed the nature of his work. Deloney's next literary effort, *Jack of Newbury*, reconciles the two careers of weaving and writing that had ended in disappointment. While many clothworkers turned to rioting and seizing grain as a

---

16 Nashe jokes that Deloney's privation forced him to resort to drinking "carded ale" (84). While Nashe refers to ale which has been mixed with other substances to make it cheaper, his joke is also a reference to Deloney's profession—wool cloth had to be "carded," or pulled with a carding implement—which had also been debased by external influences. Another contemporary writer is less generous towards Deloney and may point to his scrapes with the law. In *Defence of Conny-Catching*, Greene apologizes for the low subject matter of his text, which he likens to "triviall trinkets and threedbare trash." Greene sees the Elizabethan underworld as a subject more befitting of "T.D. whose braines beaten to the yarking up of Ballades, might more *lawfully* have glaunst at the quaint conceites of conny-catching and cross-biting" (A4r).

form of protest in the face of an unsympathetic government, Deloney turned to prose narrative. Whereas the looting of grain carts and the physical violence of rioting was a destructive display of discontent, Deloney's writing becomes an instructive form of protest, one that aims to engender a new vision of the English clothworkers as a cohesive group of individuals. In response to the perceived government passivity to the clothworkers' crisis in the late 1590s, Deloney creates an idealized version of a nation where workers are revered.[17] In *Jack of Newbury*, Deloney envisions an England whose past as well as future relies on the interests of merchants and laborers.

Deloney's focus on the cloth industry also presents an industry historically important to England's vision of itself. Hearkening back to the past by "rais[ing] out of the dust of forgetfulnesse a most famous and worthie man," the weaver John Winchcombe, Deloney lends historical import to his tale (Deloney, 3). By emphasizing that Jack is *both* "famous" *and* forgotten, Deloney indicates the tension in the position of his own fellow clothworkers. In *Jack of Newbury* Deloney presents the cloth industry as an English institution whose workers are to be valued. This sentiment would have resonated with the specific class of laborers adversely affected by recent economic troubles and yet crucial to the economic health of the nation.

The struggles that faced clothworkers in the late 1590s are rewritten in *Jack of Newbury* as a story of a prosperous and hopeful English community of rural clothworkers. In telling his story, Deloney looks to the rural past in order to challenge the urban present. Deloney chooses to position his vision of the cloth industry in the thriving early decades of the sixteenth century.[18] That Deloney shows us a portrait of an industrious and successful cloth industry with a diligent leader does not mean, however, that he conceives of his own culture of clothworkers in the same way. By considering the relationship between his earlier writings that criticize government policy and his literary work, we cannot ignore the stake he had in the fate of his fellow clothworkers and we cannot help but see that Deloney's text is a bold critique of the challenges faced by the community of workers in the 1590s. Deloney's text reconstructs the image of his profession and its contributions to England and in so doing reveals the nation's very fissures. *Jack of Newbury* might be regarded as Deloney's metaphor, his myth of a rebuilt industry and a unified nation that stands in opposition to the threatening realities faced by his fellow clothworkers.

That Deloney chose prose narrative as the mode in which to write his portrait of John Winchcombe is not altogether surprising given the rise in popularity of the prose romance and novella in the 1590s.[19] The Renaissance romances of Sidney, Greene, and Lodge signaled a shift in the reading public and reader demand rose

---

17 Insofar as Deloney emphasizes the work of the lower classes in his text, his story is consistent with what Richard Helgerson calls a narrative of "inclusion," which "works to broaden the national community" (*Forms of Nationhood*, 11).

18 Moreover, Deloney focuses on a producer of wool cloth rather than silk. The celebration of the wool industry would have had a more wide-ranging appeal because, as I argue throughout this book, wool was regarded as England's own special industry. Silk, on the other hand, was often looked on with suspicion and derision. See my Chapter 4.

19 For an excellent catalog of criticism on early modern fiction, see Relihan's Introduction to *Framing Elizabethan Fictions*.

during the last twenty-five years of the century (Salzman, 101). Following Sidney's *Arcadia* and Greene's *Pandosto*, Deloney also creates a fantastical tale at its center. Like Gascoigne's *The Adventures of Master F.J.*, Deloney's texts are set in the English countryside and include sexual escapades. Critics, however, have seen *Jack of Newbury* as ushering in a shift in prose narrative where the hero is from the middling class and his heroics are, however fantastical, within the epistemological framework of the reader. Paul Salzman recognizes the influence of romance, yet sees something distinct at work: "Deloney was bold enough to abandon the fantasy world of the chivalric romance and instead depict the world of the skilled artisan and successful merchant" (101).[20] Margaret Spufford asserts that Deloney's fiction engenders a new kind of "realistic novel" (238), while Theo Stemmler calls it the advent of the "bourgeois novel" (50). Deviating from the conventional prose romance, Deloney bases his character on a historical figure, inventing a "capitalist" hero (Beecher, 41).[21]

While *Jack of Newbury* is certainly distinct and novel in certain of its elements, it still shares many characteristics with earlier prose tales. Despite these commonalities, prose fiction as a generic category is extremely difficult to pin down. As Salzman pithily puts it, "the principal characteristic of Elizabethan fiction ... is its diversity" (6). It is precisely this diversity and slipperiness as a genre that has allowed prose fiction to fall by the critical wayside. According to Donald Beecher, these works have not yet received their due recognition for the "variety of their styles, the motivations of their authors, and the diversity of their social and ideological concerns" (11). And as Laurie Newcombe has recently argued, the diversity of the reading audience contributed to this sense of marginality: "The pleasant histories— chivalric romances and native Elizabethan romances ... that were constantly in press and reliable sellers—were singled out as cultural leftovers fit only for low-status readers, including women, servants and eventually children" (9). Constance Relihan sees the "non-artistic nature and frequently non-aristocratic subjects and characters" of prose fiction as central to its marginality as well (*Fashioning Authority*, 13). *Jack of Newbury*, with its multiple plots, characters, and chapters that can stand alone as mini-narratives, is a fine example of the diverse nature of prose and a text that caters to the diverse tastes of its audience. Deloney's fiction is structured in scenes, "often using each chapter as a narrative unit ... [and] often the end result is fragmentary" (Salzman, 108).

The "ambiguous and liminal nature" of Elizabethan fiction (Relihan, *Fashioning Authority*, 15) in general and the episodic structure of *Jack of Newbury* in particular may seem to detract from the potential efficacy in arguing for social change. However, the very diversity of the formal elements of the text echoes the wide ranging audience and results in an altogether inclusive narrative. The novel has been

---

20 See Simons for a discussion of Deloney's prose narratives in relation to medieval romance.

21 As Beecher argues, Deloney's works feature "the new mercantile man as hero surrounded by microcosmic utopias of production ... they are public personalities without inner lives, cheerful conquerors in the name of the common man, goal-oriented strivers after material wealth and social influence" (39).

regarded by theorists of nationalism as the genre that most prominently announces a nationalist agenda. Seen as "a hotch potch of the ostensible separate 'levels of style' corresponding to class; a jumble of poetry drama, newspaper report, memoir and speech," the novel "historically accompanied the rise of nations by objectifying the 'one, yet many' of national life, and by mimicking the structure of the nation, a clearly bordered jumble of languages and styles (Brennan, 51, 48). Like the nation that Deloney is presenting—one that includes children, women, courtiers and Kings—his narrative is imbued with the complexities one would expect when several, sometimes competing, forms are presented side by side.[22] Fantastical *and* real, historical *and* contemporary, *Jack of Newbury* embraces its audience and invites its readers to take it as they like it. And it is precisely the episodic structure that enables a radical reading of the text. The subplot chapters, resembling jestbooks in their tone and plots, may be compartmentalized by the reader away from the primary narrative of Jack's advancement and tribulations as a cloth maker, lending greater import to these scenes. The jestbook chapters, however, allow the text as a whole never to be too heavy-handed in its didacticism. The result is a celebration *and* critique of the cloth industry, a largely sympathetic portrayal of the clothworker who, although fallen on hard times, may find a model for working and living in Jack.

Deloney's project of glorifying the English clothworkers and advancing their cause begins in the prefatory letter to his readers. He addresses the epistle to "all Famous Cloth workers in England," to whom he wishes "all happiness of life, prosperity and brotherly affection" (3).[23] The letter reveals Deloney's aim in *Jack of Newbury*, the adulation of the cloth trade and especially its workers, when he announces his subject: "Among all manuall Arts used in this Land, none is more famous for desert, or more beneficiall to the Commonwealth, than is the most necessarie Art of Cloathing. And therefore as the benefit therof is great, so are the professors of the same to be both loved and maintained" (3). Despite the crises facing the cloth industry in the 1590s, Deloney suggests a fantastic and flourishing trade. He begins with a letter addressed to the "famous," "happy," and "prosperous" clothworkers at a time when many were disenfranchised, despondent, and poverty-stricken. The fantasy of the cloth trade as a booming industry underscores the very bleak state of the industry of the 1590s and draws attention to the workers' sorry plight.

While the "Art of Cloathing" receives top billing in this letter, Deloney reveres the artisans behind the art for providing the sustenance of a nation: The "excellent ... commoditie" of cloth is that "which hath been, and yet is the nourishing of many thousands of poore People" (3). The country's clothiers are still those who provide jobs for the working poor. Deloney's admonition that the clothworkers are "*to be both loved and maintained*" suggests that the government has not given them their

---

22 For an interesting look at "opposing" generic forms in terms of nation formation, see Helgerson, *Forms of Nationhood*, pp. 7–8. For Helgerson, "every form ... depended for its meaning and its effect on its difference from some openly or latently competing form" (7).

23 While Deloney addresses his epistle to the clothworkers, his audience was certainly broader. *Jack of Newbury* was reprinted no less than eight times in twenty-three years (Stevenson, *Praise and Paradox*, 217). The book outsold almost all other fictional texts in the seventeenth century (Stevenson, 126).

due respect, the very project proposed by Deloney in the offensive publication of 1595 (my emphasis). *Jack of Newbury* will highlight the people behind the looms, the workers who labor long and arduously to create the perfect commodity for England. To do this, Deloney writes for a common audience about matters near to their own experiences. He tells his readers that he writes "in a plain and humble manner, that it may be the better understood of those for whose sake I take pains to compile it, that is for the well minded Clothiers, that herein they may behold the great worship and credit which men of this trade have in former time come to" (3).[24] Again, Deloney emphasizes that contemporary clothworkers—a group of men whose simplicity prompts him to write plainly—have not been given the "credit" that they deserve, the credit that their historic predecessors have been given. Importantly, the clothworkers to whom he specifically speaks are "in England." He ends his letter by "commend[ing]" the clothworkers "to the most high God; who ever increase, in all perfection and prosperous estate, the long honoured trade of English Clothiers" (3). The clothworkers' virtues are to be acknowledged by England's most supreme authority: God shall see that the clothworkers aim to further the nation's "honoured trade" and come to represent all that is "perfect" and "prosperous" about England. Because no product is "more beneficial to the commonwealth" than cloth, Deloney makes clear that to value the clothworkers is to value England. These workers, he suggests, are at stake in the very definition of the nation.

One important way Deloney shows the state of the cloth industry is by imagining—and to a certain extent inventing—ideal working conditions. Deloney refers back to John Winchcombe's early sixteenth century, a time most closely linked to the guild system, and imposes on it a large workshop system and in so doing creates a utopian work environment.[25] His "house" is at once workshop and domestic space, large cottage industry and intimate center of production. With no analogous systems existing in Elizabethan England, Deloney forces his readers to *imagine* Jack's workshop, further pushing them towards a communal fantasy quite separate from their economic realities. Jack, the master of production, is experienced with and intimately tied to the product on which his employees work as well as to the employees themselves. Jack's beginnings as an apprentice to a wealthy clothier suggest his ties to manual labor. His own success—his swift rise from apprentice to journeyman to master of a large production workshop—would likely have left those of his audience who were themselves journeymen in awe.[26] While Jack keeps his

---

24 Although cloth historians agree that "clothier" designated one who was in control of the cloth manufacturing process, here Deloney uses "clothworker" and "clothier" somewhat interchangeably. "Clothier" was also used in the period to indicate "draper," or retail seller of cloth. For a thorough discussion of the role of the sixteenth century clothier in the Kentish Weald, see Zell, Chapter 7, *Industry and the Countryside*.

25 As Ladd has written, Deloney "tends to write the gild hierarchy out of the process" of the control of the trade (986). Despite the fantastical description of Jack of Newbury's workshop, it is important to note that the cloth industry in Newbury was remarkably thriving. See Money, p. 25.

26 Margolies claims that "the increasing amount of time and money required for the masterpiece prevented many journeymen from becoming masters themselves while enabling their masters to keep them as wage-earners" (145–6).

workers in the position of wage-earner indefinitely, his meteoric rise to the top of his profession allows for a working class fantasy and reveals the tensions at work in the text. As a "clothier," Jack is neither artisan nor merchant; rather he is an employer of the various artisans who labored with his materials (Lipson, *History of the Woollen*, 72).

Deloney's Jack represents a kind of clothier who owned and was in control of the production of his product, an employer who was disappearing if not already vanished from the contemporary cloth producing scene. In his civic pageant, *Himatia-Poleos* (1614), Anthony Munday describes the bygone cloth producer: "the Wooll-winder ... did carde and spinne his wooll, then weave it into cloth, full, rowe, sheare, dresse, and dye it, and sell it afterwards in his shop, performing all these severall offices thereto, by himselfe and servants" (73). Munday describes a system of production in which the clothier-worker owns both the materials and the instruments of production and sells the product of his labors. He laments that this form of producing woollen broadcloath has given way to a production process that is fractured by its many disparate points of production: the production system "hath branched it self into divers other Companies, and of one entire Trade or Mysterie, is become many" (2). The unified workshop that Deloney presents subscribes to the ideal of "one entire Trade," which knits together the industry such that the workers themselves form a unified workforce, the face of the national product.[27]

To show the benefits of the clothworkers' productivity, Deloney constructs an idealized work environment that contrasts sharply with what his readers would have been familiar. Deloney represents Jack's workshop as a "great housould" where his laborers work on all aspects of the cloth-producing process. Jack's "Ware-houses" are filled with several rooms under one great roof where the workers perform the acts of weaving, fulling, shearing, and dying of several types of cloth. Some rooms are filled "with wooll, some with flockes, some with woad and madder,[28] and some with broad cloathes and kersies readie dyed and drest, besides a great number of others, some stretched on the Tenters, some hanging on poles, and a great many more lying wet in other places" (28). Deloney's presentation of Jack's workshop, however, would have seemed unusual to his audience. Successful weavers in the late sixteenth century would possess three or four looms but larger manufacturing centers were rare (Kerridge, *Textile Manufactures*, 196).[29] Further, cloth production during Deloney's time relied on the "putting out system," which was based on the

---

27 Munday's nostalgia for the bygone days of the cloth producer who worked "by himself" is also felt by John May, the cloth tax collector to James I. May laments the passing of the age where clothmakers were part of a community of men who, at the same time that they worked independently, belonged to a brotherhood of laborers all working for a common purpose (4). For a longer discussion of Munday and May, see Chapter 6.

28 Two types of dyestuffs.

29 As Zell has shown, in the late sixteeth and early seventeeth century most of the wealth surrounding the cloth industry was in the hands of a very few large scale clothiers. Zell concludes that the reason that large scale clothiers had such an advantage over small masters was, among others, because they could operate their business on a system of debt, whereby customers would be able to pay them three to six months after the delivery of a product. Smaller masters had to rely on selling their cloth for ready money (Zell, "Credit").

distribution of wool by clothiers to spinners, weavers, and cloth finishers. Once the particular labor was completed, the clothier would pass the product on to the laborer in the next stage of production. While the cloth trade in the 1590s was fractured in its production processes, Deloney represents the past industry as a unified and flourishing one in order to imagine future prosperity for England's cloth trade.

This fantasy of production is nowhere more clearly described in the text than in the description of the laborers of Jack's house, which Deloney writes in ballad form. While giving his future father-in-law a tour of the premises, Jack shows him "all his servants at worke": "Within one room ... There stood two hundred Loomes ... Two hundred men, the truth is so / Wrought in these Loomes all in a rowe" (26).[30] The two hundred men and looms suggest the immense space of the workshop, which is further amplified by the fact that by each loom "a pretty boy, / Sate making quils" (26). In a nearby room, separated from the men, a hundred women "Were carding hard with joyfull cheere," while in an adjacent room two hundred maidens "all day did spin" (27).[31] The fantastical number of men, women, and boy workers—700— is augmented by 150 children "wool pickers," fifty "shearmen," eighty "Rowers," forty dyers, and twenty fullers (27).[32] In addition to the thousand-plus clothworkers Jack employs, he also keeps a full kitchen staff so that his workers can live on the premises like a "great houshold and family" (28). Jack's workshop is not necessarily striking for the size or the amount of production that takes place there—curiously, we are never told the specifics of that—but rather for the sheer multitude of people at work together and the variety of production. Perhaps even more stunning is the notion that the workers in Jack's factory are content; the boys make quills with "mickle joie;" the carders work "hard" while they sing with "joyfull cheere."[33] Jack's

---

30 According to Kerridge, the historical John Winchcombe was a kersey clothier rather than a weaver of broadcloth. Kerseys were wool cloths that were lighter, narrower, and less costly than traditional broadcloths. This is a minor fabrication when compared to the fantasy of the workshop: "no building in the world could have accomodated such a long row of looms" (*Textile Manufactures*, 192).

31 For a discussion of the gendered role of spinning in the early modern period, see Jones and Stallybrass, Chapters 4 and 5. See Alice Clark, Chapter 4, for a discussion of women's labor in the early modern textile industry. In the Middle Ages, women contributed significantly to the profession of weaving; by the sixteenth century, however, their work and that of children was confined to spinning because they were ostensibly not strong enough to operate the heavy looms (Alice Clark, 102–3).

32 A "Quil" is a piece of reed or other hollow stem on which yarn is wound; "Wool picker" most likely refers to the activity of separating debris from the sheep's wool once it has been cut from the animal. See my Introduction for a description of the various jobs referred to here.

33 Interestingly, the workers most demonstrative in their joy are the quillers, who are children, and the carders and spinners, occupations generally associated during the early modern period with women. The traditionally "male" clothworking jobs—weaving, shearing, and fulling—are taken more seriously here. See Mesa-Pelly, p. 87. Linton suggests that the women's singing "trivializes their labor, turning them into entertainment for the men" (68). The text suggests, however, that the male and female workers are separated in different rooms of the warehouse. See Linton and Suzuki for a discussion of *Jack of Newbury* as a narrative of masculinity and female subjugation.

workplace is enormous at the same time as it retains an intimacy associated with the domestic household. Importantly, this notion of "domestic" space suggests the workshop's status as *both* home and factory. By portraying the nation's industry through a place where laborers both live and produce, Jack's workshop represents an idealized vision of an England where cloth workers *are*, as he hopes in his opening letter, both "loved and maintained." The solidarity felt among the clothworkers in Jack's workshop, the love they feel towards him, and their high level of productivity, points to a utopian England at the same time as it reminds the readers of their own industry that was multi-faceted, plagued with problems of disunity, and threatened by the foreign other. The nation in *Jack of Newbury*, then, becomes an imagined community for Deloney's fellow clothworkers, one they may envision and to which they may aspire.

If Jack's workshop is a strange world of cloth production compared to that of his contemporary readers, it is made familiar through the very form in which he describes it—the ballad. Deloney, who spent several years of his life writing ballads to supplement his income as a silkweaver, certainly knew the popularity with which ballads were received. The description of Jack's astonishing workshop in ballad form makes it more imaginable on two counts: first, the ballad form, which often claims to refer to "actual" historical instances, gives Jack of Newbury's workshop a grounded referent in John Winchcombe's past. Secondly, the ballad creates a communal sense through its very form. While the ballad form may seem to locate the narrative as an exaggerated folklore, the mundaneness of the recounted activities—weaving, spinning, carding—return the narrative to the world of the everyday. Ballads, a cheap form of fiction, would have been accessible to a large portion of the working class audience.[34] Further, one needed not be literate to enjoy the ballads—they were very often read aloud and generally were set to music. Because Deloney's ballad is about clothworkers who are busy working at a time when so many clothmakers were not, it allows for a concrete example of what a nation of busy workers would look like. This fantasy transports the readers away from their own circumstances and enables them to imagine the possibility of a unified national industry supported by a community of clothworkers who contribute to the well being of England.

It is this emphasis on the national contribution on the part of the clothworkers perhaps more than anything else that moves *Jack of Newbury* from simply a nostalgic work by a disgruntled weaver to nationalistic narrative of activist politics.[35] As a way to legitimize the national contribution of clothworkers, Deloney emphasizes the significance of Jack's military efforts. Like a great feudal landlord, Jack gathers forces from within the ranks of his workshop to help England's efforts against Scotland.

---

34 For an introduction to the ballad see Neuberg, *Popular Literature* and Louis Wright, *Middle Class Culture*.

35 According to Margolies, Jack's labors "are a public service done by a man who puts the welfare of his country above other considerations" (149). The idealization of this labor, however, subordinates the work of government to the work of the weaver. As Dorsinville argues, "Jack's world, or kingdom, is pitted against the court, the better to manifest its superiority based upon the cardinal virtue of manual labor" (236). Jordan, however, sees such displays of Jack's superiority as role-playing.

While King Henry VIII "was making warre in *France* ... *James*, king of *Scotland*, falsly breaking his oath invaded *England* with a great army and did much hurt upon the borders" (30). Although Jack was commanded to gather six men "to meete the Queene in *Buckinghamshire*, who was there raising a great power to go against the faithlesse king of Scots," he shows up having gathered fifty men in "white coates, and red caps with yellowe Feathers ... fiftie armed men on foot with pikes, and fiftie shot in white coats also" (30). In a display of great loyalty, Jack humbles himself before the queen and emphasizes his pride in his profession:

> Most Gracious Queene quoth hee, Gentleman I am none, nor the sonne of a gentleman, but a poore Clothier, whose lands are his Loomes, having no other Rents but what I get from the backs of little sheepe, nor can I claime any cognisance but a wodden shuttle. Nevertheless, most gracious Queene, these my poore servants and my self, with life and goods are ready at your Majesties commaund, not onely to spend our blouds, but also to lose our lives in defence of our King and Countrey. (31)

Jack is the model subject, one who would lay down his life and the lives of his men to serve the king he loves. His humble yet highly articulate assertion of his position reminds the queen that he has nothing but his life to give: no lands, no rents, no cognisance.[36] A lack of "cognisance" here refers to Jack's lack of an emblem distinguishing the retainers of a noble house. Instead of a cognisance, Jack claims he only possesses a "shuttle" or a weaving instrument. It is Jack's "shuttle," however, that *is* his "cognisance" in both senses of the word: his weaving implement is both his emblem (it represents him) and his knowledge (it is through the production of cloth that he knows the world). Jack's display prompts the queen to assert that he is "though a Clothier by trade, yet a Gentleman by condition, and a faithful subject in heart" (32). On the other hand, Jack's astonishing effort—bringing along 144 more men than required—may be also seen as a vaunting display of his wealth. As Laura Stevenson suggests, Jack's effort "shows the queen that he is not just the most loyal, but the most powerful man in Berkshire" (115). These two attributes, loyalty and power, are in tension with one another as Jack usurps the function of the crown by raising a private army at the same time as he represents himself as intensely loyal to that crown. Deloney revises the role of the faithful subject to make space for one who also contributes significantly to the nation. Rather than "lands," Jack possesses "loomes" and it is with these looms that he has become wealthy enough to contribute to the nation's well being and security.

Despite the improbability that there was ever such a meeting between John Winchcombe and Katherine of Aragon, this display of mutual reliance was common even in the late sixteenth century (Lawlis, *Novels*, n. 350). Indeed, as Stevenson suggests, Elizabeth "was increasingly dependent on the loans of London merchants as her reign progressed, and the court, like the country, profited from England's trade" (107). Profit for the crown, however, did not necessarily lead to respect for

---

36 Lawlis points out that class distinctions are reversed in the formal elements of the prose in *Jack of Newbury*: "As if to reinforce his democratic vision he has persons of the lower or middle class speak in exalted language while persons of the upper class speak plainly" (*Apology*, 11).

the laborers, and the government was not always sensitive to the precarious position of the cloth industry when it called on the trade companies to lend financial support. By inserting this episode, Deloney foregrounds the common interest which binds the court and the clothworkers. That is, the continued health of the cloth industry relied on the notion that the clothworkers needed the support of the crown in order to prosper.

While Queen Katherine has given Jack and his followers her utmost approval, it is not until Jack has the attention of King Henry VIII that the clothworkers can be fully glorified. Henry comes to Berkshire on a progress and in anticipation of the king's arrival Jack clothes thirty of his men in "blewe coates, faced with Sarcenet,"[37] while he dresses himself "in a plain russet coate, a paire of white kersie breeches, without welt or gard" (35).[38] Jack ornaments his men in showy colors and expensive fabrics to demonstrate his fortune and benevolence toward his servants; their clothes signify that they are deprived of nothing. At the same time, his own attire, without ornamentation and made from traditional homespun cloth, announces his humble position in the face of his king. Yet while his clothes may assert his humility, they also tell another story: The fabrics from which his suit is made are the same fabrics that were in the sixteenth century generally associated with the English broadcloth industry: heavy, coarse, and simply made textiles. Not only does Jack labor for the clothes on his back, but he chooses decidedly English stuffs.

The king sees Jack and several of his men at a distance with their swords drawn as they defend "a company of Ants from the furious wrath of the Prince of Butterflies" (36). What ensues is a series of actions on Jack's part that at once humble him to the king and suggest contempt for his authority. When asked by the king's messenger to go before the king, Jack declines: "his Grace hath a horse, and I am on foote, therefore will him to come to mee" (36). This gesture of defiance is coupled with his argument that he would never leave his people in a time of potential invasion: "while I am away, our enemies might come and put my people in hazard as the Scots did *England*, while our King was in *France*" (36). Referring to his own involvement in the protection of England during the time of the battle at Flodden Field, Jack admonishes his sovereign for being an absent king. This, however, is not the message he asks the herald to give to the king. Rather than sending this criticism of the Henry's policies, Jack appeals to the king's sensibilities as defender of his people: "and tell his Majestie, hee might think me a very bad Governour that would walk aside upon pleasure, and leave my people in peril" (36). The king agrees to approach and upon his arrival near Jack and his "troops," they "put up all their weapons, and with a joyful crie flung up their caps in token of victorie" (36).

---

37 "A very fine and soft silk material" (*OED*).

38 Money, historian of Newbury, suggests that King Henry and his court were actually at Newbury in 1516. Wolsey was probably with the King because there is evidence that Wolsey wrote a letter on 10 September 1516 from Newbury to Sir Richard Jerningham (26). See Tribble for a reading of *Jack of Newbury* in the context of royal progresses. In 1578, Queen Elizabeth visited Norwich and was presented with a pageant and shown examples of the immigrant artisans at work spinning and knitting. According to Priestly, "her retinue brought plague and infected the town and especially the foreigners" (11).

Lest King Henry think that he is being insulted by Jack's impetuosity, "Jack of Newberie with all his servants fell on their knees, saying: God save the King of *England*, whose sight hath put our foes to flight, and brought great peace to the poore labouring people" (36). Jack's performance reveals his somewhat disingenuous humility. His behavior prior to this moment is by any standards potentially treasonous; he refuses to come to the king when asked for and insults the king's policies. Yet Jack's ultimate actions leave Henry with the impression of Jack as a true and honest subject: he prostrates himself before and exalts the king in the name of the working poor.[39] While Jack's final action seems to consolidate the king's authority over his subjects, his previous behavior—especially his comments regarding the absent king, which could be perceived as subversive—are kept from the king. And while Jack's self-association with the laboring poor places him in the king's eyes as a harmless yet productive subject, his great wealth and stake in what happens to his trade gives him a certain power. Any potential for subversion, though, might seem to be undercut by Jack's subsequent humility. Jack explains that he

> yeeld unto his Majestie all my sovereign rule and dignitie, both of life and goods, casting up my weapons at his feete, to intend[s] to be no longer a prince, because the majestie of a King hath eclipst my glorie ... and humbly I doe any service wherein his Grace shall command me. (37)

Jack's renunciation of sovereignty to the King is a gesture of deference. And, yet, it is surprising in that it suggests that Jack possessed any sovereignty at all. Jack thus presents conflicting versions of himself: he is at once a prince and a poor laborer; he worships the king at the same time as he is an outspoken critic of the King's policies; he is both subject to a sovereign and himself a sovereign.[40] Jack cannot then be confined to the role of either loyal subject or insurgent; he is both.

The episode in which the King comes to Newbury would certainly have resonated for the readers who would have recognized the King's companion, the sycophantic Cardinal Wolsey, Henry's Lord Chancellor, as the butterfly from which Jack is defending his ants. The numerous insults that Jack hurls in the direction of Wolsey seem to go unnoticed by the king. Jack tells the king that their reason for defending the Ants against the Prince of the Butterflies is because "the Butterflie was much misliked, but few durst say anie thing to him because of his golden apparel: who through sufferance grewe so ambitious and malapert, that the poore Ant could no sooner get an egge into her nest, but he would have it away" (37). The king, seemingly oblivious to the implications of Jack's fable replies simply, "[t]hese were proud Butterflies" (37). Jack's veiled comments recall the Lord Chancellor's excessive display of wealth as well as his outrageous tax policies during the 1520s. Picking up on this doubleness and "gall'd by the Allegorie of the Ants," Wolsey suggests to the King that Jack "hath not stucke this day to undoo himself onely

---

39 See Ladd for a discussion of Deloney's engagement with debates over poverty, especially vis-à-vis the guild system.

40 As Stevenson suggests, while "Jack's princeliness is allegorical fiction, his power is not ... He says he is a poor clothier, but this too is simply a pose. 'Poor' in this context loses its standard meaning, and 'clothier' comes very close to meaning 'lord'" (124).

to become famous by receiving of your Majestie" (39). Rightfully suspicious that Jack's allegory was directed against him, Wolsey is less generous in his impression of Jack as he suggests that Jack glorifies the King to advance his own reputation. By staging the Ants' defense of their hill from the Butterflies, however, Deloney is less interested in revealing Jack's desire to "become famous," than revealing Wolsey's own ambition and impudence.[41]

Understanding Jack's accusations perfectly, Wolsey claims that Jack, "being King of Ants, do carry a great grudge to the Butterflies" (37). The King of Ants' "grudge" against the Prince of Butterflies does not merely stem from the Butterfly's vanity and ambition, but also from the power that the Butterfly has over the Ants: Deloney's criticism emphasizes the grievous position of the Ants, the symbol for the clothworkers. In a peculiar departure in the text, where Deloney's tone changes from that of storyteller to that of chronicler, he describes the Lord Chancellor's vanity as well as his devastating foreign policy regarding the clothworkers:

> This Cardinall was at that time Lord Chancellor of *England* and a wonderfull proud Prelate, by whose means great variance was set betwixt the King of *England* and the French King, the Emperour of *Almaine*, and divers other Princes of Christendom, whereby the trafficke of those Merchants was utterly forbidden, which bred a general woe through *England*, especially among Clothiers: insomuch as having no sale for their cloath, they were faine to put away many of their people which wrought for them. (38)

Deloney suggests that clothworkers have fallen into poverty as a result of the market closures abroad, the outcome of Wolsey's wars on European countries. By removing the reader from the imaginative story into a larger historical narrative, Deloney forces us to consider the oppression faced by the clothworkers. The disregard that Wolsey has for the clothworkers is reflected in their fate: they are simply "put away" like useless instruments. Deloney expands the ramifications of these wars: because the cloth industry has fallen into a depression, "a general woe" is felt throughout the nation. We find a source for his complaint in a 1528 episode in Holinshed's *Chronicles*, describing the effects of the wars with Spain on the cloth merchants: "the trade of merchandize was in maner fore-let here in England, and namelie the clothes laie on their hands, whereby the commonwealth suffered great decaie, and great numbers of spinners, carders, tuckers, and such other that lived by clothworking, remained idle, to their great impoverishment" (735). The "common people" view the foreign conflicts as separate from their own cause: this war is only "between the emperour and the king."[42] Not able to sell their cloth, the once valuable commodity becomes ultimately worthless. Remaining "idle," the clothworkers are neither eating nor are they fighting for the crown. Holinshed suggests, and Deloney later echoes, that these wars affect not only the clothworkers: "the commonwealth" as a whole "suffered great decaie." As cloth goes, so goes the nation.

---

41 See McKeon, p. 225, for a reading of this passage.

42 Just before this, Holinshed suggests that during the reign of Henry VIII the masses were given relief in the form of "grain" from the continent during times of dearth. Similarly, large quantities of grain from the Baltic region were imported to England during the harvest failures of 1594–96. See Davis, *English Overseas Trade*, p. 18.

Replicating almost exactly the language of Holinshed later in his narrative, Deloney emphasizes the gravity of the situation that the clothworkers in *Jack of Newbury* face:

> By meanes of the warres our King had with other countries, many Merchaunt strangers were prohibited from comming to *England*, and also our owne Merchants (in like sort) were forbidden to have dealing with *France*, or the *Low-countries*: by meanes whereof, the Clothiers had most of their cloth lying on their hands, and that which they sold was at so low a rate, that the money scarcely paid for the wooll, and workemanship. (56)

Considering Deloney's earlier disgruntlement with foreign weavers, it may seem surprising that he laments the prohibition of "merchant strangers" in England. This complaint, however, is only to point out the true victim of the wars: the domestic cloth industry, while those involved in England's national trade suffer the effects. Despite earlier episodes in which Jack and his men pledge eternal duty to the king, here the clothworkers are not participants in his wars. Loyalty to the cloth industry, then, precedes loyalty to the crown.

Deloney's interest in referring back to earlier struggles between the clothworkers and their government reveals the extent to which clothworkers were personally invested in the crown's military action abroad. The late 1580s to the 1590s— the very years Deloney was most likely active as a member of the Silkweavers' Company—were similarly marked with depression in the cloth market due to wars with Spain (Peter Clark, 49). Though by the late sixteenth century the entrepôt at Antwerp had been in decline for many years, trade to the continent had been brisk, especially since the advent of the new draperies. Conflict with Spain during the 1580s and 1590s halted this healthy industry and drove many of the trade, including silkweavers, into poverty. While the dearth of grain as a result of disastrous harvests during the late 1590s surely compounded the poverty of domestic clothworkers, it was, as Outhwaite puts it, "only one of a succession of problems, and the duration of this whole period of difficulty coincided generally with the years in which England was in open conflict with Spain" (23).

The argument with Cardinal Wolsey, historically as well as in *Jack of Newbury*, reached a happy conclusion in a relatively short time: within two months Wolsey agreed to exclude Antwerp from the embargo and later a formal truce was reached (H.C. Bindoff, 123). Deloney dramatizes this conclusion to suggest that social protest on the part of the clothworkers had direct effect on this reversal of policy. In a letter to "all the chief clothing townes in England," Jack calls for a unified front of clothworkers to combat the depressed state of the industry:

> having a taste of the generall griefe, and feeling ... the extreamitie of these times, I fell into consideration by what meanes we might best expell these sorrowes, and recover our former commodity ... I found that nothing was more needfull herein then a faithfull unity among our selves. This sore of necessity can no way be cured but by concord ... Dear friends, consider that our Trade will mainetaine us, if wee will uphold it, and there is nothing base, but that which is basely used. (57)

The letter appears to be a romanticized re-narrativization of his letter of 1595. By drawing on his experience of writing the letter from the silkweavers, Deloney shows that words can indeed mobilize a dedicated community. While Deloney's letter landed him in Newgate, Jack's letter prompts a "faithful unity" of clothworkers—112 men representing the country's 60,000 clothworkers—to go to London and express their complaints to their sovereign. Indeed, Jack claims the clothworkers will not attain relief unless they themselves make an effort to protest their condition. Unlike the government officials who arrested Deloney in June 1595, the king, who comes to realize that the clothworkers are indispensable to the commonwealth, agrees that they shall have their "griefs redressed" (57). Believing the clothworkers to be "in the number of the best Common wealths men," the king delivers a petition to Wolsey. Remembering his quarrel with Jack and further insulted by Jack's reference to the Cardinal's lowly birth, Wolsey arrests him and all the other protesting clothworkers.[43] Finally, Wolsey grants the clothworkers their suit "so that in short space, Clothing againe was very good, and poore men as well set on work as before" (60).

In the world of *Jack of Newbury* clothworkers may complain about the impoverished state of the industry and gain the king's ear. They may write letters to mobilize, protest the sovereign's foreign policies, and still be deemed by the king "the chief Yeomen of our Land" (58). They may insult the Lord Chancellor's familial background and still be forgiven. All this may occur in the narrative because the crown values the cloth industry above all others. Yet, while the world of *Jack of Newbury* is one in which the king lauds Jack, the emblematic clothworker, it is the esteem of his fellow clothworkers that brings Jack his fame and consolidates his status as "the famous and worthy clothier of England." The text questions the sovereign as the site for the nation's unity in favor of an alternative commonwealth in which the *wealth* of the nation is founded upon the *common* people. Because the labor of the clothworkers becomes that which is most effective in defining England as a unified community, the text rejects the policies of the sovereign as being able to do the same. We might read this as a challenge to Deloney's sovereign, Queen Elizabeth and her counselors who were, at best, ambivalent to the clothworker's plight. The irony of Jack's exclamation, "God save the King of *England*, whose sight hath put our foes to flight, and brought great peace to the poore labouring people" (36), would not have been lost on the laborers of the 1590s who, although "poore," were not at "peace." Perhaps Elizabeth's father (or at least the representation of him) could bring peace to the laboring poor, but she has been ineffectual in this regard.

Deloney's text is a call for clothworkers to understand that their difficulties are similar to the plight of the workers in his story. His prefatory letter underscores that the "professors" of the "most necessarie Art of Clothing" need to be both "loved and maintained" (3). Deloney's text is a logical extension of his pamphlet of 1595 and his

---

43 Jack refers to Wolsey's status as a son of a butcher when he jokes that "if my Lord Cardinals father had been no hastier in killing of Calves then he is in dispatching of poore mens sutes, I doubt he had never worne a myter" (59). Wolsey, hearing a report of this slight, believes Jack is "infected with *Luthers* spirit" (59). See Ladd, pp. 989–90, for a discussion of the Reformation in the context of the shifting guild system. See also McKeon, p. 226, on this passage.

ballad of 1596 in that he is genuinely interested in promoting the betterment of the clothworkers of England. That his narrative is fiction should not cloud the aims of his project: to remind a government concerned with national economic prosperity that it could not take the producers of this prosperity, the clothworkers, for granted. For Deloney, text and textiles are intimately linked in that they help the reader to imagine a future beyond the status quo. Deloney's narrative does not simply celebrate the work of the clothworkers; he presents them as effective and socially transformative members of a unified nation.

PART 2
The Circulation of Subjectivity in the Cloth Trade

Chapter 3

"Vente for our English Clothes": Promoting Early New World Expansion

The legend of Walter Raleigh spreading his cloak over a puddle so that Queen Elizabeth could cross it without getting wet first appeared in Thomas Fuller's *History of the Worthies of England* (1662), more than forty years after Raleigh's death. The tale famously demonstrates not only the civility with which courtiers treated their queen, but also the generosity with which Elizabeth reciprocated courtly favors:

> This captain Raleigh coming out of Ireland to the English court in good habit (his clothes being then a considerable part of his estate) found the queen walking, till meeting with a plashy place, she seemed to scruple going thereon. Presently Ralegh cast and spread his new plush cloak on the ground, whereon the queen trod gently, rewarding him afterwards with many suits, for his so free and seasonable tender of so fair a footcloth. (133)

The story of this most dramatic episode—which may or may not have taken place[1]—has come to symbolize the lengths to which courtiers would go for their queen and the sway that Elizabeth held over the men who served her and needed her patronage. Elizabeth's reported gift to Raleigh of "many suits" suggests both gifts of clothes (the passage underscores the "good habit" to which he was accustomed) and court positions. However magnanimous Elizabeth's gift of expensive clothing may have been, it certainly was not entirely selfless.[2] As a representative of the queen's court, Raleigh would need to display the best possible apparel as a reflection of his sovereign; the suits bound him to his queen. The reward of court suits also involved a reciprocal exchange. Raleigh, an unknown at court upon his arrival, proved his loyalty to the queen who, in turn, advocated and sponsored his overseas enterprises. The money for the expeditions would be exchanged for the gift of the glory of England, in the name of Elizabeth.

I take up the tale of the cloak not to discuss Elizabethan courtiers or even specifically Raleigh, but rather to examine what this story can teach us about the moment in England's history when it began to look to the New World as a site for expansion. In order to do this we must not dwell on whether the fantastic meeting

---

1   Fuller's editor, John Freeman, says that this story "is generally discredited, but Fuller's uncle Robert Townson then dean of Westminster and later bishop of Salisbury attended Ralegh in his last hours, and may very well have heard the story from Ralegh and passed it on to the young Fuller" (Fuller, n. 2, 133).

2   As Stallybrass points out, to be a member of a household, even the court, was to wear the livery of that household. Clothing was remarkably costly and was the major form of payment at court in early modern England. See pp. 291–2.

ever occurred, but instead look at the story as an allegory for a crucial period in early modern English culture. If we imagine that Raleigh was attempting to win the queen's favor so that she would agree to support his expeditions to the New World, then the cloak and puddle take on greater significance. Like the "plashy place" that Raleigh entreated Elizabeth to step over, Raleigh and other English adventurers in the late sixteenth century appealed to their queen to endorse expeditions across the Atlantic Ocean, which would be conducted in the name of England and for the glory of the queen. Elizabeth as head of state figuratively would be making the great leap across the Atlantic to the New World. The Atlantic, however, like the puddle, could not be crossed without material assistance. Just like the "footcloth" that Raleigh spread on the ground, adventurers needed the means to convince the queen to expand westward. The "material" that many adventurers and their propagandists used to implore the queen's crossing was English cloth.

In the first section of this book, I have argued that social protest served the important function of emphasizing the germane role that domestic wool and woollen cloth played in creating a sense of Englishness. The home industry in both sheep farming and broadcloth weaving was economically central for England, but it also created a national narrative that allowed for a more symbolic understanding of marketable goods. In this chapter, I turn from the production of cloth towards its circulation abroad. Once wool left England's shores, a new understanding of England's place in the world emerged. If, as I have argued, wool cloth was crucial to the definition of England's nationhood, then the export of the textile—whether that exportation was real or imagined—further consolidated this definition. If England's representative product was "out there," the foreign lands that imported the cloth became more legible and, as a result, less threatening. Further, the export of cloth to other nations necessarily forced English subjects to imagine themselves vis-à-vis an "other," thus creating a more keen sense of "self." And, finally, the notion that foreigners would use, wear, and ostensibly come to adore English wool allowed for a fantasy of dominance so crucial to the culture of cloth. The propaganda for England's westward enterprise, in particular, shows us how the economic and social pressures of expansion were crucially tied to the representation of textiles in print.

England's voyages to the New World are largely understood to have been made to bring glory to the nation and expand its role on the world stage. The desire to search for riches in the New World and establish colonies for England surely drove the interest of many venturers. However, the voyages could not be sent forth and the colonies could not be established without substantial material support. Men who were invested in early expansion schemes to the New World knew that their expeditions needed justification and many advocated these travels by arguing that such expansion would not only revive but significantly augment the ailing domestic cloth industry. In this chapter I focus on the early promotional writers of the westward enterprise who based their arguments for expeditions to and colonization of the New World on the material benefit it would bring England. The international cloth trade, which had faltered since the boom days of the mid-sixteenth century, needed to be radically reorganized to allow for the possibility of new trading ports. In insisting that England relied too heavily on European nations, particularly Spain, for their cloth trade, promoters of the New World enterprise were able to cast the largely unknown land as an alternative possibility for the expansion of the industry. Further, the authors of tracts arguing for colonization claimed that by planting in the New World the cloth industry would be revived, both through the resuscitation of ailing production at home and through the exploitation of potential New World products related to cloth production. The writings of men in the last quarter of the sixteenth century such as Richard Hakluyt the elder, George Peckham, Christopher Carleill, Thomas Harriot, and the man who represented them all in his massive *Principal Navigations, Voyages, Traffiques, and Discoveries of the English Nation*, the younger Richard Hakluyt, all looked to the expansion of the English cloth industry as a promise of voyages to the New World.

To be sure, economic gain could not be the sole argument for sea voyages. As Theodore Rabb reminds us in *Enterprise and Empire*, "[i]t was of prime importance that overseas activity began to take on the character of a national undertaking. Colonies, explorations, and new markets brought more than profits; they also enhanced England's prestige" (100). Along the same lines, Richard Helgerson argues that "national interest alone makes a commercial venture ... a fit subject for humanist eloquence and courtly patronage. It alone makes profit honorable" (*Forms of Nationhood*, 180). Proponents for westward expansion necessarily had to link economic promise to national promise. It is my argument that for these writers, justifying expeditions to the New World through glory for the nation and justifying the expeditions through an expansion of the cloth industry were not two separate endeavors. As I have argued in my introduction, the cloth industry was imbued with crucial significance for early modern culture that reached far beyond its role as a commodity of production and exchange. Cloth was not simply one product among many that might help England's economy; it was a symbol of the nation's cultural significance. To base arguments for national expansion to the New World on the growth of the cloth industry was not simply to reduce this enterprise to an economic level. Importantly, the argument for the growth of the cloth industry was also an argument for England's well-being. Economic success and the attendant cultural superiority over other European nations were in the service of national glory and were all among the benefits that advocates for New World exploration and settlement imagined that an expanded cloth industry could have for England.

Fueled by competition with Spain to expand to the New World at the same time as it defined itself against Spain's bloody conquests, England found what seemed to be a benevolent form of colonization—bringing the gift of cloth to the New World.[3] Just as the promoters saw the New World as an abundant land that would provide the home industry with products, so did they imagine a vast population that would want to enter into trade relations. But more than a commodity by which England could

---

3   The commonplace suspicion that Spain's New World expansion was one of bloody tyranny was solidified by Bartolome de la Casa's *A Short Account of the Destruction of the Indies*, which gave the English ample grounds on which to base their colonial efforts. For a discussion of English expansion vis-à-vis Spain, see Helgerson, *Forms of Nationhood*; Scanlan, *Colonial Writing and the New World*; Mancall, *Envisioning America*, and Bess, "Hakluyt's *Discourse of Western Planting*." For a discussion of the importance of acknowledging Spain's role in early colonial efforts on the part of modern scholars, see Fuchs, "Imperium Studies."

expand its coffers, wool was the voyagers' representation of their nation to the indigenous peoples of America. As Stephen Greenblatt has pointed out, European contact with indigenous people "is continually mediated by representations; indeed contact itself ... is very often contact between representatives bearing representations" (*Marvelous Possessions*, 119). The voyagers went to the New World as representatives of their nation and queen and sought to bring with them that which signified the wealth of their nation—the gift of cloth. In order to imagine how the industry might expand, the adventurers had to project an interest in English cloth on the part of the native population, thereby attaching to them a desire for it. The would-be colonizers in turn saw this desire—however conjectural—as an indication of the expansion of the industry, the promise of economic gain, and an assertion of superiority. English venturers speculated that if the native Americans fancied the cloth, they would necessarily like to trade for it. The various garments became visible signifiers for a successful colonial effort, an outward display of England's *cultural* conquest. In contrast to what England saw as the trail of native blood left in the wake of Spanish colonial efforts, the English would display the result of their settlement efforts by clothing the natives in English fabrics. As we shall see, several writers understood that bringing English cloth to the natives would produce a civilizing effect.[4] Without knowing whether or not an American market for English cloth was really feasible in the late sixteenth century, the English nonetheless assumed a desire on the part of the native population. While the argument to expand the English cloth industry was viewed as a harmless form of colonialism when compared with what England regarded as Spain's tyrannical tactics, English ambition to clothe the naked natives reveals a complex dynamic of colonialism: the English desired to convert the indigenous population from "savage" consumption (of animal skins, furs, and— purportedly—each other) to the "civilized" consumption of English cloth.[5]

In the 1550s and 60s, wool cloth comprised up to 94 percent of England's exports and dominated the European textile market. As Lawrence Stone puts it, "the balance of trade hung entirely upon the capacity of Europe to handle, transport, and purchase the cloth of which England was an almost unlimited purveyor" (Stone, 39). For much of the century, English cloth was primarily sent to the entrepôt at Antwerp, from where it would then be carried to other European nations. Antwerp alone took a remarkable 65 percent of England's cloth exports (Croft, "English Commerce," 243).[6] Many of the goods necessary for cloth production that were unavailable in England, such as oils for finishing and plants for dyeing cloth, also flowed through the port. This singular dependence on cloth as a commodity and the reliance on the port of Antwerp ultimately proved disabling to England after the Spanish invasion

---

4   "Civilized" was not in common usage until the mid-seventeenth century. When I use the word here and throughout the chapter, I mean it to invoke the double meaning of being in the state of civility, where civility means "orderly state; social order, as distinct from anarchy and disorder" and "behavior proper to the intercourse of civilized people" (*OED*).

5   Throughout the chapter, I use "colonialism" to mean both the planting of permanent colonies *and* the cultural logic by which the colony is claimed for the nation that is settling there.

6   For a discussion of the important reciprocal relationship between London and Antwerp in the sixteenth century, see Keene, "Material London in Time and Space."

of the Low Countries precipitated the closure of the port in the 1580s.[7] After 1576, when the Spanish took the city, the port declined significantly until it collapsed entirely in 1585 when the Dutch rebels closed off the Scheldt to traffic. The Dutch Protestant revolt against Spanish Catholic invaders resulted in the dismantling of this crucial trading center. If the English were to retain the country's prominence as the chief supplier to the European cloth market, they by necessity had to reformulate trading arrangements.

The closure of the Antwerp market pushed the English to trade directly with eastern countries. Initially, the inception of the Muscovy and Levant Companies gave hope to cloth merchants who desired to expand overseas trade without relying entirely on Antwerp. However, the promise of opening the cloth trade to markets farther afield, while not entirely disastrous, did not flourish as English merchants had hoped. Russia, for instance, was unable to find use for large quantities of English textiles.[8] In his tract promoting planting in Virginia,[9] Christopher Carleill complained that the voyage to Russia was too expensive and too far; furthermore "Dutchmen are there so crept in," that Anglo-Russo trade relations were being undermined (28). The Levant countries of Turkey, Syria, and Egypt, while providing England with alum, a crucial component in dyeing cloth, did not find England's wool cloth quite as useful. George Sandys, visiting Egypt several years after the establishment of the company, remarked that "the English have so ill utterance for their warm clothes in these hot countries that I believe they will rather suffer their ships to rot in the river than continue that trade any longer" (122). Carleill further remarked that the route to Turkey necessarily put English ships in the "daunger of many States," presumably those controlled by Spain (28). Worse yet, by trading with the Levant countries, they were dealing with infidels: "it is thought a harde poinct to have so much familiarity with the professed and obstinate Enemie of Christ" (28).[10]

While economic benefit was surely the primary motivation for reorganizing trade relations in the 1580s, this motivation was often couched in religious terms. Just as Carleill treats trade with Muslim nations with disdain, trade with Catholic countries was increasingly troublesome as the Spanish oppression of Protestant nations was on the rise. In *A Discourse of Western Planting* (1584), which I will discuss in greater detail below, Richard Hakluyt the younger lamented the fact that England must rely so thoroughly on trade arrangements that involve the expanding Spanish empire.

---

7   See Youings, p. 49, for a discussion of England's dependence on cloth and Davis, pp. 14–15, for a discussion of the decline of the Antwerp market.

8   Prior to 1620 less than three percent of England's cloth exports were bound for Russia (Brenner, 364). The Barbary trade with Morocco, however, was fairly vibrant (Andrews, 101).

9   During the early years of English exploration and colonization, "Virginia" referred to most of the eastern seaboard, from present day North Carolina to New England.

10   The East India Company, established in 1599, had a similarly difficult time exporting English cloth. See Fumerton p. 181 and Shammas, p. 164. Thomas Aldworth complained that "'English cloth will not sell ... for garments they use none in these parts'" (qtd. in Fisher, "London's Export Trade," 72). The East Indian merchants bought cloth primarily as "a convenient form of purchasing power with which to obtain peppers, spices and other oriental goods" (Andrews, 263).

English trade in Western Europe had become "beggarly or dangerous, especially in all the kinge of Spayne his Domynions, where our men are driven to flinge their bibles and prayer bookes into the sea, and to forsweare and renownce their Relligion and conscience, and consequently their obedience to her Majestie" (71). What is at its core an economic problem of the disruption of overseas trade routes is cast in terms of the abusive treatment the English received by those loyal to Philip II. The English, however, were forced to undermine their national fealty and suffer harassment at the hands of the Catholic Spanish because they needed products, especially dyes, available only in regions controlled by Spain:

> In all the king of Spaines domynions our men are either inforced with wounded consciences to play the dissemblinge hypocrites, or be drawen to mislike with the state of religion maintained at home, or cruelly made away in the inquisition: Moreover he being our mortall enemye, and his Empire of late beinge encreased so mightily, and our necessitie of oiles and of colours for our clothinge trade being so greate, he may arreste almoste the one halfe of our navye, our traficque and recourse beinge so greate to his dominions. (Hakluyt, *Discourse*, 74)

In this scenario, the Spanish are depicted as aggressive crusaders who detain the English dye merchants and force them to renounce their religion. However, Hakluyt admits that the English cloth industry greatly relies on a return, or "recourse," to the Spanish controlled regions.[11] By underscoring Spain's tyranny over England's commercial efforts in Western Europe, Hakluyt fed into what may have already weighed heavily on the sovereign. England had for too long been reliant on the continent for its trade.[12] Spain's choke-hold on English trade through the Low Countries resulted in a perceived economic collapse of sorts of England's market on the continent.[13] Hakluyt, then, calls for a reconsideration of English economic policy abroad, which he imagines will result in decreasing Spain's power over the nation: "yt behoveth us to seeke some newe and better trade of lesse daunger and more securitie, of less dommage, and of more advauntage" (75). The argument to suspend trade with several European nations with whom England had a longstanding relationship, however, was a radical one. It required a serious reconsideration of

---

11 *Recourse*: "a running, flowing, or coming back, a return" (*OED sb.* 1a).

12 Although Hakluyt, in order to make a convincing case for expansion into new markets, necessarily must portray Anglo-Spanish trade as dangerous and that which must be curtailed, trade between the two countries was relatively vibrant until the embargo of 1585. The lighter New Draperies were especially popular in the Spanish markets. Spain bought a significant amount of English cloth, some of which they delivered to their New World settlements, while at least 11 percent of imports that came to London, including oil and dyes for finishing cloth, were from Spain. Trade between the two countries was particularly beneficial to England. See Croft, "English Commerce," p. 251.

13 Hakluyt also enumerates the detriments of relying on trade with other European nations. For example France imposes "daily devised" taxes; English cloth is "confiscated" on the charge of "insufficient workmanshippe;" Furthermore, the country has begun to make "better clothe then heretofore they were accustomed." Trade markets in Flanders have been destroyed by years of the "moste cruell civil warres." And trade to Russia has been too expensive with the further issue of "the disorderly dealinge of their factors" (*Discourse*, 75).

an entrenched understanding of the global cloth trade as well as confidence in the speculation that New World locales would provide the same volume and kinds of goods available on the continent. What is important to note is that in a document whose primary purpose is to promote "western planting," Hakluyt must spend a considerable amount of time persuading his audience that current trade arrangements are inadequate and/or detrimental to England's economic health.

Once we understand the perceived complications of trading cloth in European markets, it becomes clear that merchants involved in the cloth trade would necessarily look westward as a hopeful site for promoting the industry. The propagandists for New World expansion understood the crucial role that the cloth industry played in England's economy and saw in it a cornerstone for their arguments of expansion to America. It is no surprise, then, that the textual form most likely to engage with the complexities of the fissures in the overseas cloth trade was promotional literature. The difficult economic problems brought on by a collapse in the business as usual approach to trade required a radical reorganization of the way in which textiles were traded. Promotional literature, by its very nature exciting and speculative (perhaps exciting *in* its speculation) was the very form to help re-imagine and jump start the lethargic trade. While travel narratives—descriptions of voyages already taken—could certainly serve a promotional function, as we shall see in our discussion of Thomas Harriot, they are necessarily bound up in the mode of reportage (even if those reports are highly imaginative and rhetorically crafted), and thus emphasize a description of the new and often unfamiliar landscape and foreign peoples.[14] Promotional literature on the other hand was primarily persuasive. As Andrew Fitzmaurice has convincingly argued, promotional texts were written "in terms of a humanistic understanding of persuasion" ("Classical Rhetoric," 223). Most men who argued for westward expansion would have been educated in the Aristotelian method of rhetorical argumentation that had at its core the classical persuasive techniques of Quintillian and Cicero. As opposed to the travel narratives, where descriptions of new locations were valued precisely for their novelty, authors of promotional texts understood that their audience needed to comprehend the New World in terms that were entirely knowable: "In rhetorical persuasion novelty is not necessary valued; the unfamiliar has to be cast in terms of the familiar so that the audience can be emotionally attached to the subject" (Fitzmaurice, "Classical Rhetoric," 224).[15] Thomas Scanlan puts it another way: "writers of these narratives would need to render the colonial enterprise in terms that allowed their readers to embrace it as an essential part of their own story" (29).

The English "story" of overseas ventures had always been the story of the cloth trade. Promotional literature, then, was entrenched in the realm of the economic.[16]

---

14 For a discussion of the relationship of travel writing to fictive discourse, see Linton's *The Romance of the New World* and Steve Clark's introduction to *Travel Writing and Empire.*

15 In another essay, Fitzmaurice discusses the neglected area of early modern sermons as a means for propaganda for the Virginia Company in the early seventeenth century. See "Every man, that prints, adventures."

16 As Howard Jones has argued, "[n]ot until a deliberate literature of propaganda was created was the image of America made attractive" (62).

Many of the authors who envisioned expansion based upon cloth—both the travelers themselves and the propagandists—could not predict the success or failure of their proposed projects. What is significant though is how the cloth industry figured in the *imagination* of these writers. As Greenblatt reminds us, "the discourses of colonialism actually do much of the crucially important work of colonialism" ("New World Encounters," xvi). That is, though the projects that these writers anticipated ultimately failed and an English cloth trade was never established on any large scale, the imagined effect cloth would have laid the groundwork for these expeditions. The revival of the domestic trade, the erasure of unemployment, the dominance over other European countries, and the civilizing effect that cloth would have on the natives were all simultaneous fantasies of what cloth could do for England. And again, we return to our allegory: as Raleigh invited Elizabeth to tread across his "plush cloak," so too the proponents for colonialist efforts justified such an uncertain step as England's westward expansion with the complex and civilized fabric of the cloth industry.[17]

The textual materials for the earliest voyages to the New World, specifically the expeditions to Newfoundland and Virginia in the 1580s, are complex and rich texts, highly crafted, and possessing a tone of assuredness not consistent with the epistemologically nebulous nature of their subject matter. However speculative these texts are about the success of the English enterprise, they have in common the insistence that no colony would be viable without the swift establishment of trade or "traffic."[18] Thomas Churchyard's poem commemorating Humphrey Gilbert's intended westward adventure of 1578, a long panegyric ode to Gilbert and the other valiant adventurers, briefly mentions what was in many ways the principal motive for the overseas expansion:

> What charges you are at,
>   what venter you have made,
> And how you seeke to trafficke there,
>   where never yet was trade. (218–19)

As Churchyard points out, the adventurers are transformed into "venters" by their desire to trade in a place where such a system of long distance exchange did not yet exist.[19] The establishment of traffic, however, necessarily relied on the planting of

---

17 If this story is indeed more than apocryphal, Raleigh's "plush" cloak was no doubt made from luxury cloth, such as velvet, which would likely have been imported from the continent. While the native wool industry suffered in England, and attempts to resuscitate it increased, those able to afford imported silks nevertheless continued to buy it at an astonishing rate. See Chapter 4 for a discussion of imports.

18 In an early manifestation of this argument, Humphrey Gilbert, in his 1576 "Discourse of a Discoverie for a New Passage to Cataia," speculates that "we might ... have a yerely retourne, inhabiting for our staple some convenient place of America, about Sierra Nevada, or some other part" (21).

19 See Helgerson's chapter, "Voyages of a Nation," for a discussion of class issues involved in New World trade. As he argues, Richard Hakluyt the younger's *Principal Navigation* "Brings merchants into the nation and brings gentry into the trade" (*Forms of Nationhood*, 176).

a permanent colony. Richard Hakluyt the Elder, lawyer at the Middle Temple, the younger Richard Hakluyt's cousin, and adviser to merchants involved with trading ventures and other men engaged with overseas exploration, was one of Humphrey Gilbert's advisers for his westward enterprises. Hakluyt's 1578 notes to Gilbert mark one of the first attempts to justify colonization of the eastern part of North America. Previous westward expeditions did not regard North America as a destination but rather a land mass to get around. Francis Drake's 1577 circumnavigation of the globe, for instance, was—among other things—meant to assert English puissance in the Spanish inhabited waters of western South America. And Martin Frobisher's voyage of the same year was largely in the interest of finding a northwest passage to China. Hakluyt's advice, then, indicates a shift in the intent of the English voyagers towards an understanding of the New World as a land to possess and inhabit. In his letter to Gilbert, Hakluyt—presuming a successful voyage followed by immediate settlement—counsels the gentleman on the necessary conditions for a functioning plantation. Despite the practical tone of the text, Hakluyt introduces a notion that would pervade much promotional literature to come: that is, the promotion of English nationhood through the establishment of English overseas commerce. Indeed, he asserts that a colony will not be viable without the establishment of a cloth trade.

While the practical advice Hakluyt gives is directed at one man for a particular intended voyage, presumably Gilbert's expedition to Newfoundland, Hakluyt understands that his counsel will resonate beyond his specific audience. He asserts that the tract is "not unfit to be committed to print, considering the same may stirre up consideration of these and of such other thinges, not unmeete in such new voyages as may be attempted hereafter" ("Notes," 23). English promotional literature for overseas expansion was certainly in an inchoate state in 1578. Nevertheless, Hakluyt indicates a sense that there is a public project afoot larger and with a reach more wide ranging than Gilbert's particular adventure. By "committing" his text to print, he recognizes an afterlife for his advice. Just as the New World enterprise as a whole needed a literature to promote it, so did the economic arguments for that enterprise. As Mary Fuller asserts, "as commerce and navigation developed, neither could be practiced *without* writing, frequent, detailed, ongoing, and systematic" (*Voyages*, 3). Hakluyt the elder understood that arguments in print, designed for a larger audience, would be important if the promoters were to "sell" their schemes.

Initially Hakluyt's advice is concerned with martial matters as he advises Gilbert to seek settlement specifically on the coast so that a navy may be organized and an unspecified "enemie" may be detected (23). A seaboard settlement, however, would not only allow the colonizers to be "least subjecte to annoy of the enemie," but it would give access to the "shippes of England" to deliver goods necessary for the settlers and take away "your commodities." Halkuyt explains that it is necessary for the English settlers to organize trade with their home country: "If they [the settlers] shall live without sea trafficke, at the first they become naked by want of linen and wollen, and very miserable by infinite wants that will otherwise ensue, and so will they be forced of them selves to depart" (24). Hakluyt implies that lack of cloth, especially the kinds of cloth to which Englishmen are accustomed, should be the primary worry of would-be colonizers. New inhabitants of America, without a steady supply of cloth, and without the means to acquire cloth in their new home, will surely "become naked."[20] Out of this lack, other "infinite wants" will surely "ensue." While Hakluyt can only vaguely point to the other needs of the potential colonizers who will attend Gilbert on his voyage, he specifically articulates wool and linen as the capital necessities of the settlers from which all others follow. So crucial is the establishment of a cloth trade that without it, Hakluyt predicts, the colonizers' efforts will fail and they will be forced to "depart" or, worse yet, "easely they will be consumed by the Sp[aniards] by the Fr[ench] or by the naturall inhabithantes of the countrey" (*sic.*, 24). In an astonishing turn of logic, and an uncharacteristic alarmist tone, Hakluyt emphasizes the extreme gravity with which Gilbert, and those who follow him, should regard the import (in both senses of the word) of English cloth. Should they choose to live "without trafficke," the colonizers will quite simply be "consume[d]" or destroyed by the natives and/or their European enemies.[21] The shame of this, of course, will not be limited to those who fail to set up the trade (and are "consumed"). The entire project, rather, "becomes reprochfull to our nation" (24). Hakluyt, then, at the beginning of his tract, clearly lays out the stakes for his audience. New World exploration, which was to be conducted by individual men and carried out in remote and specific locations, and was therefore novel and unique, participated in an enterprise that was historically bound up in old conflicts with European nations and had as its center a new conception of England's famous cloth trade.

With the help of Francis Walsingham, the Queen's secretary and chief promoter of English exploration, Gilbert was granted a patent for six years from Queen Elizabeth, authorizing him and "his heires & assignes" to inhabit and plant lands in America that were "not actually possessed of any Christian prince or people" (Elizabeth I, 186).[22] While previous licenses were granted encouraging traffic of goods in the New World, Gilbert's patent was significant for the charge to take possession of land not otherwise claimed by another European sovereign.[23] Gilbert initially set

---

20 There is perhaps a subtext to this statement that without clothes the settlers will become "naked" like the Indians. While there were not many reports from English people of the attire of the natives in the New World, there was a cultural stereotype of the "naked savage" perpetuated by reports from other European travels. See Kupperman, *Settling*, p. 39 for the variety of meanings of "naked" in the period. In Thomas Harriot's "A Brief and True Report of the New Found Land of Virginia," he remarks that the provisions of the new lands were plentiful but they had "some want" of clothes (154).

21 While I do not think that Hakluyt took "consumed" here to mean "eaten," cannibalism was certainly a concern of would-be settlers and reports of New World anthropophagi made their way back to England. See Bartolovich, "Consumerism, or the Cultural Logic of Late Cannibalism."

22 Gilbert's expeditions to Newfoundland were authorized by Elizabeth but financed with private funds, which he drummed up wherever he could find them. Between 1578 and 1583 he sold land to various investors (Quinn, *Explorers and Colonies*, 141), "giving" 30,000 or more acres to those who offered more than one hundred pounds in cash. Twenty million acres in present day New England were dispensed in this manner (Quinn, *Explorers and Colonies*, 159). Many aristocrats including Philip Sidney were able to claim a piece of the New World even though they would never set foot there.

23 Specifically, Edward VI granted licenses allowing fishing off of Newfoundland and Ireland.

out in September 1578 with a massive fleet of 11 ships bound for the southern parts of the Atlantic seaboard. They set sail from Dartmouth, but immediately returned to Plymouth due to bad weather; the voyage was aborted altogether in November. The second of Gilbert's expeditions, undertaken nearly five years later, just one year before his patent was set to expire, was also ultimately a failure. Gilbert landed in Newfoundland, an area of North America to which other voyagers had previously journeyed, and where there was a thriving international fishing community. Although Gilbert did reach Newfoundland to claim it for England, several mishaps occurred, and Gilbert perished.[24] Nevertheless, this expedition is significant, not only for the historical patent granted by Elizabeth, but also for the impact it would have on later expeditions and promotional literature. While Gilbert may not have followed Hakluyt's advice in planting a successful colony, and did not stay to establish traffic in English wool, his expedition sparked the interest of future promoters and ensured that the discourse of colonialism would continue unabated.

The elder Hakluyt was also involved, albeit less intimately, with promotions to areas further south on the eastern seaboard. In one tract promoting colonization of lands between 34 and 36 degrees latitude, he manages in a short space to encapsulate several reasons why opening trade markets with the New World would benefit the industry. As Quinn has written about this text, "a profusion of objectives is set out ... he clearly expected a great deal of North America" (*NAW*, 61). In his tract, Hakluyt sets up what would later become the primary arguments for reviving the cloth industry in the New World:

> And to conclude by reason of the great increase of wolles in Spayne the like in the weste Indyes and the greate ymployment of the same into Cloathe in both those places with the greate decaye of our usuall Trades in all places in Europe at this tyme, And the wonderfull increase of our people here in Englande and a greate number of them voyde of any good trade or ymployement to gete their lyvinge maye be a sufficient cause to move not onlye the marchauntes and Clothiers but alsoe all other sortes and degrees of our nacion to seeke newe dyscovereyes of peopled regions for vente of our Idle people, otherwise in shourte tyme many mischiefs maye ensue. ("Inducements I," 63–4)

Hakluyt cites an increase in production and sale of Spanish wool in Europe and Spain's dominions. This, together with the "decay" of traditional European cloth trade has created an unprecedented competition for the English cloth industry. Further, according to Hakluyt, England had become overpopulated, with an abundance of

---

24 The events of the 1583 voyage are recounted in detail by Edward Hayes, a surviving member of the expedition in "A Report of the Voyage ... by Sir Humphrey Gilbert." En route to the New World, the *Bark Raleigh* (owned and funded by Walter Raleigh) deserted the expedition; after reaching Newfoundland, *The Swallow* went back to England with the sick and unwilling; and during a reconnaissance trip down the coast of America, the flagship *Delight* ran aground and sank. Returning to England in September with two ships, the *Golden Hind* and *Squirrel*, Gilbert insisted on sailing the smaller frigate, *The Squirrel*. After encountering a storm, Gilbert was reported to have said, "we are as near to heaven by sea as by land" before his ship was "swallowed up of the sea" (Hayes, 241, 242). See Edwards's "Edward Hayes Explains Away Sir Humphrey Gilbert" for an excellent argument about Hayes's retelling of the Gilbert voyage.

people without employment. These combined factors demonstrated the need to send "marchauntes and clothiers" and "other sortes and degrees of our nacion" to Virginia. What Hakluyt outlines as ways to revive the cloth industry become standard arguments of promotional literature. Competition with Spain and England's social problems attached to unemployment were visited again and again in New World propaganda. These arguments, however, are underscored by an ominous strain in Hakluyt—"in shourte tyme many mischiefs maye ensue." It is the vagaries of the subtext, the dangers associated with *not* colonizing, that serves an important role in the promoters' tracts.

The other primary mode of persuasion in the literature, hyperbolic idealism of the New World, is also registered through the cloth trade. Without having any firsthand knowledge of America, and not having much secondhand knowledge to go on, Hakluyt nevertheless suggests a thriving and unstoppable potential for trade: "in tyme such league and entercourse maye aryse, between our Staplynge Seate there and all the portes of Ameryca that incredible thinges may followe tendinge to the ympeachment of our myghtye Enimyes and to the common good of all the Domynions of this noble government" (63). Just as nebulous as the "mischiefs" that may occur if the textile trade is not expanded, are the "incredible thinges" that will arise if it is. In Hakluyt's text and other tracts for westward expansion the threat is important as the promise. This tension—the punishment and reward—is woven into the very fabric of the cloth on which so much seemed to depend.

Hakluyt's younger cousin, Richard Hakluyt, an Oxford educated theologian, took great interest in his kinsmen's writings and is well known as a pivotal figure in discourse about the New World.[25] Keen on joining the westward enterprise, the younger Hakluyt contemplated accompanying Gilbert on his ill-fated voyage to Newfoundland. Instead, Hakluyt took a leave from his theology studies at Oxford to accompany the English Ambassador, Sir Edward Stafford, to Paris as his secretary and chaplain. One of his main objectives in France became the study of French expeditions to the New World (Quinn, *NAW*, 70).[26] When Christopher Carleill, Sir Francis Walsingham's step-son, became interested in the enterprise in the New World in 1583, not much was known in England of North America, and Hakluyt's discoveries—which he sent home to both Carleill and Raleigh, who was Humphrey Gilbert's half brother, before returning in July 1584—were crucial in providing English explorers and promoters of exploration with information.[27] While gentlemen

---

25 In 1582 Richard Hakluyt published *Divers Voyages Touching the Discovery of America*, dedicated to Philip Sidney. This text, a collection of various narratives of English and continental voyages previously taken to the New World, also served promotional purposes. See Payne, p. 5. Sidney invested in July, paying for the rights to three million acres, and in a letter to Edward Stafford called Hakluyt's text "a very good trumpet" for Gilbert's voyage ("Sir Philip Sidney," 264).

26 While in France, Hakluyt was in contact with the André Thevet, royal cosmographer to the French king, who provided Hakluyt with information on past Spanish efforts in the New World as well as proposed French expeditions (Neville-Sington, 70). Further, French seaports occasionally provided harbor for Spanish ships returning from the New World. By setting Hakluyt up in Paris, Walsingham could hope to discover Spanish involvement in New World enterprises (Beeching, 18).

27 When it initially appeared that Gilbert, after his failed first voyage, was unable to fund another expedition, Carleill—with the help of Walsingham and the younger Hakluyt—

and merchants alike were willing to invest in expeditions to North America, both Raleigh and Walsingham agreed that at least some support from the crown would be necessary for sustained successful exploration.

Drawing on information that Hakluyt had gathered in France as well as from Raleigh's preliminary expeditions, in September 1584 he completed his *Discourse on Western Planting*, perhaps one of the most important promotional tracts written during the early expansion period and one of the first pieces aimed at the queen.[28] In it, the very crucial argument that England's efforts in the New World should be taken in order to promote Christianity is subordinated to the even more crucial argument that colonies be established to serve new trade markets. Hakluyt initially echoes the language of Gilbert's patent to remind his reader that the portion of America under consideration for planting—the land between 30 and 63 degrees latitude—is "in no Christian princes actuall possession" and is inhabited by "idolaters" (72). Further, he underscores that the "Kinges and Queenes of England have the name of Defendors of the Faithe" and have been charged to "inlarge and advaunce" faith in Christ (73). This mission, however, needs to be carried out carefully and deliberately, first by establishing a plantation and "learning the language of the people nere adjoyninge" (73).[29] This must be done in order to avoid the fate of a particular group of "Spanish Fryers," who failed to establish a plantation in Florida and were "miserablye massacred by the Savages" (73). At the same time that the English explorers should learn from the mistakes of the Spanish, Hakluyt ironically argues that—in order to spread God's word—they should *emulate* the Spanish who successfully set up two hundred "houses of Relligion in the space of fyftie yeres" (73).[30] Although there are limits to the extent that Hakluyt will laud the Spanish enterprise, claiming that they spread Catholicism for "filthy lucre" and "vaine ostentation" (73), he emphasizes that it was their "meanes of plantinge in those partes," that ensured Spanish success. Armed with what Hakluyt asserts is the "true and sincere Relligion," and first having established a functioning colony, the English can "distill" into the natives' "purged myndes the swete and lively liquor of the gospell" (73). The "mynds" of the natives are depicted here as empty receptacles awaiting the succor of an English God. The

---

succeeded in getting support for his own journey from Bristol financiers. He also attempted to gain support for his own expedition from members of the Muscovy Company, who had claimed rights to Northwest voyages based on its 1555 charter. Carleill was the son of a founding member of the company. See Quinn, *NAW*, p. 27. It is difficult to overestimate the close circle that the promoters for these ventures formed. Many of them were related by blood or marriage and most had served in the campaign to colonize Ireland. For a discussion of the patronage circle of these men and their service in Ireland, see Miller, *Invested With Meaning* and Quinn, *Explorers and Colonies*.

28 While Hakluyt presents a persuasive case to Elizabeth, it is important not to overstress the impact that Hakluyt assumed this tract would have on her policies. As Quinn reminds us, "it was a confidential report by a minor official which might or might not bear any practical fruits" (*NAW*, 70). The essay remained unpublished until the nineteenth century.

29 See Greenblatt, "Learning to Curse," and Helgerson, "Language Lessons," for a discussion of linguistic colonialism in the New World context.

30 For a discussion on English uses of the example of Spain, see Hart, *Representing the New World*.

souls of the presumably barren natives must be tilled by an English plantation. The "people of America," Hakluyt goes on to imagine, "crye oute unto us their nexte neighboures to come and help them" by bringing the word of the English Lord (73). An imagined understanding on the part of the native Americans that the English are their nearest neighbors projects onto them a European understanding of global geography, one that is based on trade concerns rather than saving souls. The rhetoric of economic expansion thus pervades even the most sacred of arguments in *A Discourse of Western Planting*.

A primary argument for colonization that the younger Hakluyt and others return to in their promotional materials is the extent to which planting in the New World would result in rejuvenation of the decayed English cloth trade and an increase in English employment. The issues of unemployment and itinerancy, while related to the decline in the cloth industry, were not solely the problems of the cloth industry: they had become a national blight that Hakluyt argues must be addressed—and solved to a large extent—by an increased trade with colonizers in the New World. Taking Spain and Portugal as his model, Hakluyt argues that westward expansion will increase productivity among Englishmen. Spain and Portugal's discoveries, both of materials abroad, which may be used in their nations, and their own products, which may be exported to their colonies, have provided "so many honest wayes to sett them on worke as they rather wante men than meanes to ymploye them" (82). Perhaps in an effort to arouse the queen's animosity for Spain and her desire to compete with it, Hakluyt hopes that arguing for expansion of the domestic work force will not only put England on par with its enemy, but also solve what had become a national crisis. The promised turn of fate, from a prior dearth of work to a future surplus of jobs, is an important fantasy for a nation that had seen the deleterious effects of unemployment. Hakluyt hopes that the westward expansion will deem the able poor in England "profitable members by employinge them in England in makinge of a thousand triflinge thinges, which will be very goodd marchandize for those Contries where we shall have moste ample vente thereof" (83).[31] The "ample vente" of English manufactures will indicate an increased productivity on the part of the English laboring poor but, even more importantly, a new—however nebulously defined—trading partner will emerge, signaling a turn away from dependence on European markets.

Despite legal efforts to control vagrancy, Hakluyt laments the fact that idle men still plagued England.[32] Indeed, Hakluyt claims that if left without work, these vagrants would be a threat to national security: "[M]any thousandes of idle persons are within this Realme, which havinge no way to be sett on work be either mutinous and seeke alteration in the state, or at least very burdensome to the common wealthe" (82). The result of this deluge of vagrants is that they, for lack of employment, must fall into criminal behavior, which then lands them in the overcrowded prisons. Hakluyt suggests that it is not the vagabonds' nature as criminals but rather their

---

31 See Netzloff, p. 98, for a discussion of this section of Hakluyt's text.

32 See Miller, *Invested with Meaning*, especially Chapter 1, for an excellent discussion of the discourse of "idleness" in framing New World voyages.

fundamental lack of employment that leads them into illegal activities.[33] Thus, following the lead of his cousin, he argues for the deportation of these vagrants to the New World where they will be occupied with producing goods for the betterment of England: "yf this voyadge were put in execution, these pety theves might be condempned for certen yeres in the westerne partes" (82).[34] Among the labor that the criminals will perform is that which will expand England's clothmaking industry. These men might participate in the "beating and working of hempe for cordage," the "mayneteynaunce and increasinge of silke wormes for silke and in dressinge the same," "in gatheringe of cotten whereof there is plenty," and "sowinge of woade and madder for diers" (82).[35] It is no surprise that the New World cultivation of silk, cotton, and products for dyeing fabrics are specified here; they were the very products that England had to import from the continent. Hakluyt's solutions to the unemployment crisis in England are imagined in the cloth industry of the New World—a seemingly thriving, yet undiscovered industry—which would ultimately work to repair England's reputation as the premiere producer of cloth and replace English dependence on markets abroad.

To be sure, Hakluyt's *Discourse* takes up more than the cloth industry in his text. The tract, perhaps the longest of the promotional texts, engages in topics as various as England's rights to claim the land of North America, the promise of a northwest passage to China, the potential vulnerability of Spain in the New World, and a catalog of preparations to be made if the voyage goes forth.[36] However, I would argue that Hakluyt emphasizes the boon to the cloth industry that would attend western colonization because it was the most effective means to persuade the queen, who understood the complex socio-economic factors bound up in cloth production and trade, not the least of which was national pride. In his conclusion, Hakluyt reiterates the importance of expanding the trade, but underscores how the decline of the industry from its prior position of dominance is symptomatic of the decline of England as a nation: England has "for certen hundredth yeres last passed by the peculiar commoditie of wolles, and of later yeres by clothinge of the same ... raised it selfe from meaner state to greater wealthe and moche higher honour, might and power then before" (118). In this meteoric rise of the industry, England has

---

33 By the time Hakluyt writes the *Discourse*, this argument for expansion was fairly common. In Gilbert's promotional tract for the exploration of a Northwest passage to China, he argues that expanding trade in the east will provide the opportunity "to set poore mens children, to learne handie craftes, and thereby to make trifiles and such like, which the Indians and those people doe muche esteeme: By reason whereof, there should be none occasion, to have our countrey combred with loiterers, vagabonds, and such like idle persons" (21).

34 In a promotional tract from c. 1591, Hayes and Carleill make the claim that "we in England are overburdened" with a "multitude of distressed people" that "the realme my happily spare" ("A Discourse Concerning a Voyage," 164, 161). For a discussion of the "venting" of labor, see Netzloff, Chapter 3.

35 See Leggett, p. 233, for a discussion of English knowledge of New World markets for cotton.

36 For other discussions of Hakluyt's *Discourse* see Hart, *Representing,* especially Chapter 4; Bess, "Hakluyt's *Discourse of Western Planting;*" Neville-Sington, "'A very good trumpet;'" and Andrews, *Trade, Plunder, and Settlement.*

found itself the equal of other European nations. But, with the apparent increase of Spanish clothes and trade in the West Indies, the English cloth trade

> will become base, and every day more base then other, which prudently weyed, yt behoveth this Realme yf it meane not to returne to former olde meanes and baseness, but to stand in present and late former honour glorye and force, and not negligently and sleepingly to slide into beggary, to foresee and to plante at Norumbega or some like place,[37] *were it not for any thing els but for the hope of the vent of our woll indraped, the principall and in effect the only enrichinge contynueinge natural commoditie of this Realme* ... and yf it be not foresene and somme such place of vent provided, farewell the goodd state of all degrees in this Realme. (My emphasis, 118)

Using similar alarmist tactics as his cousin, Hakluyt asserts that if the cloth trade— the "only" commodity that enriches England—is not expanded to the New World, England will once again regress to the "baseness" and "beggary" of former times. Yet, in a confusing turn of phrase, he claims that an expansion of the cloth trade will allow England "to stand in present and late former honour glorye and force." Hakluyt's text, however, has enumerated all the problems with the current state of affairs in the industry, so the "present state" of "glory" to which he refers is unclear, as is the former state, which is simultaneously one of "honour and glory" *and* "beggary." This convolution of syntax suggests the complex nature of how the industry was viewed: at home it is represented at once in disrepair and vibrant; abroad it is simultaneously in danger of collapse and dominant. By articulating both of these dynamics, Hakluyt's case is ironically more persuasive. The famous industry must be saved from itself—and this salvation will take place in the New World—if the "goodd state" of England is to continue.

While Hakluyt was certainly invested in the nationalist and economic interests of England, his zealous arguments for expanding the English cloth trade are not simply patriotic. Hakluyt was intimately connected to the Clothworkers' Company. As a theology student at Oxford, Hakluyt received a yearly pension of upwards of six pounds per annum. He received this pension from 1578 until 1587, well past his tenure at Oxford, when he surrendered it. The Clothworkers' Company, which mainly consisted of workers involved with the finishing of cloth, had invested money into Hakluyt's career and he was known as the company's scholar (Girtin, 54).[38] Hakluyt's reasons for promoting the cloth industry in New World expansion are clearly tied to his involvement in the Clothworkers' Company. Joan Pong Linton asserts that Hakluyt would "repay the Clothworkers' kindness in his colonial promotions" (62). Although Hakluyt must have felt a loyalty to the Clothworkers' Company, his promotion of the industry was not merely a "repayment" for their material support of his studies. The Clothworkers' Company was governed primarily by merchants who

---

37 Norumbega, an Algonquin word that means "quiet waters," was often the name used to indicate the region that we now call New England. Hakluyt here seems to be using it to describe the entire eastern seaboard.

38 See Mary Fuller, *Voyages*, p. 141; Girtin, pp. 55–6; and Linton, Chapter 3. The Clothworkers' Company began setting aside five pounds a year for a worthy scholar in 1551 (Girtin, 9).

were interested in longer-range markets (Ramsay, "Clothworkers," 513).[39] Their interests in finding markets in the New World coincided with Hakluyt's own desire to promote New World exploration. He was a participant in a general concern for the fate of the industry and, together with the merchants governing the Clothworkers' Company, saw a promise for a market of finished cloth in the New World. As David Armitage has written, Hakluyt's support of the Clothworkers' Company might have been rooted in the generosity that it showed to him; but his vision for the future of the cloth industry had at its heart the glorification of his nation through reinventing the cloth industry to have a larger presence in the world: "[H]is ends were ideological. The aim of his enterprise was not simply the English colonization of America but, more precisely, the reorientation of English trade away from short-range commerce in the Mediterranean and Northern Europe and toward long-distance trade, not least across the Atlantic" (53–4).

Other promoters of the westward enterprise were also convinced that employing the able yet idle English workforce was crucial in colonial efforts. In his "True Report of the Late Discoveries by Humphrey Gilbert," George Peckham, one of the Catholic gentlemen promoters of Gilbert's expedition, also saw that establishment of colonies in the New World would solve England's social ills of unemployment and poverty.[40] Peckham asserts that an interest in cloth on the part of the native population in America would result in a boom for the English cloth industry at home. Because he assumed the natives would want to consume cloth, he imagined a great "vente for our English clothes will ensue" (50). In the margin, Peckham had indicated all those who would benefit from this increase in the industry: "Clothiers. Wolmen. Carders. Spinners. Weavers. Fullers. Sheremen. Diers. Drapers. Clothiers. Cappers. Hatters. etc." The result is that "many decayed townes" will be "repayerd" (n. 43, 50). Peckham further

---

39 The Clothworkers' Company's interest in longer-range trade was in contrast with the Company of the Merchant Adventurers who wanted to expand short-range traffic. For a discussion of Hakluyt in the context of the Merchant Adventurers and the Clothworkers, see Ramsay, "Clothworkers."

40 Although the text is ostensibly a narrative of Gilbert's voyage to Newfoundland, Peckham's tract promotes colonization of the lands between 30 and 60 degrees latitude, or roughly Jacksonville, Florida to the Hudson Straight. Dedicated to Francis Walsingham, Peckham's text begins with a proper narrative of the events surrounding Gilbert's journey to Newfoundland and the circumstances of his disappearance. However, the tract then quickly shifts to persuading his audience of the value of further promotion. Peckham had to assume that investors would be wary of funding future voyages after Gilbert's expensive failures. However, by claiming that Gilbert's "adherents, associates, and freendes" plan to carry on with future explorations of the New World (41), Peckham has decided to "write this simple short treatise, hoping that it shall be able to perswade such as have been" promoters of the expeditions and also to change the minds of those who have been "detractors" of the westward enterprise (42). Although Peckham never claims he desires further exploration to recoup his investment, he did have a small fortune disappear with the failure of Gilbert's enterprise. Gilbert granted thousands of acres of land to a group of Catholic gentlemen, headed up by Peckham. Peckham's hope was to establish colonies in the New World where they would be free to practice their religion. Gilbert would have been landlord and governor of the entire region (Andrews, 190–91). See Miller, *Invested with Meaning*, for the ways in which Peckham's text uses the "trappings of patronage" to "distance the commercial component of his enterprise" (92).

points to the problem of men, women, and children who "now live heere ydlelie to the common annoy of the whole state" (50). In a sense, it is the unemployed who will save England as they set to work to support westward expansion:

> not only a greate number of men which doo nowe live ydlely at home, and are burdenous, chargeable and unprofitable to this Realme, shall heereby be sette on worke, but also children of 12. or 14. yeeres of age or under, may be kept from ydlenes, in making of a thousand kindes of trifleing thinges, which will be good Marchandize for that Country. (50)

The idle of England will benefit the nation in their production of, however ambiguously put, a "thousand kindes of trifleing things."[41] Although we cannot know what Peckham meant when he refers to the "things" which will put the idle to work, we do know that he, like other writers, understood that the production of cloth would be germane to this revival of labor. Interestingly, though, those targeted for this labor are women who will travel to America to produce cloth and clothing from stuffs found in the New World:

> [O]ur ydle women, (which the Realme may well spare) shal also be imployed on plucking drying and sorting of Feathers, in pulling, beating, and working of Hempe, and in gathering of Cotten, and dyvers things right necessary for dying. All which thinges are to bee found in those Countries most plentifully. (50)[42]

Peckham suggests that these idle and dispensable women will form the basis for a colonial cloth industry based upon materials—cotton, hemp, feathers, and dyes— not readily found in England.[43] Thus, while they may be "spared" in England, they are also *indispensable* to the forming of industry in the New World.[44] Peckham's

---

41 For a compelling discussion of the use of "trifle" in New World discourse, see Knapp, *An Empire Nowhere*. Putting the able-bodied poor to work was a common refrain of economic policy and projects of the period. See, Beier, *Masterless Men*; Hindle, *On the Parish?*; and Thirsk, *Economic Policy and Projects*.

42 Here and elsewhere it is clear that Hakluyt relied heavily on Peckham's text in writing his *Discourse*, where he says that the deported workers could be useful in "beating and working of hempe for cordage," "in gatheringe of cotton," and "sowinge of woade and madder for diers" (82). The repetition of these descriptions certainly reinforces their veracity, despite the fact that neither Peckham nor Hakluyt saw the New World.

43 Women are largely absent from discourses of colonialism. As Linton argues, "domestic and colonial promotions for the cloth trade are in fact narratives of ideal manhood" (7). See her Chapter 3 for a discussion of masculinity in Raleigh's voyage to the New World. See also Steve Clark, especially pp. 19–24, for a discussion of gender issues in travel narratives.

44 In addition to noting the problem with vagrancy, propagandists for westward colonization argued that England's overcrowding problem would be remedied by exporting people out of the country. See Fisher, "Development of London," p. 197. Edward Hayes and Christopher Carleill, in "A Discourse Concerning a Voyage" (1591?), argue that "we in England are overburdened, and as it were pestred with people. If therfore many, yea 20 thousand of our spare people ... were sent and imployed into those Contries there to inhabit ... It shoold both ease the realme of our superfluouse people, and bring much wealth & happiness & honor unto the state" (164). For a discussion of England's overpopulation as a justification for English expansion to Virginia, see George Beer, Youings, Netzloff, and Mancall.

rhetoric is nothing less than idealistic as he claims that this increase in the industry will restore "to theyr pristine wealth and estate" "all such Townes and Villages, as both have beene and nowe are utterlye decayed and ruinated" (50). In the fantasy of a new industry, the decline of entire cities in England can only be reversed through the establishment of new colonies in America.

While much attention was paid to how an expansion of the cloth trade would increase production at home, this was contingent on finding an abundance of products in the New World that would jump start the domestic industry.[45] With the 1585 voyage to the outer banks of North Carolina, English promoters for New World expansion finally had some hard evidence on which to base their assertions. In 1587, Thomas Harriot, Walter Raleigh's tutor in cosmography and surveyor on Richard Grenville's 1585 expedition, wrote his famed "Brief and True Report of the New Found Land of Virginia" largely as a promotional text for future settlers and their financers. Although the book has largely been regarded for its rich descriptions of the new land, its 1588 publication suggests that Grenville and Raleigh viewed it as "publicity ... to attract investors and volunteers" to future Virginia voyages (Quinn, *NAW*, 139). Addressed to the "Adventurers, Favourers, and Wel-willers of the enterprise for the inhabiting and planting in Virginia," Harriot begins his "report" with a description of commodities "found or to be raised" in Virginia, focusing primarily on goods related to textile production. Painting a characteristically rosy picture of this new found land, Harriot asserts that these commodities

> will not onely serve the ordinary turnes of you which are and shall be the planters and inhabitants, but such an overplus sufficiently to be yielded, or by men of skill to be provided, as by way of traffique and exchange with our owne nation of England, will inrich your selves the providers: those that shall deale with you, the enterprisers in generall, and greatly profit our owne countreymen, to supply them with most things which heretofore they have bene faine to provide either of strangers or of our enemies, which commodities, for distinction sake, I call Merchantable. (141)

Harriot takes pains to describe products in Virginia that are not regularly produced by England, such as "silke of grasse," "worme silke," "woad," and "madder." The dyestuffs, of course, were extremely important to cloth finishing, but were mostly products of other nations, who would dye English cloth and import it back to England. Silk, of course, was a luxury item for which wealthy English people had a large appetite but few native sources. To claim that the production of these commodities in the New World was plentiful meant to imagine a decrease in the reliance on foreigners for these products, some of whom were England's "enemies."[46]

---

45 For a discussion of the twin projects of finding products in the New World and desire to export English manufactures there, see George Beer, pp. 72–3.

46 The younger Hakluyt also believed that the commodities that were available by the "Steelyard" and "Eastland" merchants would be readily available in the North part of America "neere unto Cape Briton, in returne for our course Woollen clothes, Flanels and Rugges fit for those colder regions" (*Discourse*, 64). Hakluyt also saw the possibility of a trade in dyes (*Discourse*, 67).

While earlier promotional texts for New World exploration and colonization argue for the *probable* availability of products related to cloth production, the fact that most of the propagandists had not actually been to America and relied on secondhand reports or speculation, emphasizes the specious nature of their assertions. Harriot's observations of the New World, on the other hand, have the added veracity of firsthand observation, lending the promotion greater authority. The fact that Harriot begins his report with a description of the "Merchantable commodities" of Virginia would, of course, suggest that he has seen and analyzed products beneficial to England. His descriptions, however, are no less speculative and fantastical as those written by the Hakluyts or George Peckham, suggesting that Harriot knew, as the other men did, that the way to the investors' money was through an argument of an expanding cloth trade. The "report" is in effect a *projection* of the future cultivation of products previously found in Europe "*to be* yielded, or by men of skill *to be provided*," not necessarily a description of what he has actually seen. At some points Harriot imagines taking the products he has found and cultivating them to imitate their use in the Old World; While Harriot did indeed observe "grasse silke," which he emphasizes is similar to that which "groweth in Persia," he underscores that it must be "planted and ordered *as* in Persia" in order for it to be profitable (my emphasis). At other points, Harriot makes an argument for what he *assumes* is a product like that of Europe. He describes "faire and great" creatures that he takes to be silkworms. Even though it is not their "hap" to find "plenty" of the worms, he confidently asserts that "there is no doubt but if arte be added in planting of Mulberie trees" and the worms are "husbanded in that sort ... there will rise as great profit in time to the Virginians, as thereof doth now to the Persians, Turks, Italians, and Spanyards" (141). Of other products in his report, Harriot has had scarce evidence or simply has not found any at all. "The trueth is," Harriot ruefully acknowledges, "of Hampe and Flaxe there is no great store," although "there cannot be shewed any reason to the contrary, but that it will grow there exceedingly well." Woad and madder, the two dyestuffs that are "of so great vent and use amongst English Diers" and "which can not be yielded sufficiently in our owne countrey," have not even been observed in Virginia, even though he assures the reader that it may be planted there because there is "ground enough" and "it growth plentifully" in the Azores, "which are in the same climate." While Harriot's book is billed as a "true report," it is important to see it as another promotional text that understands the financial gains to be made through a decreased dependence on European and eastern markets for commodities beneficial to the cloth trade.[47]

Both the resuscitation of the home industry and the trade in products to be found in the New World were focal points for the promoters. However, a true reordering of the cloth industry could not have been imagined without a perceived need for English cloth on the part of the native population. While in many ways this was the most speculative part of the promotion, since it imagined the trade practices of an

---

47 See M. Fuller for a thorough discussion of the rhetorical techniques by which Harriot "fills in" the *lack* of his text. The superabundance of landscape and potential commodities was as important to the narratives as was the argument that the landscape was empty enough to need English colonists. See Sweet, p. 405. Steve Clark has suggested that "precisely observed particulars" in travel narrative is closely connected to "parody, high fantasy" (1).

unknown people, it was also in some ways the most effective because it brought into the picture an entirely new potential trade partner. The elder Hakluyt makes clear that it is only in a native need for the cloth that trade can be set up: "If the people in the Inland be clothed, and desire to live in the abundance as all such things as Europe doth, and have at home all the same in plenty, yet we cannot have trafficke with them, by mean they want not any thing that we can yield them" ("Inducements II," 66). Trade relations are, of course, predicated on a *lack* on the part of one of the parties. If the natives already have an abundance of clothes, they will have no need for England's trade. And here we see why it was so crucial for promoters to invent a void that could only and necessarily be filled by the English cloth trade.

In *A Discourse for Western Planting*, Hakluyt attempts to support the assertion that there is a need for English products—specifically cloth—in the New World:

> And seinge the savages of the graunde Baye and all alonge the mightie Ryver that ronneth upp to Canada and Hochelaga are greatley delighted with any cappe or garment made of course wollen clothe, their Contrie beinge colde and sharpe in the winter, yt is manifest wee shall finde great utterance of our clothes, especially our coursest and basest northerne doosens and our Irishe and Welshe frizes, and rugges: whereby all occupacions belonginge to clothinge and knittinge shalbe freshly sett on worke, as cappers, knitters, clothiers, wollmen, carders, spynners, weavers, fullers, sheremen, dyers, drapers, hatters and such like, whereby many decayed townes may be repaired. (83)[48]

The native desire for British cloth—they are "delighted" with the wool—is here subordinated to what Hakluyt regards as their need for it.[49] That is, the climate in Northern America clearly indicates to Hakluyt that the natives require English woolens. Assuming that the "coarsest and basest" of woolens will be preferable to the indigenous population than animal skins and furs, he deduces that the English poor will be put to work. In an almost hyperbolic frenzy, Hakluyt rattles off the occupations of all those involved in the production of cloth to underscore just how many jobs will be available by opening up the export of English cloth to the New World. Further, as Peckham had suggested, this "manifest" boom in the cloth industry may magically "repair" depressed cloth producing towns. The imagined solution to England's problem reaches fantastic heights here. Every worker involved in the production of cloth as well as the nation it represents will benefit greatly by Westward expansion.[50]

---

48 Doosen or dozens were coarse woolens generally associated with the cloth producing region of Devonshire (*OED*); frize or friezes were a kind of coarse woolen cloth with a nap usually on one side only generally associated with Ireland (*OED*); and rugges were a coarse woolen frieze.

49 Sweet suggests that the potential colonists "regard the indigenous inhabitants less as people to be conquered than as prospective trading partners" (405).

50 In the elder Hakluyt's "Inducements to the Liking of the Voyage," he also draws upon a similar image of success in the New World: There will be "an ample vent in time to come of the woollen clothes of England, especially those of the coursest sorts, to the maintenence of our poore, that els serve or become burdensome to the realme" (64).

Carleill, in his "Breef and Sommarie Discourse Upon the Entended Voyage to the Hethermoste Partes of America" (1583), describes how the export of English cloth to the New World would benefit the industry:

> [T]here muste of necessitie fall out, a verie liberall utterance of our Englishe Clothes, into a maine Countrey, described to be bigger then all Europe, the larger parte whereof bendyng to the Northward, shall have wonderfull greate use of our saied English Clothes, and after they shall once come to knowe the commoditie thereof. (30)

Despite Carleill's enthusiasm for expanding the nations' main export, his project is founded upon a speculative fantasy of a future fictive market.[51] By saying that North America is "bigger then all Europe," Carleill assumes that it is *like* Europe, that is densely populated, and therefore apt to provide an enormous market for English cloth. Certainly, at the end of the sixteenth century the area north of modern southern New England was at best sparsely populated. Unlike England, there were no urban centers appropriate for establishing a central cloth market along the lines of Blackwell Hall in London. Indeed, North America contained no communities even remotely commercialized to purchase wool on the scale that would serve as a substitute for European markets.[52] Carleill's second assumption that England's cloth would benefit inhabitants of northern New England is only partly wrong. While the heavy textile would certainly be appropriate material for the winter months, Carleill, like other explorers before him, did not understand the climate of North America. Contrary to what early colonizers thought, Eastern North American locations with latitudes comparable to Western Europe would not have similar climates.[53] During several months of the year English woolen cloth would be too heavy for use, assuming there would even be a market for it.[54] This leads to Carleill's final fallacy: that the natives will actually *wear* English cloth, let alone recognize its superiority. Without knowledge of what the native inhabitants of North America would do with the cloth, Carleill could not speculate with any certainty that they would prefer it above their own textiles and furs.

Carleill's presumption that the native Americans will not only wear but revere English cloth participates in the subtle but systematic oppression of indigenous North Americans by the value systems of the colonizers. George Peckham shares these assumptions. Peckham goes on to list no less than twelve occupations whose members stand to benefit from the increased cloth production. One of the reports

---

51 It is important to acknowledge that firsthand reports of Indian desire for English cloth did exist. Ralph Lane's letter from Virginia to the elder Richard Hakluyt of 3 September 1585 is one such example: "The people are naturally most curteous, & very desirous to have clothes, but especially of course cloth rather than silke, course canvas they also like wel of" (293).

52 See Fisher, "London's Export Trade," p. 72.

53 See Kupperman, "Fear," p. 215.

54 Even almost a century after the settlement of Jamestown, it seems that Englishmen still had not quite understood the notion of dressing for particular climates. In Robert Beverly's *The History of the Present State of Virginia*, he complains that "many of the Merchants and others that go thither from *England*, make no distinction between a cold, and a hot Country: but wisely go sweltering about in their thick Cloaths all the Summer, because they used to do so in their *Northern* climate; and then unfairly complain of the heat of the Country" (297).

made to Peckham is the delight the native population takes in "civilized" culture. Indeed, the clothes of the colonizers leave the indigenous population in awe:

> it is well known that all Savages, as wel those that dwell in the South, as those that dwell in the North, so soon as they shall begin but a little to taste of civillitie, will take mervailous delight in any garment be it never so simple: As a shirt, a blewe, yellow, redde, or greene Cotton cassocke, a Cappe or such like, and will take incredible paynes for such a trifle. (49)

Although the clothing that the natives see are "trifles" to the colonizers, the clothes still signify civility. That the "savages" are pleased by the clothing shows that they are capable of becoming civilized. By this logic, the desire for "civilized" clothing is equated with the desire for civilization itself. Peckham goes on to say that he has heard "sundrye times ... that the people in those parts, are easily reduced to civilitie bothe in manners and garments" (49). Here, clothing is indicative of behavior. When civilized clothing is thrust upon the natives, so will civilized manners be.[55]

As he does so often in his tract, Peckham uses the example of Spanish success as an argument for English Expansion. In the West Indies, he claims, the natives "are easily reduced to civilitie both in manners and garments. Which being so, what vente for our English clothes will thereby ensue, and howe greate benefit to all such persons and Artificers" (49–50). That the natives are "reduced" to civility suggests that, according to common usage of "reduce" in the late sixteenth and early seventeenth centuries, they would be led from "error in action, conduct or belief" (*OED*). The verb also suggests that they would be brought to "order, obedience, reason, *etc.*, by constraint or compulsion."[56] Importantly, the assumption that the native Americans could be taught to be civilized indicates that the English did not see their "savage" condition as something permanent. As Karen Kupperman suggests, "English colonists assumed that Indians were racially similar to themselves and that savagery was a temporary condition which the Indians would quickly lose" (*Settling*, 2). While Peckham may not imagine physically forcing English cloth on the natives, the superiority with which the English regarded their cloth and the assumption that the natives also would regard it as such suggests the English administration of desire. That is, an economy of compulsory exchange is set up between the English and native Americans.[57] In *Mimesis and Alterity*, Michael Taussig suggests that the moment would-be colonizers have contact with natives

---

55 An important early example of this logic is in Robert Fabian's description of the Newfoundland natives that Sebastian Cabot brought back to England after his 1497 voyage: "these were clothed in beast skins, & did eate raw flesh ... and in their demeanour like to bruite beasts, whom the King kept a time after. Of the which upon two yeeres after, I saw two appareled after the manner of Englishmen in Westminster palace, which that time I could not discerne from Englishmen" (155).

56 Linton also notes this double-meaning of "reduce" when referring to Christopher Carleill's view of Christianizing native Americans: Carleill "sees colonization as a means of 'reducing' the savage people to Christianitie and civilitie" (76).

57 Carleill similarly suggests that by trading products found in the New World for English cloth, the Indians will become civilized: "It is to be assuredly hoped, that they will daiely by little & little, forsake their barbarous, and savage livying, and grow to suche order and

and present a gift as a potential item for trade, the interaction masks violence on the part of the colonizers: "[v]iolence or the threat of violence seems displaced into rather than overcome by the gift and ... I feel a deepening confusion ... as to where gifts stop and trade begins, it being obvious that objects here take on the burden of negotiating between might and right" (94). In Peckham's imagination, the display of English cloth alone is enough to convince the natives not only to desire it, but also want to enter trade relations based upon it. Further, Peckham assigns cloth the magical ability to "subdue" the natives; cloth here, rather than the bearers of the cloth, in Taussig's words, "negotiate[s] between might and right."

Peckham and Hakluyt's proposals were essentially unfounded. Indeed, as Kenneth Andrews asserts, "readers who knew much about English industry would have found Peckham's vagaries in that respect less than convincing" (198). Certainly Peckham did not know enough about the cloth market to project the kind of success he was certain that his proposal would have. Andrews also asserts that Hakluyt's arguments in *A Discourse on Western Planting* are specious: "Hakluyt's argument that American trade would solve the [vagrancy] problem would hardly have convinced an Elizabethan cloth exporter" (204). And as Linton points out, tobacco, rather than cloth, "became the trade that first established English colonists in America," suggesting that the cultivation of an indigenous product was the only viable way to set up a large scale trade with the New World (82). Of course, promoters, with presumably little trading experience themselves, could not reliably predict that trade to an untested market would or would not be necessarily lucrative. On the other hand, Peckham and Hakluyt's idealism shows the important cultural work of *imagining* the success of commercial enterprises in the New World. Hakluyt did not make this argument to cloth merchants but rather to the queen who saw the cloth industry as more than a commodity for economic benefit; it was that which could bring England national prestige. Cloth in the New World was capable of creating a fantasy for the nation—one that could free England from its dependence on Spain, erase both criminality and unemployment, civilize the native population, all the while rescuing the failing industry.

In the Jacobean period, after early efforts for westward expansion, English travel writers still found themselves using the dilapidated English cloth industry as a way to foster interest in the New World colonies. For Robert Johnson in his *Nova Britannia* (1609), the English cloth trade must expand towards Virginia both to revive the industry and to clothe the naked and thus offensive natives. As with earlier proponents of colonization in the New World, these two goals necessarily go hand in hand. Describing the native population in Virginia, Johnson asserts that "they have no law but nature, their apparell skinnes of beasts, but most goe naked" (239).[58] The clothing of the native Indians—either animal skins or nothing at all—suggests to Johnson their relationship to nature: there is no artifice in their apparel. At the same time, this seeming rejection of artifice and preference for "nature" is their "law;" it is the rule of conduct that governs them. Their nakedness also simultaneously indicates

---

civilitie with us, as there may be wel expected from thence no lesse quantitie, and diversity of Marchandize, then is now" in the Netherlands, Italy, France, and Spain (30).

58 In similar language, written nearly twenty years earlier, Harriot reports that the Carolina Algonquians are "people clothed with loose mantles made of deere skinnes, and aprons of the same round about their middles, all els naked" (150).

both a prelapsarian innocent state of nature as well as a fallen state where nakedness must be covered. As Linton has argued in her discussion of Raleigh's presence in California, descriptions of naked natives were steeped with biblical references:

> The unmistakable scriptural reference points to the moment after the fall when Adam and Eve first know shame. Although they devise a garment of fig leaves to cover their nakedness, God teaches them instead the use of animal skins. The Edenic reference invokes a biblical typology in which God's clothing of the fallen couple finds repetition and fulfillment in the colonists' clothing of the Indians. (79)

The way in which the disturbing natural law of the natives must be remedied is through bringing the natives into the world of commercial production and exchange. As Kupperman puts it, the use of "naked" to describe the indigenous population has mercantilistic motives behind it: "The Indians, being naked, will be pleased to trade the commodities of America for English woollen cloth. Both sides would benefit from such a trade ... so that benefiting the American Indian would also benefit the English poor" (Kupperman, *Settling*, 40).

Unlike the Spanish, who had denigrated the indigenous population, Johnson argues for the intrinsic value of the colonized as partners in commerce. The goal of the English colonizers will be

> not to bring a people ... out of the frying panne into the fire, but to make their condition truely more happy, by a mutuall enterchange and commerce in this sort: That as to our great expence and charge, wee make adventures, to impart our divine riches, to their inestimable gaine, and to cover their naked miserie with civill use of foode and clothing, and to traine them by gentle meanes to those manuall artes and skill, which they so much affect, and do admire to see in us. (240)

In Johnson's scenario, the natives will be the beneficiaries of colonization: While he claims that the exchange of commerce between the natives and the colonizers is "mutual," it is at the "great expence" of the English and the "inestimable gaine" of the indigenous Americans. While the commercial exchange between the two peoples will be reciprocal—both peoples will give each other things or the knowledge to attain them—the natives will gain happiness and escape their perceived misery. Represented by their lack of clothing, their misery is that which must be covered by the blanket of colonization. The "riches" that the Indians will be given are the "divine" materials of civilization—English cloth. Cloth, then, is imbued with the dual power to civilize the heathen natives and revive the English economy. This is made even more explicit in Johnson's tract when he argues, like many propagandists for Virginia before him, that exporting English cloth to the colony will solve England's economic problems. In fact it is the key piece of the puzzle in sorting out the success of the colonial enterprise:

> But of all other things, that God hath denied that countrie, there is want of Sheepe to make woollen cloth, and this want of cloth, must alwaies be supplied from England,[59]

---

59 In *The Story of Wool*, Leggett asserts that while sheep in America are generally "associated with the eastern seaboard," sheep were actually brought to the continent

whereby when the Colony is thorowly increased, and the Indians brought to our Civilitie (as they will in short time) it will cause a mighty vent of English clothes, a great benefit to our Nation, and raising againe of that auncient trade of clothing, so much decayed in England. (245)

Although Hakluyt had made this argument—that exporting English cloth to the New World would benefit the colonial enterprise by both civilizing the natives and expanding the economy at home—nearly a quarter of a century earlier, Johnson's argument must still have had some gravity. For him, English cloth plays a crucial and seemingly paradoxical role in the colonial enterprise: the way to revive the glorious days of the "auncient" cloth industry in England is to expose the colony to English cloth; old England's past can be recovered by clothing the New World. As Linton has argued, "as colonial prospects for trade dimmed, references to the clothing of savages grew in symbolic value in the argument for colonization, revealing the distance between the symbol and the facts of commerce" (82). Like Thomas Deloney's look to the past in *Jack of Newbury* to represent a consolidated and thriving industry at the turn of the sixteenth century, the propagandist for westward expansion also relied on the strength of the cloth industry's early successes and reputation to create a fantasy of the success of the future.

This argument for expansion based upon cloth has at its core the same fantasy that prompted earlier propaganda—that the natives will be "brought to our civilitie" by English cloth. Unlike Hakluyt, Carleill, and Peckham, however, Johnson understands that there can be neither "civil" Indians nor a "mighty vent of English clothes" until the colony is "thorowly increased," until there is a substantial population of colonists. While Hakluyt and Peckham rely on the notion that the natives will want to trade for English cloth without considering that they may not have the desire or capital for the cloth, Johnson recognizes that there must be a population of English people in America before English cloth can become a viable commodity of trade. Importantly, though, the "mighty vent of English clothes" can only occur *after* the Indians are civilized through the consumption of this cloth. The civility of the native, then, is an important primary step in achieving the ultimate goal—the "raising againe of that auncient trade of clothing." In the English imagination, both in early tracts as well as Johnson's, the success or failure of the cloth industry is put uncomfortably in the hands of the natives. By the time Johnson writes his pamphlet, native consumption of English cloth does not appear to be irrefutable—he is sure that "they will in short time" become civilized through cloth, but cannot say that they already have. Johnson's refusal, like that of the other New World promoters, to believe that the natives may not want cloth and that the English cloth trade in the New World may fail, suggests the idealism with which the westward enterprise was viewed. What loomed large in the English imagination, however, was that the natives were naked, that they needed and wanted to be clothed, and that English cloth would provide this most crucial function. This imagined desire reveals the extent to which cloth became

---

by Spaniards in the 1530s. Leggett goes on to explain that after the establishment of the Jamestown colony, sheep—bred for their mutton instead of for wool—were sent to Virginia along with the early colonists (233).

viewed as a symbolically charged object able magically to solve England's financial woes and civilize the natives.

Michel de Certeau has argued that the appearance of natives is in the eye of the colonialist beholder: "he who does not understand the language," de Certeau asserts, "only sees the clothes" (79). Or perhaps more appropriate for our case, the English would-be colonizers only saw that the natives *lacked* clothes. More specifically, the natives lacked *English* clothes, the outward signifier of civility. As Linton has asserted regarding Drake's travels to California, cloth and clothing served as symbols of colonization: in the English colonial imagination, native Americans were not, "civilized by religion alone, and it remains for the English colonists equipped with cloth and clothes to civilize them in manners as well as religion" (76–7). Cloth and religion, however, should not be viewed as entirely separate entities here: the commercial exchange of cloth is the religion upon which this colonial enterprise is based. In the presentation of English cloth to the native population, cloth is imbued with meaning far beyond its reference as the potential commodity of trade. It comes to represent the English people who give it and—in the colonists eyes—the possibility of representing the natives who will consume it.[60] Invested with the potential for civilizing the natives, resurrecting the ailing home industry, and asserting England's cultural dominance, cloth takes on a supernatural, almost religious, power for the propagandists. It has the power to convert that which is not English (the natives, a failing industry, Spain's dominance) into that which is. And as Louis Wright argues, for the younger Hakluyt—the man who represented all these proponents in *The Principal Navigations*—his life's work as a writer and compiler of travel narratives certainly was linked to his training as a theologian: "[f]or the preacher, expansion became a religion. He found his texts in geography and became the evangel of trade and colonization" (Wright 525). Significantly, one crucial focus of his gospel of trade was the word of the cloth industry. Indeed, we must see Richard Hakluyt and the other propagandists as men of cloth.

---

60 In the words of Taussig, "the commodity is hardly a sign or symbol. Only in religion or magic can we find equivalent economies of meaning and practises of expenditure in which an object, be it a commodity or a fetish, spills over its referent and suffuses its component parts with ineffable radiance" (233).

Chapter 4

Treasonous Textiles:
Foreign Cloth, and the
Construction of Englishness[1]

As we have seen in Chapter 3, the imagined export of cloth to the New World engendered excitement among those involved in the westward enterprise and served as an important basis for promotion. It also functioned symbolically as the material representation of England's nationhood to the inhabitants of the New World. Thus a national identity becomes consolidated when it engages with other lands. When we turn from the export of textiles to the imports thereof, we see a shift in how this circulation of national subjectivity works. As foreign fabrics are imported into England and worn on the English body, they are perceived of as disrupting the domestic wool cloth industry. This calls into question the cultural capital of English cloth, thereby creating a crisis of national identity. Importantly, though, challenges to the domestic industry and sense of nationhood serve the purpose of forcing a further articulation and a heightened sense of the cultural significance of cloth. Just as printed propaganda for New World expansion insisted on the centrality of English cloth in making legible a national identity, so too do texts that critique the new preoccupation with foreign textiles.

The English Monsieur

In his eighty-eighth Epigram, "On English Monsieur" (1616), Ben Jonson ridicules the vainglorious pride in apparel of his subject and specifically the Englishman's obsession with clothes and accessories from France. Attired head to toe in French clothing, the Englishman becomes unrecognizable as such: he mutates into a "monsieur" through his very apparel. The speaker, however, does much more than simply deride the man's vanity. By asking his reader to marvel at the Englishman whose clothing belies his nationality, he puts into question the very identity of the English subject: "Would you believe, when you this Monsieur see, / That his whole body should speak French, not he?" (1–2) Could we imagine, the poem continues,

> That so much scarf of France, and hat, and feather,
>   And shoe, and tie, and garter should come hither
> And land on one whose face durst never be

---

1   Earlier versions of this chapter appear in the *Journal of Medieval and Early Modern Studies* and *Clothing Culture, 1350–1650*.

Toward the sea, farther than half-way tree?[2]
That he, untravelled, should be French so much,
As Frenchmen in his company should seem Dutch? (3–8)

The Englishman, though never having ventured beyond his homeland, has forsaken any signs that reveal his proper national affiliation by wearing the various French garments. He has invited foreign fashion "hither," thus becoming a foreigner in his own land. The body of the English subject, covered over with "so much" that is French, not only obscures his Englishness but also welcomes in the unsavory qualities stereotypically associated with the French: vanity and moral laxity. Jonson concludes the poem by remarking upon his subject's obsession with his tailor's wares and the display of foreign apparel: the Monsieur "must prove / The new French tailor's motion, monthly made, / Daily to turn in Paul's, and help the trade" (15–16). By parading through Paul's Walk, the middle aisle of St. Paul's Church and London's early modern catwalk for the fashionable, the Englishman tests his sartorial success.[3] Moreover, by exhibiting the apparel in a public place, the French tailor, and his "motion," or puppet, the English monsieur, perpetuate the domestic market in foreign clothes.[4]

As Jonson's epigram demonstrates, clothing and the cloth from which it was made was not only associated with specific nations, but also helped to create sentiments of nationhood through the linkage of clothing with a particular county. William Prynne asserts in his antitheatrical polemic, *Histriomastix* (1632), that "apparell" was meant, among other things, "to distinguish ... one Nation ... from another" (207). In the early modern period, national identification could be clarified by the visible medium of clothing. At the same time, however, as Jonson's epigram also underscores, clothing *confuses* national identity. While clothing may have confirmed national origin in its unworn state, the donning of apparel by actual bodies often disrupted this imaginary national clarity. Wearing foreign clothes disrupted the way of knowing one's country of origin and, perhaps more upsetting, where one's loyalty lay. The English monsieur, his very name a blurring of national fealty, is several things at once: completely domesticated ("untravelled"), utterly French, morally suspicious (carrying "the French disease"), and possibly traitorous. Jonson and other authors of early modern London who disparaged stylish men and women decried the social

---

2   "Half-way tree" may refer to "a landmark on the Dover Road" (Donaldson, n. 647).

3   Paul's Walk was notorious as "the common lounge of the idler, the Fop's Alley of the day" (Simpson 235). See Chapter 13 of Simpson, *Chapters in the History of Old S. Paul's*. A result of its reputation of a cross section of London society, Earle calls Paul's Walk in his *Microcosmography*, "the Land's Epitome, or you may call it the lesser Ile of Great Brittaine" (92).

4   Most of Act III of Jonson's *Every Man Out of His Humour* takes place in the middle aisle of St. Paul's. At one point, Fungoso, a fashion-hungry student, has his tailor "note all" of the details of a particularly fashionable courtier, Fastidious Brisk (3.5.18). See Chapter 5 of Bailey's *Flaunting* for a discussion of the play in relation to male comportment in St. Paul's. For a satirical representation of the fop and his tailor in Paul's Walk, see Chapter 4, "How a Gallant Should behave himself in Paul's Walk," in Dekker, *The Gull's Horn-Book*.

misdeeds that accompanied wearing foreign fabrics.[5] But by drawing attention to the foreignness of the clothes, the authors do something else: they present the notion that clothes are capable of both disrupting and affirming English national identity. As Ann Rosalind Jones and Peter Stallybrass point out, "the innovative force of fashion was associated both with the dissolution of the body politic and with the exorbitance of the state's subjects" (1). Importantly, though, it is the very "force of fashion" that can work to consolidate a sense of nation. The threat of the other, and specifically the threat of the other's *clothes*, works to confirm the importance of the English cloth industry for its subjects.

While the English Monsieur's finished suit of clothes and the haberdashery of French items that accessorize it are highlighted to satirize this fashionable Everyman's foolishness, the cloth from which these suits were made was the primary culprit in debasing the nation. In the late sixteenth and early seventeenth century, the importation of silk, satin, and velvet from the continent had reached an all time high.[6] After wine, the primary imports of the sixteenth century were silks and velvets from Italy (Davis, 27). By the late years of that century, luxury cloth imports from Spain, as well as from France and Italy, had increased six-fold and were the most prominent class of imports (Stone, 49). By the turn of the century there was a growing complaint from those involved in the manufacture of English cloth: The increased consumption, both at home and abroad, of textiles from France, Spain, and Italy, contributed to a crisis for the English domestic wool industry (Bowden, 186). As the depression in the cloth industry in the late sixteenth and early seventeenth centuries was in part blamed on the craze for foreign fashions, grievances against the consumption of foreign textiles were almost always also complaints about the decline of the wool trade at home.[7] The literature of the period that takes up the subject of foreign fabrics—primarily satirical texts and polemical sermons—reveals the extent to which the disruption of the cloth trade had become a national concern. Indeed, the popular writers of the time were in effect echoing the preoccupations of the authorities who were troubled by the precarious position in which the domestic industry had been placed by the burgeoning trade in foreign cloth. As Jane Schneider has asserted, "[s]tate-makers ... welcome, and often manipulate, the moral and religious revulsion that fashion tends to provoke" (109). The assault in print on those that bought and wore foreign clothes also announced the damage these actions inflicted on England's nationhood.

---

5   While London and its denizens were most often the target of satire, the city became a synecdoche for the rotten state of England itself. As Manley states, "the urban market, and especially the growth of London, played an important role" in the transition from a feudal to capitalistic culture. "The long-distance luxury trade ... may in fact have contributed" to this shift (*Literature and Culture*, 68).

6   Prior to 1603, when James repealed the sumptuary laws, wearing luxury fabrics was regulated. For discussions of the social ramifications of these laws see Jardine, *Still Harping on Daughters*; Newman, *Fashioning Femininity*; Bailey, "'Monstrous Manner;'" Jaster, "Of Bonnets and Breeches" and Vincent, *Dressing the Elite*. The seminal study of sumptuary legislation in England remains Baldwin, *Sumptuary Legislation*.

7   See Newman, p. 111.

In the hands of these writers, the cloth from France, Spain, and Italy represented leisure, decadence, disease, and—most crucially—dissolution of the virtues associated with English textiles such as charity, hospitality, and humility. Foreign fabrics on English bodies were not only an affront to the cloth industry, but also blurred the line between English and foreign.[8] Unabashed consumption of the fabrics from the continent compelled writers of the period to associate those who wore foreign fashion with the scandalous qualities of the country of origin. Papistry and lasciviousness were linked with silks and satins from Spain and Italy, venereal disease and ostentation with French fabrics. Donning the fabrics and fashions from these countries invited the corruption into England. The perception of the Continent was thus transformed into an imaginative geography of morality wherein a foreign nation became legible through its characteristic iniquities. If these writings represent the Continent as shadowy regions of vice, they also cast England as an untainted island of virtue. Domestic wool cloth, considered a visible manifestation of moral superiority, was the material through which early modern writers often negotiated questions of national selfhood and foreign otherness.[9] In focusing on the threat of foreign textiles, a fundamental concern for the economic health of England's trade relations is written over as a narrative of uncertainty and anxiety about national distinctions. In representing England, texts and textiles are intimately linked in their ability to articulate national identity.[10]

The literature most apt to take up the critique of foreign fashions and fabrics is satire. This particular textual mode is as complex and wide-ranging as the multiple genres of prose (both non-fiction and imaginative), verse (epigram, ballads, and so on) and drama in which it was written.[11] The neo-classical strain of satire that became so popular in the 1590s and is most closely associated with Hall, Guilpin, Marston, and Donne, owed a great debt to the highly crafted rhetoric of the Roman satirists Horace, Juvenal, and Persius. These Elizabethan writers, whose texts were both

---

8   Jones and Stallybrass demonstrate how yellow starch, made with imported saffron dye, also turned the English wearer into a foreigner. See their Chapter 3 in *Renaissance Clothing and the Materials of Memory*.

9   As Hunter asserts, "[t]he foreigner could only 'mean' something important, and so be effective as a literary figure, when the qualities observed in him were seen to involve a simple and significant relationship to real life at home" (13). I would argue that the same dynamic is at work here in seeing foreign products as somehow immoral. The notion that the foreign product is dangerous is understandable to an English audience when it is put in relation with the domestic cloth product.

10   The word *text*, meaning written word, comes from the Old French *texte*, meaning "the scripture," and the Medieval Latin *textus*, meaning "gospel." The Latin *textus*, meaning "the style or tissue of a literary work" helps us to make the connection to cloth. Woven fabric or textile, is from the Latin *textil-is*, signifying "woven."

11   The criticism of satire is as contentious and wide-ranging as the literature itself. See, in particular, Kernan, *The Cankered Muse* and Selden, *English Verse Satire* for early discussions. For more recent criticism see Manley, "Essential Difference: The Projects of Satire" in *Literature and Culture in Early Modern London*; Connery and Combe's introduction to *Theorizing Satire*; Bogel, *The Difference Satire Makes*; and McRae, *Literature, Satire, and the Early Stuart State*.

derivative and learned, most often wrote in verse and understood that the didactic nature of satire needed the crafted arts of classical persuasion to be convincing. In appealing to the emotions through *pathos*, authors were able to incite feelings of laughter and gentle ridicule, of ire and derision. Attending to the imitative nature of Elizabethan satire is crucial is terms of understanding its meaning.[12] However, following the recent work of Andrew McRae in *Literature, Satire, and the Early Stuart State*, in this chapter I would like to look at satire beyond the restrictive "neo-classical standards and conventions" that inform traditional formal studies of the mode; in the early modern period—much as in our own—satire became "as much an attitude or an inflection as a literary genre" (2, 3).[13] Rather than limiting our discussion to texts that were self-conscious of their status as "satire," I would like to expand the frame of reference to include texts that were written without formal restrictions and often for a broad audience. In critiquing those who wore foreign textiles, ballads, sermons, and prose narratives were as effective as formal verse satire.[14] As McRae asserts, "satire is malleable, adaptable and sometimes most incisive when it fails to announce itself" (8).[15]

The texts that I take up in this chapter might be termed a "literature of complaint."[16] While these texts do not necessarily stand in the shadow of Roman predecessors (although some do), they are nevertheless quite self-conscious in their didacticism, highly imaginative in their wit, and complex in the stance of the speakers and assumptions about audience.[17] According to Raman Selden's helpful

---

12 See Baumlin, p. 467, for a discussion of the intertextuality of satire.

13 McRae's important study takes up satire as an expansive mode, including libelous ballads and pamphlets, and discusses it in relation to early Stuart politics. Also see Croft, "Libels, Popular Literacy and Public Opinion," for a discussion of the connections between libel and satire.

14 While it may seem curious to correlate sermon and satire, I would suggest that popular sermons of the early modern period owe a great rhetorical debt to popular satire and vice-versa. In their focus on critiquing social problems and behavior, they share similar aims. McRae asserts that satire "is concerned with acts of revelation rather than strategies of fabrication, and with attacks on agreed sins rather than particular sinners" (5). I would argue that sermons, especially those spoken to a large public audience, work in virtually the same vein. For a discussion of the connections between Puritan polemic and dramatic satire, see Crockett, Chapter 4. For an early discussion of the rhetoric of complaint and homily, see Peter.

15 While McRae emphasizes the permeability of the definition of satire, a conventional reading of satire assumes an epistemological grounding in what that category means. As Bogel asserts, "on nearly every important front, then—motive, rhetorical alignments, moral structure, generic identity—criticism of satire has insisted on its clarity, its stability, and its ultimate if not apparent lack of ambiguity" (4).

16 Traditionally, critics have generally regarded complaint as a medieval phenomenon quite different from the formal satire of the Elizabethans. See, particularly, Peter, *Complaint and Satire in Early English Literature*.

17 While the formal verse satirists constitute a group of writers as do the "University Wits," those who wrote complaint cannot be classified in so tidy a group. See Prescott, "Humour and Satire in the Renaissance," p. 289, and Manley, "London and the Languages of Tudor Complaint" and "Essential Difference: The Projects of Satire" in *Literature and Culture in Early Modern London*.

definition, complaint "is conceptual, allegorical, impersonal, moral and corrective. Its backdrop is a noble and ideal past. Its foreground is judgment, death, retribution" (48). Moreover, it is important to see that complaint is specific, tied to the historical contexts of a particular moment. As Edward Rosenheim has remarked, satire "consists of an attack by means of a manifest fiction upon discernable historical particulars" (31).[18] The move to historicize satire has in a sense liberated it from the strictures of a purely aesthetic criticism. But, as McRae astutely argues, this formulation assumes "that a text will present itself unproblematically as a satire" (9). The literature of complaint of the trade in luxury imports is by no means a cohesive group with obviously similar forms and aims. Those who complained about the English obsession with foreign clothes often did so with witty conceits, as with Thomas Dekker's *Seven Deadly Sins of London*, or in elaborate allegorical narratives, as we shall see in Robert Greene's *Quip for and Upstart Courtier*. Just as often, though, these complaints were straightforwardly funny and descriptive in their biting ridicule, as we see in many of the ballads and other poems. The least "literary" of the texts that decry the wearing of foreign fabrics—moral texts such as Philip Stubbe's *Anatomie of Abuses* and overtly religious tracts, such as the sermons preached at St. Paul's—are no less rhetorical in their crafting and biting in their invective. The complaints against wearing foreign clothes, however, find common ground in their aim to expose a social ill, pass judgment on the types that participate in the practice, sometime to offer a corrective, all the while setting their critique against the "noble and ideal past" of the domestic cloth industry.

An Englishman's Suit is Like a Traitor's Body

The English had long represented themselves in print as concerned with fashions. As early as 1562, Andrew Boorde satirized what he saw as a particularly English obsession with attire:

> I am an Englyshman, and naked I stand here
> Musyng in my mynd, what rayment I shal were
> For now I wyll were thys and now I wyl were that
> Now I wyl were I cannot tel what
> All new fashyons be pleasaunt to me. (A3v)[19]

The accompanying woodcut famously represents an unclothed Englishman with shears in his hand (see Figure 2).

The significance of this emblem, as the anonymous author of the *Hic Mulier* (1620) pamphlet suggests nearly a century later, is that the Englishman "had liberty with his shears to cut from every Nation of the World one piece of patch to make up

---

18   Although Rosenheim writes specifically on Swift and eighteenth century satire, his first chapter, "The Satiric Spectrum," is helpful in more broadly defining and theorizing satire.

19   Foreign visitors to England also noted the hunger for newfangled fashion particular to the English. See Rye, *England as Seen by Foreigners in the Days of Elizabeth and James the First*, pp. 71 and 90.

Fig. 2   Andrew Boorde, *The First Book of the Introduction of Knowledge*,
               **1562 (A3v). This item is reproduced by permission of The
               Huntington Library, San Marino, California.**

his garment" (276).[20] In *The Seven Deadly Sins of London* (1606), Thomas Dekker
also refers to this image, indicating its status as a stock emblem for representing the
absurd sartorial habits of the Englishman:

> Wittie was that Painter therefore, that when he had limned one of every Nation in their
> proper attyres, and being at his wittes endes how to drawe an Englishman: At the last (to
> give him a quipp for his follie in apparell) drewe him starke naked, with Sheeres in his
> hande, and cloth on his arme, because none could cut out his fashions but himselfe. (59)

---

20 The aim of *Hic Mulier* is to condemn and satirize the "man-woman," she who insists
on dressing decadently and without regard to gendered attire. The author invokes the image
of the naked Englishman to suggest that not even his folly in fashion can compare to the
"[m]iscellany or mixture of deformities which ... is loosely, indiscreetly, wantonly, and most
unchastely invented" by these women (276).

Both the author of *Hic Mulier* and Dekker are aware that the image in Boorde's text is meant as a "quipp," a clever barb to poke fun at their countryman's folly, while they also invoke the question of nationhood in their reading of the image. In his insistence on looking elsewhere for his apparel, the Englishman must necessarily remain naked. England, then, represented by the emblematic figure, is left bare, exposed, and vulnerable. It is only by clothing himself in foreign attire that the Englishman can be dressed at all, and it is the dressing in the clothes of "strangers" that puts English national identity into crisis.

Importantly, the authors who are troubled by the image of the Englishman with shears in his hand, poised to cut himself a foreign garment to his liking, point to the agency of the figure. In Boorde's ditty, the Englishman insists that he "*wyl wear*" "this" or "that," depending upon his "musyngs." The author of *Hic Mulier* underscores the "*liberty*" the man has "to make up his garment," while Dekker points out that only the Englishman "*himselfe*" has the ability "to cut out his fashions" (my emphases). The utter freedom for a man to choose the clothes that he wears enables him to choose the national identity with which he associates. In an age where subjects had the liberty to purchase foreign goods at an unprecedented rate, the ability to define national identity could not necessarily be controlled by the Crown. Discourse surrounding the purchase of foreign clothes thus becomes heavily moralized, pitting a national expansionism—in the subject's acceptance of and desire for foreign goods—against a national protectionism—in the desire of the Crown and moralists to promote domestic wares. One might expect to find in the literature of the period a celebration of the individual's agency to "cut from every Nation of the World," to become whoever he or she desires, be it French, Italian, or an amalgamation of many nations. In the period's topical literature—particularly satire, ballads, and religious polemics—we find almost without exception that the adoption of foreign fashions is derided for the disruption it causes to an imagined national solidarity. Repeatedly, we see in the texts that foreign cloth is sinister in its power to undermine England's virtue and the symbolic rectitude of the domestic wool industry.

While many writers reveal the obsession with foreign fashion to be a harmless foible, a seventeenth-century ballad, entitled "The Phantastick Age" (1634) connects the wearing of foreign fashions to the more sinister transgression of vanity and monstrosity:

An English man or woman now,
   (I'le make excuse for neither),
Composed are, I know not how,
   Of many shreds together:
Italian, Spaniard, French, and Dutch,
Of each of these they have a touch.
   O Monsters,
   Neutrall monsters,
   Leave these foolish toys. (156)[21]

---

21 See also Heywood's *Rape of Lucrece*, for a description of the Englishman who accepts all foreign fashion.

In their desire for the latest European styles, these modish men and women have fashioned themselves into "monsters," something unnatural and decidedly *not* English. They are constructed of so many foreign "shreds," that they—like Jonson's Monsieur—have completely obfuscated their origins. That they have a "touch" of many nations implies that they have a trace of each within them; it also might suggest—according to contemporaneous usage—that they are "injuriously" affected, "blemished, stained, or tainted" with these nations (*OED*). This seems plausible given that in Jacobean drama we see the connection between concern for foreign fashion and disease. In John Webster's *The Duchess of Malfi* (1614), for example, among the mad men intended to torment the Duchess is "an English Tailor, craz'd i' th' brain / With the study of new fashions" (V, ii, 50–51). Even in vice-ridden Italy, the English tailor stands out as particularly deranged. Thomas Coryate, based on his travels to the continent in the early part of the seventeenth century, asserts that compared to the modest and uniform styles of the Venetians, the fashion of the English is "much inferiour" indicating their unstable mental state.[22] Referring to the stock image of the naked Englishman with his scissors, Coryate says that the Englishman has been painted "starke naked with a paire of shears in his hand, making his fashion of attire according to the vaine invention of his braine-sick head, not to comelinesse and decorum" (398). The point might be further pressed to suggest that possessing a "touch" of these nations is likened to being physiologically contaminated by them. The full title of Dekker's aforementioned pamphlet indicates the notion that sinful behavior—most prominently figured as vanity indicated by the obsession with clothes—was associated with infection: *The Seven Deadly Sinnes of London: Drawne in Severall Coaches, Through the Seven Severall Gates of the Citie Bringing the Plague with Them.* The sins of the inhabitants of London are thus depicted by Dekker as not indigenous to England, and the disease that they bring— the plague—has the possibility to decimate the population with its spread.

In the period's literature, the discourse of physical disease easily slips into that of moral corruption. John Marston's "A Cynick Satyre" from *The Scourge of Villanie* (1598) suggests that the gentleman donning foreign attire invites both physical infection and evil into England:

> Seest thou yon gallant in the sumptuous clothes,
> How brisk, how spruce, how gorgiously he showes,
> Note his French-herring bones, but note no more,
> Unlesse thou spy his fayre appendant whore
> Is this a *Man*? Nay, an incarnate devill,
> That struts in vice, and glorieth in evill. (17–21; 26–7)

The gallant in fancy fabrics "struts in vice," suggesting that the clothes in which he parades around London represent evil itself. At the same time, these words indicate

---

22 In *The Merchant of Venice*, among Portia's suitors is Falconbridge, an English baron. Portia asserts that he is an abhorrent choice for a husband because he can speak "neither Latin, French, nor Italian." Worse still, he is "oddly dressed," indicating his strange temperament: "I think he bought his doublet in Italy, his round hose in France, his bonnet in Germany, and his behavior every where" (I, ii, 69–70, 73, 74–6).

that by wearing foreign clothes he struts vice in; that is, through his clothes he smuggles corruption into the city.[23]

The foppish man's choice of clothes and his accompanying prostitute also suggest that he has a venereal disease; the collocation of the pox and excessive interest in foreign fabrics is a common trope in satirical literature. The fabric from which his suit is made, herring-bone, is a silk or velvet from Lyon having a herring-bone pattern. The proximity of the words 'bone' and 'French' would have been an obvious joke to Marston's audience as an ache in the bone was a well-known symptom of the pox and the most common name for the disease in England was *Morbus Gallicus* or The French Disease.[24] Returning to Jonson's "English Monsieur," we see that the speaker wonders if the Monsieur's father, "when he did him beget" had "the French disease, with which he labours yet" (9, 10). The "disease" with which the monsieur "labours" is both his overt concern for fashion and also clearly the pox, which is evidenced through this concern. The disease is written on his body, not in scabs, but in scarves, silks, and feathers imported from France.

While satirical texts generally focus their attention on London gallants, fashionable women were not impervious to the corrupting influence of clothing. In *Pleasant Quippes for Upstart Newfangled Gentlewomen* (1595), Stephen Gosson reveals the communicable dangers that are woven into the textiles:

These hoopes, that hippes and haunch do hide,
    and heave aloft the gay hoyst traine,
As they are now in use for pride,
so did they first beginne of paine:
    When whoore in stewes had gotten poxe,
    This French devise, kept coats from smocks. (9)

The speaker suggests that the ostentatious farthingales, the apparatus made from whalebone that puffed out the skirts of ladies' kirtles and also prevented the dress from dragging on the ground, were invented by the French as a result of symptoms of the pox. The women who contracted the disease in whore-houses ("stewes") wore the farthingale to keep their dresses ("coats") from the undergarments ("smocks"), which were thought to carry the disease.[25] In criticizing English women for adopting this fashion, the speaker suggests that wearing French accessories is indicative not only of vanity, but also of the disease's entry into the social body of England.

While there was concern that imported fashions and fabrics introduced venereal disease when they crossed national borders, once in the country these fabrics were

23 The word "strut" indicates a performative, ostentatious style of walking and, as Bailey points out in her discussion of early modern actors who "jet" (a similar verb) in their fancy clothes, we see the "dangers of players playing it up, rather than simply role-playing" "Monstrous Manner" (266).

24 See my "Luxury and Lechery" for a discussion of naming the disease in Early Modern England as well as a discussion of the connection of excessive concern with foreign fashion and the pox. See also Harris's *Foreign Bodies*, p. 14, for a discussion of the rhetorical construction of social ills as foreign.

25 An alternate reading of this passage would indicate the farthingale keeps men ("coates") from the prostitutes and their diseases. I thank an anonymous reader for pointing to this.

then capable of corrupting the *moral* fabric of England itself, exposing the land to the sins of the city. Just as "pox was the reality that undermined many of the pretensions of urban life and symbolized its vice and falsity," so too did foreign luxury fabrics (Pelling, 104). In *Michaelmas Term* (1605–1606), Thomas Middleton links sexually transmitted disease specifically with the silks that country girls wear when they come to the city to be whores: "So farewell wholesome weeds, where treasure pants, / And welcome silks, where lies disease and wants" (I, ii, 53–4). In giving up modest country clothing in favor of the urban uniform of luxury goods, one must necessarily open oneself up to the lechery associated with the fabric. The French disease, whether sartorial or physical, was regarded as a sin of the city, so it was mainly those in urban areas or those susceptible to the lure of the city, that fell victim to the disease.[26] Pocky and mad, diseased and monstrous, the fashion-hungry English person comes to be portrayed at best as infected, and at worst, inhuman.

Imbued with the symbolic power, as Jones and Stallybrass put it, to "take an existing nature and transnature it" (4), clothing was seen as being capable of questioning the ontological status of the wearer and transforming him or her into that which was unknowable. For polemicist Philip Stubbes, "most of our fond Inventions, and newfangled fashions, rather deforme us, then adorne us: disguise us, then become us: making us rather to resemble savage beastes and brutish monsters, then continent, sober and chast Christians" (67). Both Stubbes and the author of "The Phantastick Age," who names those obsessed with fashions as "neutrall monsters," indicate the physical and moral transformation that occurs when donning foreign apparel. Embracing foreign clothes, one also embraces the vices associated with that country. The word *monster*, as it was used in the early modern period, denoted an animal or plant that was seen to be unnatural, from the Old French *monstre*. The word, however, was also derived from the Latin *monstrum*, which meant a divine portent or warning. Bringing together these two definitions, we see a suggestion that those who wore foreign fabrics not only were deviant, but also served as a warning to those who viewed them: the wearers' *demonstration* of foreign clothes on the English body alerted observers to the *demon* or *monstrosity* that they had become.

Thomas Dekker's *The Seven Deadly Sins of London* also associates deviance with continental clothes but importantly emphasizes the implications of wearing foreign cloth for English nationhood. Individual acts serve to usher in a crisis of national proportions. In the chapter called "Apishness," Dekker claims that wearing foreign fashion is akin to treason:

[A]n English-mans suite is like a traitors bodie that hath beene hanged, drawne, and quartered, and is set up in severall places: his Cod-peece is in *Denmark*, the coller of his Duble and the belly in *France*: the wing and narrow sleeve in *Italy*: the short waste hangs over a *Dutch* Botchers stall in *Utrich*: his huge sloppes speaks *Spanish*: *Polonia* gives him the Bootes.[27] (59–60)

---

26 See Watts, pp. 128–9 for a discussion of the more morally sound behavior of rural folk.

27 Jones and Stallybrass invoke Dekker's Englishman to assert that while clothes could be considered treasonous, they also "condensed the geography of England's trading relations" (1).

Dekker refers to the particularly English practice of simultaneously wearing various styles of clothing and fabrics derived from several countries, figuratively dispersing the Englishman's body all over Europe. By invoking the punishment reserved for high treason (hanging, drawing, and quartering), this sartorial deed is identified with a crime against the state. The donning of clothing from several countries both disassembles the English body and dismantles a unified nation.[28] Discussing this passage, Karen Newman asserts that "the mingle-mangle of English fashion is displaced onto national 'others' and xenophobia worked out through a spectacular and psychically useful synecdochic substitution of the traitor's body for the nation-state" (125). While the confusion of English fashion is "displaced" onto other nations, resulting in a xenophobic representation of Europe, it is important to emphasize that in Dekker's passage the foreign, and therefore suspect, "suit" remains *in* England *on* the Englishman's body, thereby emphasizing the main source of anxiety. Not only has the other been *willingly* allowed into England through the cloth trade, but this action also calls into question the national sympathies of the Englishman. We might, as Newman does, compare this to the representation of the English nation-state, as the body politic with the sovereign as the head and the nation's subjects as the body. If the subjects are figuratively dispersed all over the world, England itself becomes fragmented. Thus, Dekker's simile hints at what was at the heart of the debate over foreign clothes: treachery to English industry and English identity.

To underscore the extent to which Dekker's text associates clothing with national identity, and how this national identity is corrupted by the foreign, we might compare his text to that of another author who was interested in how national identity is constructed by foreign relations. Dekker's text closely resembles E.K.'s critique in the dedicatory epistle to Edmund Spenser's *The Shepheardes Calendar* (1579). The "author" complains of the bastardization of the English language by the incorporation of foreign words and phrases:

> [O]ur mother tonge, which truly of itself is both ful enough for prose and stately enough for verse, hath long time ben counted most bare and barrein of both. Which default when as some endevoured to salve and recure, they patched up the holes with peces and rags of other languages, borrowing here of the French, there of the Italian, every where of the Latine, not weighing how il, those tongues accorde with themselves, but much worse with ours: So now they have made our English tongue, a gallimaufray or hodgepodge of al other speches. (503)[29]

Like the Englishman, whose body has been "set up in severall places" through the appropriation of the fashions of many countries, here E.K. indicates a similar phenomenon with the English language. Both authors similarly list the countries that are corrupting the English, and both imply that the inclusion of such foreign

---

28 For an excellent discussion of the relationship between the body and nationalism, see Scholz, *Body Narratives*.

29 Spenser's image of other bits of other languages filling English like "rags" points to the connection between literature and cloth. See Cady, for a discussion of this passage in relation to language and disease. Paper in the early modern period was made from old rags and thus texts had a close, material connection to textiles.

influences does damage to England's name by compromising that which can be seen as representing England: for Dekker this is cloth, for E.K., the vernacular.[30] More importantly, both authors point to the crisis to which the inclusion of the foreign leads. The fragmentation of what was once English into a geographically dismembered entity leads to an epistemological predicament: the English language/body becomes unrecognizable and unintelligible through the foreign corruption of text/textile.[31]

John Lyly, in the prologue to his play *Midas* (1592), more broadly suggests that the nation itself—like the English language and subject—irrevocably is affected by foreign influences: "Trafficke and travell hath woven the nature of all Nations into ours, and made this land like Arras, full of devise, which was Broad-cloth, full of workmanshipp" (Prologue).[32] Woven into a tapestry as a result of the mingle-mangle of foreignness in England, the nation must renounce its former status as "broad-cloth," with its attendant virtue of "workmanshipp." The hodge-podge that England has become as a result of the infiltration of the stranger's wares is associated with "devise" rather than honest labor, the artifice and contrivance of tapestry rather than the purity of homespun wool.[33]

Just as secular writers like Lyly and Dekker pointed to the crisis of national affiliation that wearing foreign fabrics implied, London preachers saw the wearing of foreign clothes as an indication of moral decay. In Nathanaell Cannon's sermon delivered at St. Paul's Cross, *The Cryer* (1613), he reminds his audience of sinners that wearing foreign fashions amounted to putting one's pride on display, thereby outwardly demonstrating one's unsuitability for heavenly salvation: "For of what Nation and Country doth not your City borrow pride? and for your fashions as they are many, so they are monstrous: I would the Lord that when you goe to take measure of your wide and flaunting garments, that then your soules would remember the way to heaven which is said to bee narrow" (30). Cannon cleverly implies that the fantastic width of the various garments that men and women of fashion wear (cartwheel ruffs, peascod-bellied doublets, French bum rolls, Dutch slops) will literally not fit through the narrow gates of heaven.[34] It is the pride, however, that is woven into the fabric of the bombastic foreign clothes and that is the true reason that one cannot get to heaven wearing a French farthingale. This English heaven has a dress code: foreign fashions are not appropriate.

In another sermon preached at Paul's Cross entitled *The Celestiall Husbandry: Or, The Tillage of the Soul* (1611), William Jackson reprimands those concerned with the whims of changing fashions: "The next fallow ground, that I would have you to peruse over, is the fashion-mongers of our time; I meane the sonnes of pride:

---

30 In *Forms of Nationhood*, Richard Helgerson discusses Spenser's project of forming an English nationhood through the English language. See especially the introduction and Chapter 1.

31 In addition to stirring up anxieties of national affiliation, both clothes and language could often cover over one's class status. See Scholz, p. 18.

32 I thank Carla Mazzio for bringing this passage to my attention.

33 According to Jardine, tapestries were "a particularly ostentatious art form" in the fifteenth and sixteenth centuries (*Worldly Goods*, 399).

34 Matthew 7:14: "but small is the gate and narrow the road that leads to life, and only a few find it."

to day an English-man, to morrow a French-man, the third day a Spaniard, then a Turke, and last of all a Devill" (27). Jackson points to the now-familiar phenomenon of those who shift their national affiliations as quickly as they change their clothes, leaving their Englishness behind. But while Dekker sees this appropriation of foreign clothes as a transgression against the nation, Jackson sees it as a sin against God. Like Philip Stubbes and his fellow sermonist, Nathaneall Cannon, Jackson underscores the monstrosity of such activities. Crucially, Jackson's sermon, as well as Cannon's, was spoken outside St. Paul's Church, where men of religion were in close proximity to the men of fashion who gathered inside the church to display their latest purchases in Paul's Walk, the middle aisle of the church.[35] The place where one heard the word of God abutted the space where one expressed preoccupation with apparel, thus juxtaposing the theatrics of the sermon with the spectacle of the tailors' wares.[36] In this sense, the men of cloth competed with the men of silks and velvets.[37] According to Jackson, embracing the fashions of other nations becomes a direct route to hell. Wearing clothes from different nations draws the fashion-monger further away from Anglicanism and down a slippery slope to moral decay and heresy. Jackson suggests that by changing into French clothes the Englishman becomes, "a Frenchman," a more worldly and less spiritual Christian; donning attire from Spain converts one to "a Spaniard," or a Catholic; and changing into the apparel of "a Turk" makes one an infidel, one step away from transmuting into "the devill" himself. The "fallow" soul of the vainglorious must be "tillaged" by the "celestial husbandry" they find in God (D2r, title page). While Jackson's emphasis on changing fashion at first glance is consonant with Dekker's critique, we find that his ultimate goal is in saving souls rather than the integrity of the nation.

Or is it? The business of religious polemic becomes complicated when we understand that Jackson was a pensioner of the Clothworkers' Company, the trade company representing those involved in the finishing of domestic woolens and thus was very much concerned with the business of cloth.[38] While his rant against the men who wear foreign fashion highlights their moral corruption, his financial interest in the domestic cloth industry also suggests that his motives for writing such invective against foreign clothes may not be so godly. The "Englishman" cannot transform into the "devill" unless he purchases cloth from other nations, which will mean that

---

35 The audience for the sermons preached at Paul's Cross—the pulpit set up in a corner of St. Paul's churchyard—was notable for both its size (up to 6,000) and diversity (commoners mingling with nobleman). See Herr, *The Elizabethan Sermon*, p. 24.

36 Maclure points to the commonalties that the sermons at St. Paul's Cross shared with the early modern stage as well as the competition the sermonist felt for audience. See Maclure, *The Paul's Cross Sermons*, p. 4. More recently, Crockett has discussed the similar cultural work that plays and St. Paul's Cross sermons perform in early modern London in *The Play of Paradox*. See especially Chapters 2 and 3.

37 The sermonists were also competing with booksellers, who set up their stalls in and around the churchyard. See W. Sparrow Simpson, *Gleanings from Old S. Paul's*, pp. 266–7, for a list of booksellers near St. Paul's in 1582.

38 The Clothworkers' Company was primarily governed by merchants interested in promoting the sale of cloth to markets beyond Europe. See my Chapter 3 for a discussion of this company in the context of the desire to increase the export of wool broadcloth.

he is *not* purchasing English cloth and therefore not upholding the home industry and the clothworkers who support Jackson himself. Jackson's dedicatory epistle, "To the Worshipfull Companie of Clothworkers," concludes by commending the guild company: "yee have, and doe well, yet I beseach you to increase more and more: whereby your name may be more spread on earth, and your glory greater enlarged in heaven" (*2v). By denouncing and hoping to impede the wearing of foreign clothes, Jackson is working to uphold the labor of the domestic workers, to whom he is financially indebted and whom he blesses with prosperity. The road to wickedness through one's choice in apparel was, for Jackson, the result of the religious affiliation of the clothes' country of origin as well as a repudiation of the domestic wool industry.[39]

As Jackson's interests might express, the fabric from which foreign clothes were made was the real source of anxiety and potential criminality in the minds of those striving to uphold the domestic cloth industry. A pair of slops in the Spanish style could have been made anywhere, including England. It is when the garment is made from Spanish taffeta that it becomes identifiable with the country of origin and therefore becomes at least figuratively treasonous. Government officials and economists decried the importation of fabrics for upsetting the trade balance. At a time when the English broadcloth industry was struggling and domestic cloth exports were dipping, it simply did not make sense to import silks.[40] As Stone suggests, "[a]ll statesmen and publicists were agreed that the import of superfluous luxuries should be rigidly pruned" (43).

Whereas government officials and economic thinkers saw importing as the undoing of the economy, they were perhaps shortsighted in their assumption that they could halt the march of consumer desires. Demand for luxury goods was not only an unstoppable phenomenon, but it was deemed by some as advantageous to England's economic health. John Stow, for example, represented the positive side of London's role in the importing of commodities from beyond England's shores: "London bringeth singularly these good things following. By advantage of the situation it disperseth foreign wares (as the stomacke doth meat) to all the members most commodiously" (2.212). Somewhat surprisingly, we see a similar argument from Daniel Price, a sermonist who asserts that trade does indeed "mutually inrich al kingdomes, making the proper commodities of one county common to a nother" (B3v). He singles out "our silkes from *Spaine*" as a particularly beneficial commodity. Just as the Merchant Adventurers, the guild that exported domestic cloth to markets abroad, understood the impossibility of stopping the importation of foreign cloth, they also saw the economic opportunity in regulating it. Importing silks was crucial to making up for the merchants' sluggish cloth exports. As B.E. Supple explains, cloth exports to Northern Europe could be "made to 'finance' (by barter or the

---

39 For a discussion of the nationalistic nature of early modern sermons, see Maclure, p. 118.

40 Virtually all raw silk was imported into England, even into the seventeenth century. Responding to this, in 1606 James I ordered the planting of ten thousand mulberry trees to relieve unemployment. See Linthicum, *Costume in the Drama of Shakespeare and His Contemporaries*, p. 113 and Alice Clark, *The Working Life of Women in the Seventeenth Century*, p. 140.

setting-over of bills of debt) the import of luxury cloths from Italy, France, and Spain, which were originally sent not directly to the lands of final consumption but to the fairs at Nuremberg and Frankfort" (91). The company that dealt primarily in overseas transactions saw that the international trade of cloth was just that: a negotiated give-and-take, rather than a unilateral transaction. After all, international trade could only work if exports (which English officials did want to expand) were consonant with imports, and consumer demand prescribed both sides.

These voices, however, did not represent the majority sentiment when it came to trade relations, and most governmental authorities sided with the domestic guilds in their desires to restrict imported cloth. Such issues are raised throughout the sixteenth century, but they became more pressing as the century progressed. As early as 1576, we find literary writers criticizing what seemed to be the greedy practices of the merchants. In his satire *The Steele Glas*, George Gascoigne, in the voice of his narrator Satyra, catalogues the social wrongdoings of the time, highlighting the scandal of promoting the purchase of foreign cloth:

> And master Merchant, he whose travaile ought
> Commodiously, to doe his countrie good,
> And by his toyle, the same for to enriche,
> Can finde the meane, to make *Monopolyes*
> Of every ware, that is accompted strange. (162)

The practice of importing "strange" commodities is quite literally at the expense of promoting the products that will "enriche" and "doe" England "good." Gascoigne claims that the merchants have a responsibility to their nation: they "ought" to promote domestic wares. The practice of promoting foreign products works against loyalty to the county by detracting from England's economic prowess. The satire of the merchants who import foreign "wares" is for Gascoigne a criticism of those who import foreign cloth. He warns the men in London, especially soldiers home from foreign campaigns, to beware the lure of the silk merchants: "Let not them, pul thee by the sleeve / For sutes of silke, when cloth may serve thy turne" (159). Here the merchants are figured as duplicitous, hiding in the shadows, tugging at the sleeve of the susceptible soldiers home from the wars and possibly puffed up with pride. Gascoigne suggests that to be enticed by the merchants is to be disloyal to the country for which these men were fighting. Rejecting "sutes of silk" is the righteous and patriotic action befitting an English soldier, while patronizing mercers' shops was a simultaneously unpatriotic and immoral activity. As Barnabe Rich laments, "*Sinne* hath her *Silkmen* and *Mercers*, that doth serve her of *lace, silke, sattin, velvet, cloath of silver, cloath of gold* ... *Sinne* hath her *Merchants*, that will transport the commodities behooveful for the commonwealth, into forraine countries, and will return backe again *toies* and *trifles*" (B1v–B2r). Silkmen and mercers, those who traffic in luxury goods, are seen as evil agents who peddle their vice-ridden fabrics in England. Woven into the clothing is the vice of pride, which carries with it the disease and corruption. Thus, avoiding foreign fabric, seen as "toies and trifles," served a dual purpose—one would uphold the integrity of the nation though rejecting vanity associated with the foreign cloth as well the disease nominally assigned to them. By avoiding luxury textiles one could also avoid lechery—the two words were synonymous in the early modern period.

English Cloth: "A True Subject"

While the import of foreign luxury cloth was troubling in its disruption of England's cloth trade, it was distressing for other reasons too: foreign textiles perpetuated the craze for sumptuous fabrics, thereby causing a decrease in the *cultural* value of domestic cloth. While the success of the cloth industry throughout much of the sixteenth century was a source of pride and a locus for organizing fantasies of national solidarity, the consumers' turn away from the domestic industry was a blow to the unified vision of the nation based upon domestic cloth. Philip Stubbes, in *The Anatomie of Abuses* (1583), indicates this sentiment when he asserts that foreign fabrics were only acceptable as long as they stayed out of England:

> those [continental] countries are rich and wealthy of themselves, abounding with all kind of precious ornaments, and rich attire ... and therefore if they weare them, they are not to be blamed, as not having any other kinde of clothing to cover themselves withall. So if we would contente our selves with such kinde of attire as our owne countrie doeth yeeld us, it were somewhat tollerable. But we are so captivate in Pride, that if it come not from beyond the seas, it is not woorth a straw. And thus we impoverish our selves in buying their trifling Merchandizes, more pleasant than necessary, and inritch them, who laugh at us in their sleeves, to see our great follie in affecting of trifles, and parting with good wares for them. (69–70)

Stubbes's assumption that Europeans wear silks and satin because that is all they have, however specious, points to a primary reason the domestic cloth industry was in crisis: English people, particularly those with ready money, were decreasingly interested in wearing domestically produced cloth.[41] While Stubbes, like Jackson and Cannon, is mostly angered by the display of vanity that wearing foreign fabrics signifies, at the same time that buying foreign luxury goods "impoverish[es]" the soul, it also financially impoverishes the country. Consumers have rejected "good wares," those products provided by England, in favor of foreign "trifles," diminishing their own moral makeup as well as that of the English economy. Importantly for Stubbes, a simple solution to the vice of pride in England is for English people to embrace their own industry, to "content" themselves with the products that are "yeeld[ed]" by England itself. If the English will not wear their own cloth, then how is the industry, and indeed virtue, to be upheld?

---

41 In a 1622 letter to his top advisors lamenting the fallen state of the cloth trade, James asserts that "it is very fit to commend the wearing of Cloth of Our Kingdomes to other Nations, by Our owne example at home, We would have you consider by what meanes the Cloth and Stuffes made of the Woolls of these Our Kingdomes, may bee more frequently worne by Our owne Subjects, to what sorts of people, to what purposes, and in what manner it were fit the wearing thereof were enjoyed."

This question is at the heart of Robert Greene's *A Quip for an Upstart Courtier, or a Quaint Dispute Between Velvet Breeches and Cloth Breeches* (1592).[42] In this popular satiric pamphlet two anthropomorphized pair of breeches dispute their respective positions in England (see Figure 3).[43]

To briefly summarize the plot: A young man, going for a walk in the country, falls asleep and has a dream in which two pair of breeches—one made from cloth and the other from velvet—argue about who has more right to represent English values. The dispute is ultimately decided by a selection of jurors representing a cross-section of professions in England who happen upon the scene.[44] Velvet Breeches represents both the importation of foreign fabrics and the accompanying degradation of morals of the Londoners who wear them. Conversely, Cloth Breeches upholds the virtues of the English industry and celebrates the morals of the men who resist the temptations of city life. Significantly, this dispute takes place in the country—away from the infecting influence of the court and city. And it is at least partially the rural setting that allows English Cloth Breeches to triumph over his foreign, urban counterpart. Greene's text participates in the expression of a sentiment prevalent in late sixteenth century England: It is morally righteous to turn away from the city with its foreign and therefore dangerous influences towards the purity of the English countryside. Greene calls for a rejection of the city (London) in favor of the country (England) in order to spurn the foreign influences that have infiltrated the urban space.[45]

It is crucial to Greene's text that Velvet Breeches is not native to England. His foreignness creates the crisis in traditionally English values. In his dedicatory epistle to Thomas Burnaby,[46] Greene asserts that his tale is an allegory for the damage that vanity has done in England: "How since men placed their delights in proud looks and brave atyre, Hospitality was left off, Neighbourhood was exeiled, Conscience was skoft at, and charitie lay frozen in the streets" (209). While the "brave atyre"

---

42 Greene's late texts, *Quip* and the conny-catching pamphlets among them, are increasingly concerned with the state of moral decay in London. See Crupi, *Robert Greene*.

43 This text went through seven printings in 1592 alone. It was reprinted after that in 1606, 1620, 1622, and 1635. See Stevenson, *Praise and Paradox*, p. 209.

44 The events in Greene's text were borrowed wholesale from an earlier text, *The Debate Between Pride and Lowliness*, probably written by Francis Thynne and published in 1577. The antiquated language of the source text suggests that it may have been written several years prior to that date. The Shakespeare Society printed the text in 1841 and the editor, J. Payne Collier, reports that there is but one extant manuscript of the work in existence and that *The Debate* was prepared for print, but probably never published for sale. Greene, Collier suggests, possibly happened upon a copy of the source.

45 Here I invoke the double meaning of "country" that Raymond Williams points out in *The Country and the City*: "In English, 'country' is both a nation and a part of land; 'the country' can be the whole society or its rural area" (1). Rather than reading Greene's text as participating in a discourse of satire that questions the national sympathies of those who wear velvet, Jaster claims that "by idealizing the humble, Greene subtly suggests that those who have little should be satisfied with that" (208).

46 Thomas Barnaby (or Burnaby) was a friend of Greene's, who considered himself Barnaby's adopted son. Greene associates his dedicatee with all that is commendable about the English: he is a "father of the poore, a supporter of auncient Hospitalitie, and enemie to Pride, and to be short, a maintayner of Cloth breeches" (210).

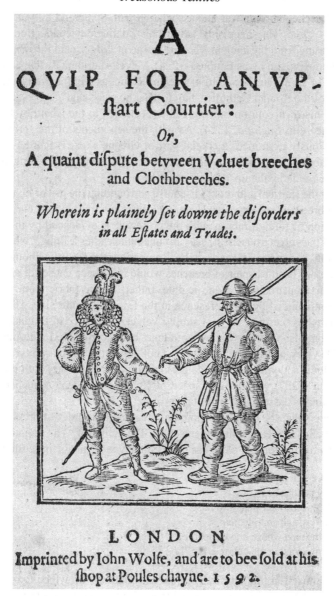

A

QVIP FOR AN VP.

ſtart Courtier:

Or,

A quaint diſpute betvveen **Veluet breeches** and Clothbreeches.

Wherein is plainely ſet downe the diſorders in all Eſtates and Trades.

LONDON

Imprinted by Iohn Wolfe, and are to bee ſold at his ſhop at Poules chayne. 1 5 9 2.

Fig. 3 **Robert Greene, *A Quip for an Upstart Courtier*, 1592 (title page). This item is reproduced by permission of The Huntington Library, San Marino, California.**

associated with foreign textiles undoes English morals, Cloth Breeches is portrayed as the material "such as ... our great Grandfathers wore, when neighbour-hood and hospitalitie had banished pride out of *England*" (222). Cloth Breeches represents a long-standing tradition in England of hospitality that is threatened by the corrupting forces that entered the country with foreign fabrics.

Velvet Breeches' foreignness and association with Spain and Italy is made clear throughout *A Quip*. He sheepishly admits his continental connections: "I (poor snake) am sprung from the ancient *Romans*, borne in *Italy* ... cald into *England* from my native home (where I was famous)" (224). Velvet's heritage is rich, emphasizing the tradition of vanity in the world of ancient Rome, as well as the connections to the Papistry of the Roman Catholic Church. That he was "cald" suggests that he did not come by his own volition but was rather beckoned to the island by the "young Gentlemen heere in *England*" (224). As with the sentiments of the sermonists and satirists previously examined, a crucial part of Greene's text is that he claims that sumptuous fabrics and their attendant vices would not be present in England unless they were *invited* in by the upstarts of London.

Recalling the satirical and moral discourse surrounding the use of luxury textiles, these velvet breeches are also seen as unnatural in their "marvellous curious[ness]." The association of foreign fabrics with the grotesque is evidenced by the narrator's first vision of the velvet trousers: he sees an "uncouth headlesse thing," which, despite the fact that it "had motion," seems to be "some monster" (220). Although the sight of an ambulatory headless pair of breeches would have been cause for alarm in and of itself, their monstrosity is made legible, rather, by the fabric from which they are made compounded by their presence in the English countryside. The character of Cloth Breeches sees that it is not simply Velvet's existence in England that is so scandalous, but also that he "camest not alone, but accompanied with multitude of abhominable vices, hanging on thy bumbast nothing but infectious abuses, and vaine glory, selfe love, sodomie and strange poisonings, wherewith [he] hath infected this glorious Iland" (227). The sinless space of England has been "touched," by the "infectious abuses" associated with Italian velvet.

As Greene suggests, the men who buy velvet cloth in order to dress the part of the court-dweller also emasculate themselves. The author of "The Phantastick Age" similarly claims that foreign cloth has usurped the young men's masculinity:

> Our men were in precedent days,
>   to manly actions bent.
> They did not seek their names to raise
>   By cloathes, and complement.
> Now he's the man whose brave apparel
> Defends him in a taverne quarrell. (157)

By clothing himself in fine fabrics, the man has nothing with which to represent his name or defend himself *except* these fabrics. Philip Stubbes similarly claims that wearing sumptuous attire actually detracts from bodily strength: "For be sure, this pampering of their bodies makes them weaker, tenderer, and nesher, then otherwise they would be if they were used to hardnesse, and more subject to receive any kind of infection or malady" (95–6). Donning the luxury fabrics in Stubbes' estimation results in a softening of the physique. For seventeenth-century writer Richard Brathwait, "delicacy in the *habit*, begets an *effeminacy* in the *heart*" (278). With all this "pampering," the man who wears such clothes places his masculinity into question.[47] And again we return to the notion that the cloth one wears leads to disease. The "weakening" of the body through fine stuffs, places one at risk for infection.

The presence of Velvet Breeches in the English countryside would have also been a reminder of the dangers to men who might leave their rural homes. The men most likely to fall prey to the ostentation of foreign fabrics are those young men from the country seeking a life of courtly luxury and decadence. Dressing in sumptuous apparel, as David Kuchta reminds us, was necessary in order to fit in among aristocrats: "elite masculinity was defined in part as properly sumptuous display, as living up to the sartorial experience of the crown" (234). Gascoigne's *The Steele Glas* refers to this practice: the youth coming to the city to seek advancement "is faine to sell, his landes for courtly cloutes, / Or else sits still and liveth like a loute" (D4r). The young men simply have no choice but to sport foreign fabrics if they are to succeed as courtiers. Despite the fact that they will sacrifice financial security—based in land ownership—for the courtly uniform of velvet, silk, and satin, their clothes ultimately cannot hide their roots. Greene reminds us that the men who wear velvet breeches "have no show of gentility but a Velvet slop, who by pouling or selling of land that their fathers lefte will bestowe all to buy an office about the court" (236). The tragedy ultimately lies in the rejection of a virtuous country life in favor of one of ostentation and debt:

A clownes sonne must be clapt in a velvet pantophle, and a velvet breech, though the presumptuous asse be drownd in the Mercers booke, & make a conney of all his lands to the usurer for commodities: yea the fop must goe like a gallant for a while, although at last in his age hee begge. (238)

In this newfangled system of exchange, land must be swapped for "commodities" and erstwhile rustics transformed into temporary gallants in exchange for a lifetime of beggary. While visiting England, Frederick Duke of Wirtemberg noticed that the women of London were preoccupied with their clothes "to such a degree indeed, that, as I am informed, many a one does not hesitate to wear velvet in the streets ... whilst at home perhaps they have not a piece of dry bread" (8). The corruption that enters in with Velvet seeps into more than just England's moral fabric; it infects and disrupts an entire economic system and leaves the people destitute.[48]

If, in *A Quip for an Upstart Courtier*, Velvet Breeches is represented as an ominous foreigner invited into England by morally suspect young men and ready to spread disease throughout the island, Cloth Breeches is a vision of humble domestic morals. Even the difference in their gaits is telling: while Velvet pompously "strouted up and down the vally as proudly as though they had there appointed to act some desperate combat,"

47 See Kuchta, "The Semiotics of Masculinity in Renaissance England" for an excellent discussion of the relationship between masculinity, class status, and clothing. Although Stubbes seems to deride all men who wear "soft" fabrics, Kuchta finds in courtesy literature that "effeminacy was found in the affected misuse of signs by vain upstarts" (238). See also Bailey, "'Monstrous Manner.'"

48 See Bailey "Monstrous Manner" for an excellent discussion of state concerns regarding "the meaner sort," particularly men of the lower orders who dressed in sumptuous fabrics.

Cloth Breeches comes on the scene "more soberly marching, and with a softer pace" (221, 222).[49] In meeting Cloth Breeches, we see that he is everything that Velvet is not. While Velvet is accented with "the best Spanish Satine," "gold twist," and "knots of pearle," Cloth Breeches are "plaine," "without either welt or garde," "of white Kersie, without a slop, the nether-stocke of the same ... and onely seamed with a little coventry blewe" (222). At a time when men were wearing as many sumptuous materials as they could possibly afford at the same time, it is remarkable that both these breeches and the netherstockings were made from the same humble cloth, without decoration ("welt or garde") or bombastic garments (a "slop"), and in simple colors (white and a "little" blue). Just as the evils of Velvet Breeches are made knowable through the naming of his countries of origin, so Cloth Breeches' humility and moral value is understood through the association with Kersey and Coventry, two English places known for their quality cloth. The "quaint dispute" to which the title refers is the important issue, not only in the text but in early modern cloth culture as well: "whether Cloth breeches are of more worth, and which of them hath the best title to bee resident in *England*" (250). While Cloth claims that Velvet has damaged his good name, and thus England's itself, Velvet feels Cloth is impinging upon his right to "honor" the gentlemen of London with his "countenance" (a puzzling word choice for a pair of trousers). The text, then, poses this crucial question to the jury of men assembled to decide the debate between Cloth and Velvet breeches and to the reader: Is it preferable to allow the popular market in foreign cloth to expand at the expense of the domestic industry so important to England's self-definition?

The jury, not surprisingly, rules in favor of Cloth Breeches.[50] In their estimation, the respective values and iniquities connected with Cloth and Velvet are enough to decide who is most fit to represent England:

> [W]e do find that Cloth breeches is by many hundred years more antient, ever since *Brute* an inhabitant in this island ... [Cloth is] a companion to kings, an equall with the nobility, a frend to Gentlemen and yeomen, and patrone of the poore, a true subject, a good housekeeper, and generall as honest as he is ancient, Whereas Velvet breeches is an upstart come out of *Italy*, begot of Pride, nursed up by self-love, & brought into this country by his companion Nufanglenesse: that he is an enemy to the Common-wealth, and one that is not in any way to be preferred in equity before cloth breeches. [Therefore in generall verdict we adjudje Cloth breeches] to have don him no wrong, but that hee hath llawfully claimed his title of Frank tenement, and in that wee appoint him for ever to bee resident.[51] (294)

---

49 This description of Velvet Breeches's gait brings to mind Greene's description of himself as performatively wearing luxury fabrics in *The Repentance* (1592): "At my return to England, I ruffeled out in my silks, in the habit of a *malcontent*" (20).

50 In the fascinating selection of jury members, which takes up the bulk of the text, each man who comes on the scene represents a particular occupation and in turn has his occupation critiqued by the two pair of breeches. The subtitle to *A Quaint Dispute* is *Wherein is plainely set down the disorders in all estates and Trade.*

51 The ending of Thynne's text is astonishingly different. While the jury is out deliberating, a group of men come and, in an imitation of Bacchus and his revelers, tear Cloth Breeches quite literally to shreds: "So that they were defaced in a throw, / And peece by peece so very small itorn, / That there nys man so conning that couth know, / Or gesse what garment they had ben beforn" (64).

Just as Velvet claims connections to the ancient and vain Romans, Cloth boasts a lineage back to the time of Brutus, Britain's first king and namesake. By linking Cloth Breeches with Brutus, Greene suggests that he is as famous and as worthy to represent England as that valiant Trojan. Further, Cloth, who is regarded equally with "kings," "nobility," "gentlemen," "yeomen," and the "poore," unites rather than divides the nation. With this final judgment, we also return to Thomas Dekker and Philip Stubbes' understanding of what the clothes one wears say about nationalist sympathies. Italian velvet is an "enemy to the commonwealth;" wearing it is likened to treason. Cloth is "a true subject;" to wear it demonstrates a show of support for the country that manufactures it. The length of Cloth's appointment in England—"forever"—precludes him from ever being threatened by outsiders again.

With the banishment of Velvet Breeches we are to assume that English virtues will be restored. Removing the stranger will reinstate the cultural superiority of Cloth Breeches and dispel all the greed, corruption, and loose morals associated with foreign cloth, thereby making the Englishman recognizable and whole again. By relinquishing the textiles of treason and choosing to wear domestic wool, the Englishman may finally become "a true subject." Moreover, England can be restored to its former glory by the simple act of choosing cloth whose virtue is woven into the very fabric. Once again the nation can revert to the time "when neighbour-hood and hospitalitie had banished pride out of *England*." And, of course, in this fantastical dream narrative this can all be so. But despite Greene's idealized representation of Cloth, the text cannot disguise the important fact that cloth is itself dependent upon the market for its successful triumph in England. Although in the national imagination, wool broadcloth might have stood for English virtue, the fabric possessed no intrinsic value beyond its economic power to render solvent England's economy. English domestic cloth, like its despised foreign counterpart, must ultimately be reduced to a commodity. And while the importation of foreign fabrics had disrupted the economies of England's most important industry in very real ways, the gravity of this disruption manifested itself as an affront to the symbolic properties of the textile. We see in Greene's text, then, as well as in those of other satirists and sermonists, a material attempt to emphasize the values so important to England at a time when the value of England's materials was under assault.

PART 3
Staging the Cloth Crisis

Chapter 5

The Fleecing of England, or the Drama of Corrupt Drapers: Thomas Middleton's *Michaelmas Term*

"*What makes the Gentleman complaine of his Wooll which lyes on his hand? The clothier complaine of his dead sales? The Merchant complaine on his losse? All but falshood.*"
    —John May, *A Declaration of the Estate of Clothing Now Used Within This Realme of England* (1613)

"*He cannot be a good Draper which is not first a good man.*"
    —William Scott, *An Essay on Drapery* (1635)

While the challenges faced by the wool broadcloth industry were legion in the early modern period, they were typically regarded as pressures external to the manufacturing of the product. Despite the many crises that the cloth industry faced—the harvest failures, the influence of immigrant weavers, the closure of markets abroad, and the popularity of imported luxury textiles—there was still a sense that the domestic product was essentially reputable, that English cloth was inherently good. Indeed, it was the insistence on the worthiness of cloth that allowed authors to articulate such vehemence against the elements that threatened it. And importantly, the pervasive belief in the integrity of the cloth industry was the basis for imagining how that industry might overcome the various challenges it faced. To return to the popular formulation I delineate in the introduction: the ancient and famous industry had fallen into a state of decay; but the industry would recover *because* it was ancient and famous. In this chapter I examine what happens to the image of English cloth when challenges come from *within* the manufacturing system and I explore the damage that is done to the reputation of English wool when the domestic production and sale practices of wool are regarded as corrupt. In particular, I focus on the figure of the London draper who is depicted in the period's literature as concerned with his personal profit rather than the good of the industry and, by extension, the nation.

Those who bought English wool from drapers in early modern London had to be wary of any number of deceptions that were understood to be prevalent among the shopkeepers: If the cloth was not stretched too much, then it might have been cut too short; if the wool was not given a false gloss, then the shop might have been so obscurely lit that the quality of the cloth was impossible to discern. While the producers of this cloth were the original source of the corruption, the frequency with which the drapers knowingly bought adulterated cloth proved them to be complicit in the crimes against the consumer. The result was that early modern London drapers contributed to the demise of the good reputation of the nation's venerable cloth industry. Just as I have argued in previous chapters that the cloth crises of the late sixteenth century disrupted the well-established image of England's noble trade, so too did the drapers' practices contribute to the demise of such an image. The claim that England's cloth was the finest in the world simply collapsed beneath the heavy fact that corrupt cloth was *knowingly* produced, sold, and exported by England's own. And while King James enacted several pieces of legislation to battle the decline of the nation's most important industry, the terrible reputation given to wool broadcloth remained a source of shame for England.[1] The sellers of this cloth, London's drapers, became a primary source of blame for wool's woes. The draper, whose primary job it was to sell wool to the domestic buyers, was the face of the cloth industry for many Londoners. Although his primary role had less to do with the manufacture, packaging, or large-scale selling of wool, he may very well have been the principal merchant of cloth with whom the city dwellers would have come into contact. The draper transformed the largely rural and attenuated wool production industry into a localized urban trade. He would have represented England's wool for hundreds of shoppers and his shop or stall in the busy London marketing districts would have been the site for contact with England's most famous product. While the symbolic properties of cloth were national in scope, the capital city and its denizens were often those who reified and challenged these properties.

Originally *draper* signified one who was involved in the manufacture of cloth.[2] By the time Edward III granted the letters patent to the Drapers' Company in 1364, the term primarily signified one who was involved in the sale of finished wool cloth to domestic customers and secondarily one who ordered raw wool to be manufactured into drapery for sale in his shop or stall (Girtin, *Triple Crowns*, 22).[3] Despite this general understanding of the term, by the end of the sixteenth century the role of the draper was multifaceted and often disjointed. The daily business of the Drapers' Company itself, one of the 12 great guild companies, dealt less with the ins and outs of the cloth trade and more with affairs of urban and national politics (Girtin, 192). The crown, for example, continually called upon the drapers to help fund foreign martial endeavors, such as Essex's expedition to Cadiz in 1596 to which the Drapers gave £460. The Drapers were also required by the crown to purchase nearly 800 quarters of grain from overseas in 1597 following a year of bad harvests and, in 1606, to contribute £1152 to a loan for King James (Girtin, 194, 198). Moreover, the Drapers were embroiled in several scandals, from the serious—the Company was accused of concealing lands they owned without disclosing the titles—to the more mundane—several drapers were alleged to have mistreated their apprentices. As Girtin says about the last decade of the sixteenth century, "the Court of the Drapers had become so involved in administration, and in their financial cares, that they

---

1   During the first 25 years of the seventeenth century there were no fewer than 15 proclamations concerned with the decline of the cloth industry.

2   "Draper" and "clothier" were originally essentially synonymous, except that "clothier" was associated with the provinces rather than London. (Girtin, *The Triple Crowns*, 22). Those who participated in the sale of luxury cloth were called "mercers."

3   The main reason that the charter to sell cloth was given to the Drapers was so that fraudulent practices among many of those involved in the cloth industry would be eradicated and that the selling of cloth would become centralized. The ironies of this will become clear.

were temporarily no longer concerned with human relationships" (191).[4] While its monetary obligations led the Company away from focusing on matters of cloth, those members who did continue to sell cloth also expanded their business. As A.H. Johnson notes in his magisterial *History of the Drapers' Company*,

> many of the smaller Masters had abandoned their trade for that of other Crafts and the more opulent had completely burst the narrow bounds of the old Gild. If they still did a large business in the wholesale trade in cloth, they did much more. They had become great merchants, dealing in every kind of article, both of export and import, and sharing with members of other Companies the opportunities offered by the new ventures of the day. (2:240)[5]

While the role of the Drapers' Company had certainly undergone significant changes in the late sixteenth and early seventeenth centuries, it would be incorrect to say that no drapers continued in the traditional business of selling cloth in London shops. Indeed, Johnson concedes that the majority of the freemen of the Drapers' Company "continued their work as sellers of cloth retail or wholesale according to the size of their business" (2:239–240). And to the early modern Londoner, the profession of the draper was still associated with selling cloth. In describing London's Watling Street, just east of St. Paul's, Stow explains in his *Survey of London*, "that at this present [1603], the inhabitants thereof are wealthy Drapers, retailers of woolen cloathes both broad and narrow, of all sorts, more than any one street of this citie" (1:346).[6]

While the role of the draper, and particularly that of the Drapers' Company, was clearly undergoing a transformation around the turn of the sixteenth century, what is less obvious is the extent to which the average Londoner recognized this. The literature of the period—both non-literary and imaginative—seems to locate the selling of cloth decidedly in the drapers' shops. And more importantly for our purposes, these texts insist that the shops were hotbeds of corruption and the men who ran them were deceptive and immoral. It is difficult to detect just how rampant this corruption was among urban drapers. However widespread the problem actually was or to what extent it affected the daily lives of the London cloth buyers may never be known. As fraudulence in the manufacture of cloth was given sustained attention by government officials, there is reason to believe that the problem was real and persistent enough to demand constant legislation. And in the period's literary output there is a keen sense that adulterated wool was sold at an alarming rate. Some satires, some moralistic treatises, some economic documents, the texts all share a sense that the wool industry had disintegrated and drapers were in large part to blame for this state of affairs. Although the texts reveal a common interest in exposing the drapers'

---

4 See Girtin, *The Triple Crowns*, especially Chapter 10, "The Years of Difficulty."

5 With the increase in the trade of cloth to the Low Countries and Spain, many drapers became involved with the Merchant Adventurers or other trading companies, such as the Eastland, Levant, and East India Companies. During Elizabeth's reign, fifty-two drapers belonged to an overseas trading company (Hunting, 71–3).

6 In J. Cooke's play, *Greene's Tu Quoque or, The City Gallant* (1611), Staines, a financially ruined gentleman, idealizes the life of a liveried serving-man who "weares broad-cloth, and yet dares walke Watling-street, without any fear of his Draper" (vii, 685–6).

practices, the aims of their projects do not appear to be of a piece. The sermons and texts of a religious nature aim to expose the moral ills that false practices elicit and to call for reform, while the more secular texts seem less interested in the *reform* than the *exposé*. Both sorts of texts, however, reveal the extent to which the corrupt draper had become a widely known cultural stereotype, akin to the greedy usurer or the morally bankrupt gallant, and central to the demise of the cloth industry.

Although the figure of the draper was depicted in print as symbolically responsible for all the corruption associated with the domestic cloth industry, drapers are generally not given sustained treatment in more properly literary texts. In *Michaelmas Term* (1605–1606), however, Thomas Middleton dramatizes the embarrassment that had become of England's riches through his main character, Ephestian Quomodo, a cozening wool draper.[7] Quomodo is known for his efforts to bamboozle money out of rural gentry, and the play revolves around a particular scheme to trick a young gentleman from Essex out of his lands and estate. Many critics have taken this merchant as a representative of all corrupt and usurious London citizens. For example, Theodore Leinwand asserts that "Quomodo is a rich London draper whom we see, not in the role of a trader, but as a usurer and a swindler" (*The City Staged*, 53); Harry Levin lumps Quomodo in with Middleton's other "money grubbing shopkeepers" (143); Ruby Chatterji associates Quomodo with the Vice figure of medieval morality plays (350); A.L and M.K. Kistner have asserted that Quomodo is a representative of the "all devouring city" (65). And several authors, while acknowledging Quomodo's illicit behavior, fail to mention his trade altogether. Gail Paster, in her introduction to the latest edition of the play, does see the importance of his profession, but asserts that "Quomodo's occupation has the effect of making the merchant seem representative of the commercial forces most responsible for sixteenth-century London's rapid growth into a huge cosmopolitan city" (42). In insisting that Quomodo is representative of the corrupt citizen, a sort of usurous everyman, critics have ignored what is particular about his mode of corruption. While Quomodo may certainly be seen as representative of the swindling London merchant, it is my contention that Middleton attends carefully to his particular profession *as a draper* and that his trade is central to the play's action. Quomodo's duping of the country gentleman, then, must be read in the context of the means by which he does so: through an elaborate commercial transaction based on the exchange of cloth.

Scholars of early modern city comedy have continually seen that the dramatists, in Brian Gibbons's words, "articulated a radical critique of the Age" (17). Gibbons, however, in perhaps the earliest study of city comedy as a sub-genre, believes that city comedy in general does not engage in any meaningful way with actual material economic situations of early modern London.[8] He asserts that the plays are more concerned with questions of social morality than in offering "evidence of actual conditions at the time. What they present is a keen analysis in moral terms first and last. Such a concern is clearly less ephemeral and more profound than any economic analysis, and accounts for the permanent value of the *genre* as dramatic art" (Gibbons, 29). Gibbons posits that concentration on "economic analysis" would diminish the

---

7   See Paster, Introduction, pp. 8–10, for a discussion of the play's date.

8   Gibbons seems to follow Knights, who believes that Middleton's plays in particular have "limited usefulness as 'social documents'" (Knights, 261).

"profundity" of these plays, thus detracting from their "permanent value." In this formulation, discussions about the economic questions of the day would necessarily preclude drama from surviving as "art;" since the art has survived, the drama therefore must not have given an accurate picture of the "actual conditions of the time." This is, of course, ridiculous. But what is more troubling is Gibbons's formulation that the moral and the economic are mutually exclusive. A play, in his schema, cannot possibly say something important about moral attitudes if it offers an economic analysis. City comedy, however, constantly probes the connection between economics and morality. It lays bare the notion that the world of commercial exchange is deeply and necessarily entangled with human behavior. As Susan Wells has articulated,

> many city comedies present an image of a world organized around accumulation, and raise serious questions about this world, without focusing the audience's attention on accumulation or greed, without losing the comic tone of the play, and thus its contact with the traditions of the popular feast. The play develops *through* unbridled accumulation, as various characters try to outwit and swindle each other; it is a transparent assumption of the play. Thus, greed may be posed as the central ethical problem of the play, but the conventional answers—charity and contentment—press upon our attention less than the play's image of the lavish and carefree material life of the festive marketplace. (54)

The moral iniquities so often at the heart of the plays seem, then, to suggest the plays' interest when they actually belie it. The energy of city comedy, and what makes it unique, is the sense that this action must be produced *in this city, at this time*, and *under these circumstances*. And, more often than not, the particular circumstances of the plays are wrapped up in the world of commercial accumulation and exchange. In Jean-Christophe Agnew's influential study of the early modern theater vis-à-vis the market, he argues "how the English stage developed formal, narrative, and thematic conventions that effectively reproduced the representational strategies and difficulties of the market place" and "how the stage then furnished its urban audience with a laboratory and an idiom within which these difficulties and contradictions could be acted out" (12). Staging economic realities transforms them. Certainly putting the economic world of London on display would seem contrived given the "formal, narrative, and thematic conventions" of the theater. But this does not mean that engagement with the market is somehow subordinated to the human dramas of the play. Rather, the hallmark of city comedy in general and Middleton's plays in particular is that their staging of the marketplace allows for a complex understanding of the ways humans interact within that system of exchange.

But why should city comedy be the mode in which the critique of the figure of the draper is so keenly articulated? The answer may lie in the special role the draper had in the urbanization of the cloth industry. The quotidian life of the Londoner and the sights and sensations of his or her encounters with merchants often shape or at least appear in the narratives of city comedy. City comedy participates in what Douglas Bruster has called a "materialist vision": "the collective focus of many dramatists on the essence of the physical world and its often demanding claims upon the foundations of urban existence" (38). The "demands" placed on the city dweller by the "physical world" certainly include how he or she negotiates the acquisition of goods. Shopping, whether for foodstuff or cloth or barrels, was—just as it is now—a principal activity of urban living, and often involved a concern for the quality of products. Bruster goes on to say that in city comedy "the materialist vision was characterized primarily by an obsession with the integrity of commodity and the seemingly inevitable hazards of ownership" (41). When the "integrity of the commodity" was called into question, this was largely seen as a symptom of city life. And while the Medieval period put emphasis on kinship system and bonds of trust, with increased urbanization came an erosion of "trust between individuals and families." Negotiating the dangerous landscape of possibly corrupt goods "must have eroded such established patterns of behaviour" (Richardson, 13).

As the locus for the early modern Londoner's contact with the cloth industry, the drapers' shops had an important function in how the national industry was represented and understood. The draper himself, whether honest or corrupt, was the face of that representation. In his creation of the deceptive woolen draper, Middleton stages his culture's stereotypes and fears about that occupation that were prevalent in other kinds of texts. Attending to the cultural understanding of the draper in the late sixteenth and early seventeenth centuries by exploring the textual representations of his occupation not only provides a context in which to read Quomodo, but also reveals the extent to which Middleton explored his audience's savvy of the marketplace. However, Middleton's play is in many ways more effective than the non-dramatic texts at offering a critique because the audience *sees* the drapers' deception in action. Moreover, Middleton's text is effective in presenting a corrective of the draper's immoral behavior. In offering a resolution to the problem of the corrupt draper—by banishing corrupt cloth selling practices—Middleton stages a solution, that which other texts fail to envision. While the solution is a local one, it allows for a revival of integrity to the national product.

"They Mean Deceit"

In his monograph, *Society and Politics in the Plays of Thomas Middleton*, Swapan Chakravorty asks a crucial question: "[h]ow true to life was Quomodo?" (51) Chakravorty, however, never ventures an answer and I suspect could not have done so without a full study of the context of the drapers' corrupt practices in early modern London. What follows is an attempt to offer a cultural understanding of the deceptive draper, which will provide some grounds to explore the query further.

The early modern draper was accused of several iniquities, but perhaps none was as pervasive as keeping his shop or stall poorly lit, ostensibly so that the customer would not be able to see whether the cloth he or she was buying was of inferior quality.[9] As early as 1583, Philip Stubbes articulated what must have already been regarded as common practice: "[t]hey have their shops and places where they sell their cloth commonly very darke and obscure, of purpose to deceive the buiers ... They mean deceit, and lay snares to intrap the feet of the simple" (*Second Part*, D7r–v).

---

9   As Paster notes, a 1608 repertory from the court of Alderman prohibited shopkeepers from "hanging curtains before their shop windows 'to diminishe obscure or shadowe their lighte whereby such as have come to buye their wares have bene much wronged and deceived'" (*Michaelmas Term*, n. 20, 55).

While this particular deception certainly benefited the drapers, as it allowed them to sell low quality cloth at a higher price, Stubbes's language emphasizes the victims of this cunning—the innocent, or "simple" buyers of the cloth. Moreover, Stubbes's moralistic tone suggests that the drapers participate in this practice not only, or even primarily, for a greater profit, but rather because they aim to "deceive the buiers" and take perverse pleasure in this alone. In this formulation, the drapers are seen as stock characters out to gull the latest simpleton. In his 1592 satirical text, *A Quip for an Upstart Courtier*, Robert Greene uses a less moralistic but no less accusatory tone to describe the London merchant's *modus operandi*, which is primarily to "fetch in young Gentlemen by commodities under the colour of lending money" (276): "And so for you [sic] Draper, he fetcheth them off for livery cloth and cloth for six monthes & six, & yet hath he more knacks in his budget, [10] for hee hath so darke a shop that no man can wel choose a peece of cloth it so shadows the die and the thred, a man shall bee deceived in the wool" (277).[11] Greene echoes Stubbes's estimation that the draper's purpose in keeping a dark shop is only partially to sell inferior goods, here falsely dyed cloths with poor thread quality, at higher prices. The darkly lit shop is part of the draper's repertoire for entrapping young gentlemen into usurious commodity swindles.

In the period's literature, then, a dark shop necessarily signifies greater moral iniquities. In his 1612 sermon, *The White Devil*, the preacher Thomas Adams asserts that "insufficient wares" will "appeare good to the buyers eye" because merchants have both "a darke window and an impudent tongue ... Sophistry is now fled from the schooles into the shops: from disputation to merchandizing: he is a silly Tradesman that cannot sophisticate his wares, as well as he hath done his conscience" (183). The rhetorical tools of persuasion and argumentation, once the language of the law courts, have been co-opted by the drapers who must disguise their faulty wares with obscure lighting and sell these same commodities through duplicitous language. The drapers emerge as the used car salesmen of the early modern period. Finally, as William Scott reveals in *An Essay on Drapery* (1635), written more than fifty years after Stubbes's text, the practices of the corrupt draper are seen as a social and moral blight on the London scene: "It is to bee lamented, that men have too darke, shops: but more, that they have too darke mindes; let them remember who it was which said, *There is nothing hid which shall not be made manifest*" (Scott, 21).[12]

---

10 Knack: "A trick; a device, artifice; formerly often, a deceitful or crafty device, a mean or underhanded trick" (*OED sb²* 1).

11 The context for Greene's accusations against merchants is as follows: in his text, two anthropomorphized pair of breeches, one cloth and the other velvet, debate which of them has greater prerogative to reside in England. The second part of the text involves the selection of the jury, men from a cross section of early modern classes and professions, to settle the matter. During *voir dire*, the suitability of many of the possible jurors is critiqued, as their practices are deemed morally questionable. I discuss *A Quip for an Upstart Courtier* at length in Chapter 4.

12 Scott also reveals the benefit in low lighting for drapers' shops. See p. 21. According to Thrupp in the introduction to Scott's pamphlet, there is no conclusive evidence as to the identity of the author. He may have been a member of the Merchant Taylors' Company, but he was probably not a cloth manufacturer (Thrupp, 11).

In addition to keeping dark shops, drapers were also associated with deceptions in the weight and length of the cloths. Although the drapers were not involved directly in the manufacture of the wool cloths, the common assumption was that drapers knew that cloth was adulterated or finished in a corrupt manner, and thus were abetting the iniquitous clothworkers.[13] The Drapers' Company was responsible for cloth inspection at Blackwell Hall, the primary London cloth market, and if they found that a piece of cloth did not meet the regulations of length, the cloth would have been confiscated and a fine would have been imposed on the seller of the cloth. If a draper himself was revealed to be selling cloth that did not conform to the restrictions, he was fined by the guild directly. As Hunting points out, drapers were guilty of this practice from early in the sixteenth century: in 1516 alone up to fifty-six drapers at Blackwell Hall were fined for using short measures (69). Stretching cloth seemed to be as serious a concern as cutting it too short.[14] Stubbes claims that drapers,

> after they have bought their cloth, they cause it to be tentered, racked, and so drawne out, as it shall be both broader, and longer than it was when they bought it almost by halfe in halfe, or at lest by a good large sise. Now the cloth being thus stretched forth in every vaine, how is it possible either to endure, or hold out, but when a shower of raine taketh it, then it falleth and shrinketh in, that it is a shame to see it. (Stubbes, *Second Part*, D7r)

Although it is unlikely that the draper himself would have had the means (the tenters) to stretch the cloth, Stubbes's description suggests that he is ultimately to blame because he has "cause[d]" the cloth to be stretched. The draper then knowingly sells the cloth to the innocent customer who, after having his cloth made into a suit of clothes, will become the pitiable victim when his overstretched clothes will shrink or

---

13 The legislation surrounding the regulation of length in cloth was directed specifically at the manufacturers; drapers are never named in the legislation. "A Proclamation Enforcing Statutes for Wool Cloth Manufacture" (20 January 1592) complained that the "weavers" and "tuckers" of Devonshire kersies [dozens] "have of late in vented their own gain means to defraud the laws therein heretofore made" (102). They make the kersies "too light" and "use false stays." The tuckers are accused of "minishing and cutting off parts of the cloth" and employing "extreme racking and stretching of them to ream them to a far greater breadth than the cloth can bear" (102). The proclamation was a response to complaints by Dutch merchants who noticed the debasements in cloth, only evident after the bolts had been opened (*Tudor Royal Proclamations*, n. 2, 102). The Merchant Adventurers argued that they had to buy the cloths sealed up, and that they therefore should not be held responsible. "A Proclamation for the true winding or folding of Wools" (18 June 1604) noted that foreign objects, such as "sand, stones, dust, pitch, tarre, clay, yron, leade, double markes, shorlocks, cummer, and many other deceivable things" (82), were being placed in bolts of cloth "whereby the Fleece may be more weightier" (84). The punishment for continuing to include foreign items in the cloth was spending ten days in prison and, afterwards, being pilloried in the marketplace "with a Fleece of Wooll hanging about his neck" (83).

14 See Ramsay, *English Woollen*, p. 11, for a discussion of the legislation surrounding the excessive stretching of cloth. The original Drapers' Hall, destroyed by the fire of 1666, was built in St. Swithin's Lane on a tenter ground, the site where cloth was laid out to stretch (Hunting, 9).

fall apart in a rain storm.[15] Robert Greene places even more blame on the draper who he sees as requesting the clothmaker to manufacture inferior cloth: "hee *imposeth this charge* to the Clothworker that he draw his cloth and pull it passinge hard when he sets it upon the tenters, that he may have it full bredth and length, till threed and all teare and rent in peeces" (Greene, 278, my emphasis). While the clothworker is, in Greene's words, the "minister" for the draper, the clothworker's deceptions are only to "execute" the draper's "subtlties" (278). Since the draper has the ultimate contact with the cloth before it goes to the consumer, his act of not only knowingly buying, but actually ordering adulterated cloth, is far and away the most grievous cloth-related crime.

Working in tandem with the clothmakers who produced the faulty cloth, the draper helped constitute the network of suspicious tradesmen who were interested in their own personal profit rather than the good of the industry. A 1613 proclamation "for the True Working and Dying of Cloth," asserts that "the Trade of Clothing hath been much discredited by the corrupt desires and practices of some Clothiers, Merchants, Drapers, and Dyers for their own private gaine, in making and selling of false Clothes, overstrained with Tenters, and other unlawfull Engins, and burnt and spoiled with the hot Presse" (301).[16] The use of the hot press, a mechanism that compressed the cloth between two hot metal plates, thereby creating a smooth and glossy finish, was derided as another fraudulent practice perpetrated by the drapers. According to Greene, the draper causes "the clothworker so to presse" the cloth (Greene, 278), which, according to a 1620 proclamation outlawing the practice, gives it a "false and deceitful luster." Not only was this practice explained as a "discredit of the Merchant," but more importantly it was seen as contributing to "the dishonour of Our Nation" ("A Proclamation for the Ordering of the Use of the Hot Press," 470). Although the device seems to have come into use in the early seventeenth century, clothiers were accused much earlier of generating the same effect by using a sort of liquid or gum on the cloth to create a false gloss. Stubbes underscores the deleterious effect this practice had on the textile trade:

> Some [weavers] put in naughty wool, and cause it to be spun & drawne into a very small thred, and then compounding with the fuller to thicke it very much, and with the Clothier also to sheare it very lowe, and with some liquide matter, to lay downe the wooll so close,

---

15 John May's *A Declaration of the Estate of Clothing now Used within This Realme of England* (1614), reiterates this concern: "In our owne Countrie, where much of our Wooll may be vented, the falsehood of clothing is so common, that everie one striveth to wear any thing rather than cloth: if a gentleman make a liverie for his man, in the first showre of raine it may fit his page for bignesse" (38). May suggests that it is the faulty quality of cloth that turns Englishmen away from their home product. For more on the rejection of wool in favor of foreign clothes, see my Chapter 4. See Chapter 6 for a full discussion of May's important text.

16 This proclamation called for greater oversight on cloth. All cloth that was to be sold in London and its liberties was to be "viewed and searched" at Blackwell Hall, London's principle cloth market. See, Ramsay, *English Woollen*, pp. 32–3, for a discussion of the importance of Blackwell Hall.

as you can hardly see any wale, and then selleth it as though it were a very fine cloth indeed. (*Second Part*, D7v)

Although Stubbes here does not name the draper as the primary perpetrator of this offense, the list of those involved in the practice—the weaver, fuller, and clothier—suggest that the final stop in the process will be the draper's stall, where the deceptively smooth cloth will land in the hands of the unsuspecting customer.[17]

The drapers' dark shops, where falsely measured and deceitfully finished cloth was sold to the consumer, were ground zero for complaints against all those involved in corrupt manufacturing of wool.[18] Drapers and other London merchants were so widely and so pervasively perceived of as swindlers that they came to be aligned with petty thieves. In Adams's *The White Devil*, the preacher laments the "web of theft" that is "woven in a shop or ware-house" by the cloth seller (183). The draper "rob[s]" his customers

by a false weight, and no true measure, whose content or extent is not justifiable by law; or the cunning conveyances in weighing or meating: such as cheat the buyer: are not these pretty trickes to picke mens purses? ... Now had I not as good loose my purse on *Salisbury plaine*, as in *London Exchange*? is my losse the lesse, because violence forbeares, and craft pickes my purse? The high-way theefe is not greater abomination to God, than the shop-theefe: and for man, the last is more dangerous: the other we knowingly fly; but this laughs us in the face, whiles he robs us. (183)

Adams' clever collocation of shopkeepers in London cloth stalls and cutpurses in the uninhabited plains of Wiltshire suggests that both knowingly operate in a criminal underworld and that the intent of drapers is the same as thieves: to "picke mens purses." However, the true sinister operator is the draper, who presents his customer with the face of honesty and plain dealing while he sells faulty goods. As Millar Maclure points out, the corrupt merchant was a "stock figure" of derision among early modern sermonists:

There were, of course, crooked merchants ... but ... [the sermonists'] complaints are stereotyped, repeated by rote: merchants show one thing and sell another; they use false weights and measures; they conceal the faults in their goods, sell 'bad and naughty wares.'

---

17 Mercers, those who sold luxury cloths, were continually accused of giving their silks a false gloss, often by the application of a gummy substance, which would cause the cloth to shine. In *2 Henry IV*, Mistress Quickly—in an attempt to help Snare and Fang apprehend Falstaff—tells the officers to seek Falstaff out: "he is indited [invited] to dinner to the Lubber's Head in Lumbert [Lombard] street, to Master Smooth's the silk-man" (II, i, 27–9).

18 Another common complaint about cloth was that good wool was adulterated with inferior yarn. The 1592 proclamation cited above laments that some manufacturers produce a poor product "by deceitful mixing of their yarn and false weaving of their cloths" (102), and Stubbes reveals that "some mix good wooll, and naughty wooll togither, and using it as before, they sell it for principall good cloth when it is no thing lesse" (Stubbes, *Second Part*, D8r). In a *Treatise of the Vocations* (1612), Puritan preacher William Perkins combines all the aforementioned deceptive practices in the general figure of the "the merchant." See White, 192.

The preachers invoked the dark shop, the impudent tongue, the whole process of *caveat emptor* almost mechanically; it was the thing to do. (133–4)

Although the litany of deceitful practices associated with the drapers, in particular, were stereotypes and "repeated by rote," they nevertheless tell us something important about the early modern understanding of the draper. We see that he was widely regarded in the culture as a pivotal figure in the denigration of the cloth industry and that this image of his corrupt practices was sustained over several decades surrounding the turn of the sixteenth century.[19]

Go for Wool and Come Back Shorn

In *Michaelmas Term*, Middleton highlights Quomodo's profession at the outset. The play's action opens on a London street scene as Cockstone and Rearage, two gallants, discuss the latter's potential marriage match with "Master Quomodo / (The rich draper's) daughter" (I, i, 59–60).[20] Quomodo's wealth is immediately established, as is the ostensible means by which he attained that wealth. Just afterwards, when Quomodo enters the scene, Rearage retreats, saying, "'Slid, master Quomodo!" (I.i.72) Cockstone chides him: "How then, afraid of a woolen draper?" (73) Rearage's explanation that Quomodo "warned me his house and I hate he should see me abroad" (74–5) tells us why *he* should be apprehensive about the father of the woman he desires to woo.[21] Cockstone's question, however, while suggesting that it is preposterous to fear a draper, ironically and comically presents one of the play's key themes, and one that the audience would no doubt have understood: one *should* be wary "of a woolen draper." To underscore why one should fear the draper, his corrupt trade practices are clear from Quomodo's first words as he enters with his two sidekicks. In this important scene, Middleton establishes Quomodo early on not simply as a corrupt merchant, but as a corrupt *draper*, with his specific draper's schemes:

> QUOMODO. O my two spirits Shortyard and Falselight—you that have so enriched me—
> I have industry for you both.
> SHORTYARD. Then do you please us best, sir.

---

19 As Fisher reminds us, the adulteration of cloth was very real, even though the manufacturers did not necessarily promote it primarily to deceive the buyers. Although writers blamed the fraudulence on the "wickedness that flourished in the hearts and minds of the manufacturing classes," most "debasement of materials and workmanship" was a result of manufacturers trying to "keep costs low" ("London's Export Trade," 70–71).

20 This and all subsequent references to *Michaelmas Term* will be taken from the most recent edition (2000), expertly edited by Gail Paster. Theodore Leinwand has edited the play for the forthcoming *Oxford Middleton*, but it has not been printed as of the completion of this manuscript.

21 As with many characters in city comedies, the gallants' names are comically allegorical. The name Cockstone suggests that he is sexually well equipped, while Rearage's name connotes a gentleman in debt. Sexuality and financial trouble are two of the play's principal interests and are often intertwined.

QUOMODO. Wealthy employment.
SHORTYARD. You make me itch, sir.
QUOMODO. You Falselight, as I have directed you—
FALSELIGHT. I am nimble.
QUOMODO. Go, make my coarse commodities look sleek,
    With subtle art beguile the honest eye.
    Be near to my trap-window, cunning Falselight.
FALSELIGHT. I never failed it yet.
QUOMODO. I know thou didst not. (I, i, 76–86)

In calling upon Shortyard and Falselight, Quomodo addresses the two men who serve him. But he also lauds them as the two corrupt practices that have benefited his trade and have made him "rich": selling his "yards" of cloth "short" and employing "false" "light" in his shop. When Quomodo tells us he "has industry" and "wealthy employment" for both Shortyard and Falselight, he indicates that he has errands for his servants. But if we also understand he is addressing the practices that the characters' names represent, then we see that Quomodo "has industry," or has business "*for*," or because of, these practices.[22] This entrance would no doubt have been met by laughter on the part of the audience as Shortyard and Falselight's monikers would have resonated for any even remotely aware of the stereotypes surrounding drapers. That Quomodo's "servants" are so named suggest the extent to which, by 1605, the drapers' deceits would have crept into the cultural fabric of dramatic comedy.[23]

Just as keeping dark shops was the most common accusation hurled at drapers in the period, so in *Michaelmas Term* does this deception emerge as central to Quomodo's fraudulent business practices. Quomodo's specific address to Falselight, to do as he has been "directed," reveals that he engineers where and how the light shines in his shop. And Falselight's response, that he is "nimble," shows an agility of movement and an acuteness of mental faculty, two qualities important to Quomodo's deceptions. Quomodo implores Falselight to "make my coarse commodities look sleek." By illuminating the shop "falsely," that is, by obscuring the light that enters through the "trap-window," the unsuspecting customer will be "beguile[d]" as the cloth will appear deceptively shiny, obscuring the defective material.[24] Quomodo's

---

22 Leinwand reads this scene for its homoerotic innuendos, claiming that the exchange between the three indicates that they have "shared a sexual as well as economic bond" ("Redeeming Beggary/Buggery," 56). Shortyard's name clearly points to the draper's deception of cutting cloth so it would be inordinately short. The name also suggests that he is less than sexually well-endowed. His "yard" (slang for penis) is "short."

23 *Michaelmas Term* was first performed at Paul's by Paul's Children. Although this was a private theater, and thus more expensive than its public counterparts, that is not to say that members of disparate social classes could not see plays there. For a discussion of the heterogeneity of audience members in the private theaters and the implications thereof, see Leinwand, *The City Staged*, p. 45 and Chakravorty, *Society and Politics*, pp. 25–6.

24 Sampson notes that a "trap window" was a "hinged window or movable penthouse which could be lowered to dim the light in the shop" (*Michaelmas Term*, n. 87, 378). Trap windows were associated with malfeasance, as the following contemporaneous texts demonstrate: in Thomas Dekker and John Webster's *Westward Ho* (1607), the Italian merchant Justiniano describes cuckolded husbands who "weare their hats ore their eye-browes, like

suggestion that manipulating the smoothness of the cloth's appearance is a "subtle art" implies both that the practice is artificial or unnatural and that to deceive the "honest" consumer takes a skill that only a crafty draper with his "cunning" helpers may have. That Falselight has "never failed" Quomodo in his "cunning" reveals that his shop is perpetually dim, that his commodities are always falsely represented. The persistent use of fraudulent shopkeeping tactics, then, comes to be symbolized by Falselight throughout the play. Each time Quomodo calls his name he draws attention to his own deceit. And Falselight's responses, "I'm ne'er out o'th'shop, sir" (II, iii, 237) and "over your head, sir" (II, iii, 414), indicates the omnipresence of such chicanery.

Quomodo is not the only draper reliant on poorly lit shops in London: later in the play when Quomodo finds his wife Thomasine gossiping in his shop, he asserts that his dark shop is kept bright enough that he can see her: "Why, Thomasine, go to! My shop is not altogether so dark as some of my neighbours', where a man may be cuckolded at one end while he's measuring with his yard at t'other" (II, iii, 35–8). In claiming that among the drapers' shops his is not the most darkly lit, Quomodo proposes a sort of relative immorality. While "beguiling" does occur at his shop, it is *only* that of the consumer. Still, the scenario that Quomodo envisions—a draper's wife cheating on her husband at one end of the store while he either (1) measures out cloth with his yard stick or (2) has sexual intercourse at the other end—demonstrates the ways in which commercial deceit ushers in a host of other moral offenses.[25] Indeed, later in the play when Quomodo attempts to dupe a gentleman into thinking that Falselight and Shortyard are wealthy citizens, he remarks to himself that "a dark shop's good for somewhat" (III, iv, 197–8). The ill-lighted draper's shop, for Quomodo, represents all possible iniquities, and to the audience confirms that the drapers "have too darke mindes."

It is therefore crucial to establish Quomodo as a fraudulent draper for the play's main action to have the humor, gravity, and resonance it does. The crux of the play concerns a commodity swindle wherein Quomodo gulls a landed gentleman by compelling him to take a bond on a large amount of wool cloth in an effort to force the gentleman to forfeit his lands. The gentleman, Easy of Essex, is newly arrived in London and has lost all his money at dicing. Present at the gambling house is Quomodo's servant, Shortyard, who befriends Easy by posing as Blastfield, a gentleman with substantial credit and influence in London. Shortyard/Blastfield claims that he will lend Easy money and that "Master Quomodo the draper" will "furnish"

---

politick penthouses, which commonly make the shop of a Mercer, or a Linnen Draper, as dark as a roome in Bedlam" (I, i, 154–6). In Middleton and Rowley's masque, *The World Tossed at Tennis* (1620), the figure of Simplicity complains that the eyes of the figure of Deceit "look like false lights, cozening trap-windows" (184).

25 For discussions of sexuality in Middleton's plays and *Michaelmas Term*, see Heller's *Penitent Brothellers* and Leinwand's "Redeeming Beggary/Buggery in *Michaelmas Term*." Thomasine, often privately observing her husband's devious schemes, is the moral voice of the play. Physically positioned on the stage's balcony, she takes on a Godlike omniscience. When Quomodo tells her to depart from the shop because "there's a buck to be struck" (i.e. there is a gentleman to be gulled), she asserts in an aside that "I'll watch above i'th'gallery, but I'll see your knavery" (II.iii, 83, 85). Despite the darkness of Quomodo's shop, Thomasine will be able to discern his immoral behavior.

him with a loan (II, I, 95, 96).[26] Quomodo convinces the cash-poor Easy to co-sign a bond with Shortyard/Blastfield on "a commodity of cloth" worth two hundred pounds (II, iii, 185–6).[27] Quomodo convinces the gentlemen that they will be able to sell the cloth at a huge profit, pay the draper back, and have money to spare.[28] Quomodo is not just a generic merchant-swindler in this play; he is, specifically, a draper who uses the tools of his trade, bolts of wool cloth and cunning in the selling thereof, to trick Easy and we are to suspect other gentlemen who have recently arrived in London. While Quomodo himself asserts that "we undo gentlemen daily" (II, iii, 59–60) and that "gentry is the chief fish we tradesmen catch," the means to hook the gentlemen and reel them in is Quomodo's mastery at deception in his own trade (I, i, 134).

The long and complex scene (II, iii) in which the commodity scheme is arranged, relies on the audience's familiarity with the particular offenses stereotypically perpetrated by drapers. Moreover, the scene's humor assumes knowledge of the world of the London marketplace on the part of the audience. The gulling of Easy is able to go forth because he, unlike the other characters and audience members, is unable to see the obvious warnings of a scam, thus creating an uneasy alliance between the savvy city audience and the play's corrupt merchant. When Shortyard/Blastfield brings Easy to Quomodo's shop to borrow money from the draper, the scene resembles countless other merchant shops in city drama. Quomodo calls out the common street cry of merchants, "What lack you, gentlemen?" and promises that they will "[s]ee good kerseys or broadcloths here" (II, iii, 100, 101).[29] However, Middleton's audience is never allowed to forget that Quomodo's shop is the seat of fraudulence.

---

26 The name "Blastfield" indicates what Shortyard is doing to Easy: attempting to "blast," or ruin, his "field," or status as a landowner. The deception of a higher social class, to which Blastfield's name clearly points, is, as Leinwand suggests, consonant with the trope of gulling in city comedy (*The City Staged*, 53).

27 As Paster notes, "tak[ing] up a commodity of cloth" pointed to a common practice in early modern London: "The practice of taking up commodities ... to obtain ready money was a device used to avoid usury laws. Gallants would buy something worthless ... in order to turn it, with a loss, to cash" (*Michaelmas Term*, n. 186–7, 106). For a discussion of this play in relation to the tradition of the commodity swindle in rogue literature, see Chakravorty, *Society and Politics*, p. 49, and Knight, p. 98. In her introduction to the play, Paster says that most commodity swindles in early modern drama involved "far trashier goods than" wool (11). As Bowden discusses, many country gentlemen became involved in wool dealing, indicating "that there were few better investments available in Tudor and Stuart England" (84).

28 It appears that the scheme to have Easy and Shortyard/Blastfield sell Quomodo's cloth to a third party violates the Drapers' Company's *Book of Ordinances*, which states that "ye shall nether bye nor sell nor non other person in your behalf for you, eny maner wollen cloth" (qtd. in A.H. Johnson, 1:261). Hunting asserts that the *Book of Ordinances* "was the bible of the Drapers' guild and it reveals a well-disciplined organization; a fraternity fully conscious of their duties, proud of their rituals and determined to uphold trading standards as well as the personal integrity of their fellows" (64). Quomodo's business practices suggest that he has violated the oath each member of the Drapers' Company has to take when he is made free of the Company and agrees to the contents of the *Book of Ordinances*.

29 Kerseys were fulled to a lesser extent than broadcloths (Coleman, 421). They were narrower and cheaper as well; three kersies were equal to one broadcloth (Ramsay, *English Woollen*, 13).

The draper's shop is situated under the "[s]ign of Three Knaves" (II, iii, 98) and, as Quomodo himself points out, the darkness of his shop makes it difficult for him to see his own customers: "Your worship must pardon me, 'tis always misty weather in our shops here. We are a nation the sun ne'er shines upon" (104–6).[30]

In trusting Quomodo, whom he takes to be "an honest true citizen," Easy reveals his acute naiveté in the inner workings of the London marketplace (II, i, 93). What everyone *except* Easy knows is that drapers are not to be trusted and that, although citizens, they are rarely thought to be "honest" or "true." At first, to test Easy, Shortyard/Blastfield feigns resistance to the scheme: "The mealy moth consume it! Would he ha' me turn peddler now? What should I do with cloth?" (II, iii, 197–8) Privy to the poor quality of cloth that Quomodo sells, and the deception to which he must resort to unload his goods, Shortyard/Blastfield expresses concerns that anyone buying cloth from a draper should have. Further, Shortyard/Blastfield's expletive comically suggests the possibility that Quomodo's cloth is, indeed, moth-eaten. Before Easy can mull over Shortyard/Blastfield's skepticism, Quomodo jumps in to answer the concerns: "There's no merchant in town but will be greedy upon't and pay money upo'th'nail; they'll dispatch it over to Middelburg presently and raise double commodity by exchange" (II, iii, 201–4).[31] If the merchants will not take the cloth, however, Quomodo reminds them that other drapers in town will buy it because "'tis Term-time, and Michaelmas Term too," the drapers' busiest time of year (II, iii, 204–5).[32] The cloth, Quomodo further claims, is as good as "present money" (II, iii, 210), striking a nerve with the gentleman, who must have cash in order to sustain the life of a London gallant. Easy cannot risk marring his unestablished reputation. He needs the cash because he has "already invited all the gallants to sup with me tonight" and "'Twill be my everlasting shame if I have no money to maintain my bounty" (II, iii, 135–6, 138–9). Concurring with Quomodo's rationale, Easy asserts that possessing cloth "comes in as fit a time as can be" (II, iii, 208). Easy continually parrots Quomodo's words, the language of the draper, to "convince" Shortyard/Blastfield that taking the bond is the prudent course. He repeats that the cloth is good as "ready money at the merchants'" and that "the winter season all falls in as pat as can be to help it" (2.3.225–7). In repeating Quomodo's language, Easy, who ostensibly has no prior knowledge of the marketplace or the transactions that comprise it, claims linguistic, if not actual, access to the world of commodity exchange.

Nevertheless, Quomodo understands that Easy's limited knowledge of commercial goods must at some level be bolstered by a material knowledge of what

---

30 Paster notes that this phrase is a "comment on English weather which also evokes common phrases for deception" (*Michaelmas Term*, n. 105–6, 103).

31 "Upon the nail": "On the spot, at once, without the least delay. Chiefly used of making money payments" (*OED* "nail," 8a). After the closing of the entrepôt at Antwerp, Middelburg was the port and center for England's international trade in the Low Countries.

32 Drapers would have done most of their business during the law terms, primarily Michaelmas Term, which was the longest term and followed a recess. Michaelmas Term was notorious as the period when urban crimes were most prevalent. For a discussion of the setting of the play during Michaelmas Term, see Chatterji, pp. 351–2; Kistner and Kistner, p. 61; and Chakravorty, "Middleton's *Michaelmas Term*."

he is purchasing. The cloth must be felt, even though—to recall Thomas Adams' words—we know his "insufficient wares" will "appeare good" because they are is accompanied by "a darke window and an impudent tongue." Discussing the quality of his cloth with Easy and Shortyard/Blastfield, Quomodo invites the two men to touch the cloth themselves:

> SHORTYARD. Where's this cloth?
> QUOMODO. Full and whole within, all of this piece, of my religion, Master Blastfield.
>   Feel't, nay, feel't and spare not, gentlemen; your fingers and your judgment.
> SHORTYARD. Cloth's good.
> EASY. By my troth, exceeding good cloth; a good wale 't'as.
> QUOMODO. Falselight.
> [*Enter* Falselight]
> FALSELIGHT. I'm ne'er out o'th'shop, sir.
> QUOMODO. Go, call in a porter presently to carry away the cloth with the star mark.
> (II, iii, 230–39)

Quomodo claims that the cloth is "full" and "whole" and all the cloth is like the piece in front of them in caliber. In these assurances, the draper reveals the common concerns of the cloth buyer—that the cloth was often shorter or more stretched than it seemed or that it was of inconsistent quality. Quomodo's promise of the excellence, on his "religion," points to the morally suspect and disingenuous nature of the stereotypical draper. While the oath to "religion" is ironically comical, to fully understand the humor in this scene, we have to attend closely to the timing involved in Quomodo's beckoning of his servant. Immediately after Shortyard and Easy praise the cloth for its high quality, and Easy himself swears "by my troth" that it is a "good cloth," Quomodo—by hollering "Falselight"—reminds the audience that Easy is being duped. Easy might be able to feel the pressed and therefore smooth cloth, but he certainly cannot see it. Further, we have a sense that Quomodo's trickery is not just reserved for the easily duped. It is his *modus operandi*: when Quomodo calls his servant, Falselight responds that he is "ne'er out o'the shop," implying the regularity with which Quomodo participates in his literally shady dealings. Finally, in sending Falselight on the errand to call a porter to convey the "cloth with the star mark," Quomodo publicly proclaims that the cloth possesses a mark or stamp that would ensure that it has been searched and is of acceptable quality.[33] Neither Easy nor the audience members, of course, *see* the mark. Indeed, this errand is carried out by the obscure Falselight.

The play's other unseen merchants are hardly less dishonest in their business practices, implying that no arm of the cloth trade is without its villains. Shortyard, for example, initially suggests that Easy borrow money from the fictitious mercer, Master Gum. This merchant is so named because mercers, trading in silks and

---

33 The stamping or marking of cloth was a primary oversight technique. The 1592 Proclamation "Enforcing statues for wool cloth manufacture," charges weavers to include their shopmark on the cloth, which would hold individuals accountable for fraudulence. The 1603 Proclamation "for reformation of great abuses in Measure," which called for the standardization of weight and length in cloth, insisted that inspected cloths be "printed and marked with the letter J crowned" (25). See Ramsay's Chapter 4 of *The Wiltshire Woollen Industry* for a discussion of the cloth mark.

velvets, also were known to misrepresent the sheen of their cloth, applying a gummy substance to the cloth to give it a false gloss. After Easy and the disguised Shortyard are in possession of the cloth that Quomodo assures them they will sell quickly and at a great profit, Shortyard proposes that they sell the cloth to either of two allegorically named merchants: Master Beggarland and Master Stilliard-down, two brothers between whom "there's little difference" (II, iii, 241–2). Stilliard-down's name suggests falsely heavy weight in cloth as the steel yard, a cloth balance, would be held "down."[34] The name "Beggarland," while not highlighting a particular deceit in cloth, does point to the activities with which Quomodo makes his money: tricking "land" from country gentlemen and turning them into "beggars."[35] The names assigned to these two fictitious merchants, taken with "Master Gum," underscore that all cloth merchants are swindlers, with "little difference" between them. Then we have Falselight's alias, the cloth merchant "Master Idem" whose name means "same." He is, in effect, indistinguishable from all the other merchant swindlers. Ultimately, the play seems to leave us with the hopeless scenario that all London cloth merchants are deceitful. Easy, the victim of all this treachery, is told after his arrest to "look out an honest pair of citizens" to help him out of his predicament. "Alas, sir," Easy says with exasperation, "I know not where to find 'em" (III, iii, 49–50, 51). As a newcomer to London, Easy literally does not know enough people to find someone to ask for help. At the same time, he suggests that there is no such thing as an "honest merchant" in London, that there are none to *be* found. While Middleton may seem to generalize the corruption of all citizens, it is important to recall that all these corrupt men—Gum, Stilliard-down, Beggarland, and Idem—are *fictional* in the world of the play, and it is Quomodo or one of his "spirits" that has conjured them up. It is the draper himself who is solely responsible for Easy's undoing. Easy reminds us of Quomodo's singular corruption: "Master Quomodo is all, and the honestest [citizen] that I know" (III, iii, 54–5). He is, in fact, the only merchant represented in the play.

One reason Easy is so, well, easy to convince of this scheme, is that he is newly arrived from the country. He, unlike the other characters and indeed the audience, is unaware of the various ways in which drapers deceitfully buy and sell cloth of poor quality. He has a proclivity to see London as a booming town of mercantilism and does not understand the fluctuations of the market and the deception involved in the sale of unwanted goods during depressed times. He, put simply, is unsuspecting. At the same time, I would argue, he relishes the chance to participate in the commercial

---

34 Paster points to another interpretation of the name: "'Stilliard' is the obsolete spelling for 'steelyard', itself an apparent mistranslation of the German *stahlhof*, hall for cloth merchants. The Steelyard was the headquarters on the north side of the Thames for the Hanseatic merchants from the thirteenth century until their expulsion in 1597. Thereafter the site became a tavern" (*Michaelmas Term*, n. 242, 109).

35 "Beggarland" might also be read as a term of contempt, according to contemporaneous usage of "beggar" suggesting "mean or low fellow" (*OED s.v.* "beggar," 6a). The combination of "beggar" with "land," however, points to a more complex meaning, especially within the context of the play. Quomodo admits to the practice of swindling country gallants—"we undo gentlemen daily"—while the Country Wench's father recalls his own ruin at the hands of merchants: he came to "man-devouring" London, "surfeited away" his "name and state," and now finds himself "a beggar" (II, iii, 59–60, II, ii, 21, 23, 25).

exchange of goods, an activity previously unavailable to him as a country gentleman, as evinced by his willingness to repeat Quomodo's language. This urge to act the part of a cloth broker is indicative of the upsetting of economic stratifications based upon traditional social roles. As Kistner and Kistner argue, in *Michaelmas Term* "the old socio-economic hierarchy, based on a productivity of the land, steadily disintegrates while a system based on a cash nexus and earnings unrelated to production takes its place" (61). Paul Yachnin argues that this shifting of socioeconomic systems is the purpose of the characters in the play. Gallants and merchants are

> allies, united in a radical project to change the shape of society so that they may achieve a more prominent place. Gallants and citizens alike seek to appropriate the wealth, power, and status of the older order by converting land and 'place' into 'goods'—commodities, that is, which can be owned, traded, and transformed. (94)

Yachnin's assertion, however, is complicated by the character of Easy who clearly wants to have it both ways: he is a part of the older landowning order at the same time as he wants to dabble in "goods." To be let in on the inner-workings of the cloth trade, the most extensive commercial trade in England, allows Easy to escape his unwanted position as a cash-poor gentleman. While some might argue that this shifting of roles would be distasteful for a landowner—even if he is broke—Easy's excitement to take on the role of wool broker seems clear as he pushes Shortyard/Blastfield into the deal. Easy is ready to betray or at least augment his role of gentleman to attain that which, as a destitute landowner, eludes him in London: "present money." As Paster explains, Easy is eager to be liberated from the "rustic confinement of his country estate" ("Quomodo," 169).[36] Easy, however, is not simply content to be a country gentleman turned city gallant. He wants to leave behind the world of the gentry, where money is tied up in land, and enter the commercial realm of "porters' backs and women's bellies" because "they bear men and money, and that's the world" (II, iii, 343, 344–5).

Thus, it is neither Easy's presumed friendship with Shortyard/Blastfield nor his country civility that compels him to sign the bond, but rather his desire to participate in mercantilistic activites. In fact, the entrapment of Easy is hardly an entrapment at all. Quomodo's initial rejection of Easy's signature on the bond because he is *not* a citizen persuades Easy practically to insist on signing the bond:

QUOMODO. Have you sent for a citizen, Master Blastfield?
SHORTYARD. No, faith, not yet.—Boy!
EASY. What must you do with a citizen, sir?
SHORTYARD. A custom they're bound to a-late by the default of evil debtors; no citizen
    must lend money without two be bound in the bond; The second man enters but for
    custom sake.
EASY. No? And must he needs be a citizen?

---

36 Paster believes that Easy's retreat into London is "probably meant to remind us ironically of those ... who flee court or city for the sensation of liberty in Arden" ("Quomodo," 169). Chakravorty asserts that "it is the desertion of the country rather than the invasion of the city which converts the ploughman's sweat into a silver bonus for lawyers and loan sharks" in city comedy (*Society and Politics*, 48).

SHORTYARD. By th' mass, stay, I'll learn that.—Master Quomodo!
QUOMODO. Sir.
SHORTYARD. Must the second party that enters into the bond only for fashion's sake, needs be a citizen? What say you to this gentleman for one?
QUOMODO. Alas, sir, you know he's a mere stranger to me; I neither am sure of his going or abiding; he may inn here tonight and ride away tomorrow. Although I grant the chief burden lies upon you, yet we are bound to make choice of those we know, sir.
SHORTYARD. Why, he's a gentleman of a pretty living, sir.
QUOMODO. It may be so. Yet under both your pardons I'd rather have a citizen. (II, iii, 255–76).

Listening to this conversation, Easy learns that the prestige attached to being a gentleman, even one of "pretty living," carries no weight for him in the commercial world, even if the citizen's signature is merely "for fashion's sake." The landed gentleman, with estates in the countryside, becomes "a mere stranger," akin to a foreign other. Wealth represented by property is meaningless in the London milieu where prudent transactions are preferably carried out with "those we know."[37] Quomodo understands that Easy's fascination with the world of commerce is as keen as his own with the world of the country estate. It is precisely *because* the signature is "for fashion's sake"—it is part of the customs of the exotic world of London's mercantilism—that Easy knowingly and willingly enters into the bond.[38] Additionally, it is Easy's desire to be known in London, to become more than a "stranger," to be trusted, to be a worthy citizen, that makes him insist that Quomodo "not disparage [him] so" and let him sign the bond (II, iii, 277). As Bruster has articulated about the importance of commercial transactions in the late sixteenth and early seventeenth centuries,

> [t]he idea of buying and selling, of exchange for profit and socially approved surplus value all took on heightened levels of significance in the two decades surrounding the turn of the century. In presenting commercial transaction as a natural, inescapable phenomenon, the market assumed an ever noticeable place in the foreground of urban life. (14–15)

---

37 As Wells argues, "the commercial privileges of citizens are introduced in traditional terms: they are means of binding together the inhabitants of the city, signs of communal responsibility. But those terms are deceptive ... the traditional relations of co-signers and sureties, presented as expressions of custom and mercy, are traps to cozen Easy out of his inheritance. The traditional communal ideology has been invoked, but not validated" (Wells, 50).

38 Quomodo's unusual name has been given some critical attention: Richard Levin posits that it refers to an actual person with the last name "Howe," as "Quomodo" is the Latin translation of the English "how" ("Quomodo's Name," 46). As Lehr points out, his first name, Ephestian, can be traced to the Greek word for "citizen": his name "lends itself to clever constructions, such as 'how' (to be) a citizen" (17). In the context of Easy's anxiousness to be fashionable by entering the bond with Quomodo, his name takes on an allegorical meaning where "quo" "modo" represents "how" (things are) fashionable, akin to the French "a la mode." I thank Richard Helgerson for this suggestion.

For Easy, signing the bond is a symbolic act that transforms him from a detached country gentleman into a naturalized city dweller who now has material capital and debt, two significant signs of city life.[39]

Insisting on signing the bond, of course, is Easy's undoing. His naiveté concerning the vicissitudes of the cloth market and its shark-like merchants is what Quomodo relies upon to ensnare his prey. Falselight, now disguised as a cloth porter, re-enters *"with the cloth"* (s.d., 383) and announces that "[a]ll the cloth's come back again" and that "the passage to Middelburg is stopped and therefore neither Master Stilliard-down, nor Master Beggarland, nor any other merchant will deliver present money upon't" (II, iii, 385, 388–91). Intermittent closure of cloth markets in the Low Countries was not unusual in the late sixteenth and early seventeenth centuries. In 1598, for example, a group of Merchant Adventurers asked the Privy Council to suppress cloth sales to Middelburg to prevent the sale of cloth there by interlopers (Supple, *Commercial Crisis*, 24).[40] As a country gentleman, Easy would have no way to know the reasons that the trade in wool might have been halted, or even necessarily the importance of Middelburg. His ignorance in affairs of the cloth trade, and his simultaneous desire to enter into those trade relations, enable his gulling. The large quantity of cloth is left in a lifeless heap onstage, symbolically demonstrating Easy's impotence in matters of the market. The cloth must be sold at a loss to Master Idem, a disguised Falselight. And despite the fact that Easy and Shortyard/Blastfield must take "three-score pound" for two hundred pounds' worth of cloth (II, iii, 459), Easy is somehow content. He is rid of the cloth, which proves his participation in London's commercial world, and can now go along "to the next tavern and see the money paid" (II, iii, 465–6).

Easy's desire to jump into affairs of the cloth trade without really knowing the intricacies of this world results in the loss of his lands in Essex. After "Blastfield" disappears, Easy is left solely responsible for the bond on the cloth, plus another seven hundred pounds that the fictitious Blastfield has borrowed from Quomodo. Easy is arrested by Shortyard—now disguised as a sergeant[41]—and taken to Quomodo, at which point Shortyard/Sergeant warns him that "you have fell into the hands of a most merciless devourer, the very gull o' the city" (III, iv, 79–80). Quomodo is likened to a "gull," here signifying "throat or gullet" (*OED sb* 4.1). And while Shortyard's warning is meant to terrify the country gentleman, his words support the stereotype surrounding London drapers: that they are insatiable in their

---

39 What Easy does not have is credit, something he admires in the gallant "Blastfield:" "It seems yare well known, Master Blastfield, and your credit very spacious here it's' city" (II, i, 98–9). See Ceri Sullivan for a discussion of the importance of the discourse of credit to the early modern merchant.

40 Citing Martin W. Sampson's edition of the play, Paster indicates that the trade route to Middelburg would have been stopped by pirates or perhaps by Spanish forces (*Michaelmas Term*, n. 388, 115). It is more likely, given the complicated nature of Anglo-Dutch cloth trade relations in the early sixteenth century, that the stoppage would have been instigated by the English government due to competition between London merchants.

41 Shortyard and Falselight each have various disguises in the play (Shortyard: Blastfield, a sergeant, a citizen; Falselight: the cloth porter, Master Idem, a yeoman, a citizen), which indicates the depth of their deception. Their originary roles as deceivers (Shortyard and Falselight) easily mutate into others.

greed and "merciless" in their practices. It is, of course, Easy who is the gull in the more common use of the word. Quomodo requires Easy to repay the money; when he cannot, Easy must forfeit his land, which he finally does still believing that he is dealing with an honest draper. Quomodo admits to Easy that honesty is a worthy quality in a man—"O what's a man but his honesty"—but entering into a bond is serious business: "the more you break bonds, the more they'll leap in your face ... I would never undertake to be gossip [godparent] to that bond which I would not see well brought up" (III, iv, 150–153).

While Quomodo may chide Easy for not looking to his bond, Easy's primary infraction is not signing his name to the bond, but rather trusting those whom he should know better than to trust. The play suggests, then, that Easy has no business participating in a London cloth trade that is unscrupulous. As long as he remains trusting of strangers and unaware that the cloth market is famous for its infamy, Easy cannot effectively participate in the commercial world of cloth. Unlike Rearage, Easy does not know enough to be "afraid of a woolen draper." Despite this, I would propose that the play does *not* suggest that individuals should not attempt to overstep their social class, that the gentry should stay in the country, and that merchants should not aspire to own country estates.[42] Rather, Middleton seems to assert that as long as the gentry are honest and trusting, they cannot participate in the realm of the corrupt cloth merchants. We are meant, I think, to see Easy as more than another new city gallant-cum-gull. His honest desire to participate in the world of cloth mercantilism, however poorly conceived, is highlighted to reveal the specific corruption of that world, to which he is so poorly suited.

Despite the duping of Easy, and the audience's complicity in that act, the play ultimately seeks retribution against the wool draper and allows for Easy's triumph. Quomodo, who has faked his own death to see how his friends and family will respect his memory and manage his newly acquired estate, is astonished at what has transpired in the short time since his "passing."[43] The liveried members of the Drapers' Company who attend his "funeral" discuss him as a man "enriched by shifts, / And cozenages" (IV, iv, 17–18).[44] His son, Sim, celebrates inheriting the Essex lands and is "glad he's gone" (IV, iv, 41).[45] His wife, Thomasine, woos Easy during the funeral procession and immediately marries him. And Easy regains his land, which has fallen into the hands of Shortyard. Easy's triumph at play's end elevates him to the uneasy position of the play's hero.[46] This turn of events, while

---

42 For a discussion of social mobility in *Michaelmas Term*, see Martin, p. 27.

43 This plot device echoes that of Jonson's *Volpone*, also published in 1606.

44 This is the only appearance by another draper in the play. We do not see Quomodo participate in the fellowship of Drapers. He doesn't consort with other drapers and, although we are to assume he is a member of the Drapers' Company since he is a shop owner, the only time we see him claim membership is when he fantasizes that he will "be divulged a landed man / Throughout the livery" (III, iv, 6–7).

45 Quomodo also has a daughter, Susan, who is the subject of the conversation at the beginning of the play between Cockstone and Rearage. For a discussion of the family unit in Middleton, see Brissenden, "Middletonian Families."

46 See Heinemann, p. 91; Manley, *Literature and Culture*, p. 447 and Corvatta, p. 97, on the ambivalence of having Easy triumph at play's end.

surprising to Quomodo, is necessary for the adequate resolution of the play. The comedic device of the trickster tricked was popular with audiences watching the city comedies.[47] Seeing *this* particular trickster being tricked would likely have been especially satisfying for the theater's audience. Quomodo represents the cunning of cloth merchant practices with which Middleton's audience would be not only familiar, but be pleased to see punished on stage. Just as I have argued that Quomodo's profession as a draper and fraudulence thereof are crucial to a full understanding of the play, so too is it important to see the retribution against him *as a draper*. The admonishment at play's end of Quomodo—as well as the banishment of his two sidekicks, Shortyard and Falselight, who are emblematic of the deception of the cloth industry—does not just restore order to the play's action. More culturally crucial, it restores integrity to the draper's profession.

The last lines of the play, when each of the play's villains receives his punishment from the city judge, demonstrate what it will take to restore order in the cloth industry and in England:

> JUDGE. Thou art thine own affliction, Quomodo. Shortyard we banish, 'tis our pleasure.
> SHORTYARD. Henceforth no woman shall complain for measure.
> JUDGE. And that all error from our works may stand,
>   We banish Falselight evermore the land. (5.3.163–7)

With the forced removal of Shortyard and Falselight, "error" and false "measure" will too be removed. Quomodo, significantly, is not banished. The play does not suggest, then, that all drapers must go, just those who use corrupt practices. Although he is his own "affliction," he is not prohibited from keeping shop. But without Shortyard and Falselight, he will not be able to dupe his customers. Quomodo's sidekicks, then, transform from characters into their allegorical associations—false measurement, error in work, deceptive representation of cloth. The ambiguity of their place of banishment—from "the land"—might be seen as a forced exile not just from the City, but from England. The national reputation of cloth can only be restored with the ousting of false practices. The simple act of "banishing" corruption reconstitutes mercantilistic integrity to the wool trade.[48]

And we return to Chakravorty's question: "how true to life was Quomodo?" The short answer is that we can never know. Since we have very little evidence of actual drapers performing their quotidian functions, there is admittedly scant information on which to base our claims. Paster suggests that Middleton's characterization of the draper "involves some historical ironies," primarily that "the textile industry was in fact a highly regulated one" and as a result the characterization of the draper's "deceptive practices" would not be entirely accurate (Introduction, 42). However, the swell of legislation cracking down on corruption in cloth manufactures continued

---

47 See Harry Levin, p. 129 and Stock and Zwierlein, p. 12.

48 The Drapers' *Book of Ordinances* cites that "if any of this Fraternity be of misrule *or misbehaviour either in word or deed or be* of Evil Fame or Condition ... he shall be sent for to Come afore his Wardens. And by them to be Corrected as their discretion giveth them" (qtd. in A.H. Johnson, 1:269). Apparently, Quomodo comes before a judge, not the warden of the Drapers' Company.

unabated in the early years of the seventeenth century, suggesting that fraudulence marched on with little respect for the laws. Still, it is difficult to imagine a draper keeping shop on Watling Street who would embody all of Quomodo's vices. As Leinwand asserts, the "discrepancy between the play's London and the spectator's, or the play's scheming merchant and a city Alderman, is large enough to suggest that the play is not merely a reflection of contemporary London" (*The City Staged*, 53) or that Quomodo would be recognizable as an *actual* cloth seller. So, if the representation of Quomodo is not "true" to the portrait of a London draper, then he is at least "true" to the *cultural representations* of the draper. As we have seen in the discourses surrounding the profession—royal proclamations, satirical texts, polemics, and sermons—drapers were fraudulent in their business practice, underhanded in the representation of their wares, morally questionable in their demeanor, and primarily interested in carrying out deceit. In this respect, Quomodo certainly fits the bill. What they are not, however, is punished for their deeds and stripped of their ability to continue their malfeasance. In this sense, Middleton's draper is a gross misrepresentation.

Chapter 6

Politics on Parade:
The Cockayne Project and
Anthony Munday's Civic
Pageants for the Drapers

"It was never knowne that true government did at any time decay any trade, but rather caused it to increase and flourish, by this means much more Cloth will be made, better sould, and more desired and sought for: and to conclude, supplie all necessarie wants, which this worthi (but overwronged) trade hath long time indured."

—John May, *Declaration of the Estate of Clothing*, 1613

The display of corrupt drapers' practices in *Michaelmas Term* on stage suggests both that Middleton understood his audience would see the relevance of his subject matter and that, importantly, this subject matter would get a public viewing. It is of course difficult to know how many people watched this play or how many fully grasped the careful critique of the London draper. Nevertheless, that the critique took place theatrically gives weight to the fact that the crisis of the cloth industry was much more than just a passing interest of a few disgruntled writers. Moreover, the setting of *Michaelmas Term* in London and its performance on a London stage demonstrates that the wool trade was understood as an urban concern as much as a provincial one. As I have been arguing throughout *The Culture of Cloth*, the fissures in and the fate of the industry had become a national problem, one that was imagined on a grand scale: in city and country, affecting rich and poor, and allowing English subjects to see their industry as something that extended beyond the borders of their island nation.

In this chapter I move from the dramatic representation of the domestic cloth trade in the theater to the staging of these problems on the public streets of London, where the crisis was writ large in civic pageantry. The tidy conclusion of Middleton's *Michaelmas Term* where order is restored in the cloth trade, betrays the absolute disorder that was occurring in the industry, especially in the ten years or so following the play's production. The cloth industry was so plagued with troubles that in 1613 James ordered a report to be written on the "Estate of Clothing" in England in order to better understand how to approach the problems. The author of the document, John May, found such severe iniquities among merchants and producers that James was prompted to enforce regulations on cloth so extreme that the industry was paralyzed. During the time that the cloth trade was facing its worst depression, two Lord Mayors who were also members of the Drapers' Company, were elected in succession, likely as a response to the growing misery surrounding their profession. The civic pageants performed to commemorate their respective inaugurations criticize the King's support of the ruinous Cockayne project at the same time as they celebrate the glory of the cloth industry. Written by Anthony Munday, the pageants look to the venerable history of England's broadcloth and underscore the pathetic state that the industry had fallen into thanks in no small part to the King. The result is a radical nostalgia that raises the past to lambaste the present. In this chapter, I trace how the cloth crisis manifested itself in print: May's text exposes the extent to which the industry had fallen into decay; government publications, particularly royal proclamations, demonstrate the offical attempt to rectify the decline of the industry; and Munday's pageants offer a critique of these failed attempts. Through this trajectory we find a consistent attempt to reclaim the cloth industry's, and England's, glorious past.

A View of the Present State of Cloth

In 1613 John May, Deputy Alneger to King James, wrote *A Declaration of the Estate of Clothing Now Used within This Realme of England*, a report of the dilapidated state of the cloth industry, for James's Alneger General.[1] The lengthy document catalogs the various abuses found in the industry—from fraud in length and weight, to abuses in pressing cloth, to the unorthodox weaving of different types of wool, to the corruption of the drapers who sell the cloth. None of his findings would have been particularly surprising given the widespread understanding of this corruption. But the scope of his project—"the estate of cloth"—and its breadth—"within this realm of England"—suggest that the problems in the industry had reached a critical point, one that needed to be addressed on a national scale.

If May's text is a crucial historical document for the study of the cloth industry and its degradation during the early modern period, it also helps us to understand the connection between the wool industry and national sentiment during this period. Wool, in May's estimation, is as old and famous as England itself: "The antiquitie of Woll within this Kingdome hath beene, beyond the memorie of man, so highly respected for those many benefits therein" (1). Like the origins of the ancient island of England itself, wool and its "benefits" are "beyond" man's "memory," taking on the status of myth. Contrary to the stuff of legends, though, wool remained an important source of national pride. What is "beyond memory" is also visible through the continual production of wool; wool has a special status as a legend and a material reality. The wonder of wool, May seems to say, is that it is still with us. Even if we cannot recall its glorious early days, we can celebrate the commodity today: "So that no kingdome whatsoever can speake so happily of this benefit as this realme, who findeth it the rich mans increase, and the poore mans comfort, in such an excellent nature, the quantitie so much as serveth all nations in the world, and the qualitie so good, as is chiefly desired of all" (2). By establishing the crucial function that cloth serves at both the local and national level, across the economic strata, indeed across the world, May reminds his reader that England simply cannot flourish without a

---

1   The alneger was the officer appointed to examine wool. James's Alneger General, Prince Lodowick, was also a member of his Privy Council. "Clothing" here signifies the textile rather than apparel.

thriving cloth industry. And it is only by approaching the history of the cloth industry in such grandiose terms that the devastating consequences of its present "estate" can be fully understood.

According to May, the cloth trade in England has fallen into ruin because those involved in the production and sale of wool have turned their backs on cloth as a national symbol for all time in favor of viewing it as a commodity that makes money for the moment. The contemporary clothmakers and merchants, in their quest for profit at the expense of honest business practices, have failed to understand both their place in history and their potential legacy:

> But corrupting time ... not onely infected some of this Fraternitie with the knowledge of deceit, but also stirred other intruders in this trade, who greedie of such apparent gain, obtained by the well deservers, usurped the name of Clothiers, without the knowledge of the true course, but well studied in fraud, which practice they intended should supply their want of knowledge, to equal that gain formerly obtained, more respecting their present profit than all future good, nor making conscience of the meanes, so they possest the matter. This viperous sort doth too much increase in these daies, the onely breeders of all enormities in this trade & Commonwealth, & like caterpillers destroy the fruits of the earth. (5)

The deceptive members of the cloth trade are depicted here as "infect[ing]" the cloth industry as "intruders," and "vipers." Not only does May emphasize the sinister qualities associated with fraud in clothmaking, but also the unchristian manner with which the manufacturers carry out this malfeasance. Likened to Satan in the Garden of Eden, who lured Adam and Eve to sin so that they would "breed" a race of sinners for Satan's great profit, the false members of the cloth trade also ignore "future good" in favor of destroying the cloth industry—"the fruit of the earth"—in order to breed their own profits.[2] A principal culprit here is "corrupting time": by attending to the profitable present, rather than a legendary past or glorified future, the fraudulent cloth workers and merchants usher in a host of other iniquities.

May's primary purpose in writing this document is to enumerate the various problems with the production and sale of cloth in England. But May also peppers this official document with a heavy-handed moralism. Just as the religious polemicist Philip Stubbes's text blasts the interdependent corruption of the clothmaker and the draper, so does May's document take on the appearance of religious invective when it delineates the faults of England's cloth manufacturers:

> Now as herein the Clothier and maker is taxed, the Marchants and buyer cannot escape untouched ... There is no more difference betweene a bad Clothier and a bad merchant, than betweene a theefe and his receiver; for as the one commits unlawfull crimes, the other maintained it by concealements, nay more, procures him thereunto ... But God, who is the upholder of truth, wil one day bring these hidden mischiefes to light, and turne this wicked gaine to shame and losse. (7–8)

---

2   In referring to "caterpillars" here, May might also allude to the silk worm, whose product was regarded as destroying England's domestic wool trade as a result of the import of luxury fabrics. For more on early modern attitudes surrounding the silk import trade, see my Chapter 4.

The criminality of the cloth merchant who sells corrupt goods is not only in his aiding and abetting of the deceptive clothmaker, but also in "procuring" the clothmaker through perpetuating the market in faulty cloth. The score will be settled, however, by God, the almighty alneger himself. Even if the customers or the earthly cloth inspectors cannot detect the rampant fraudulence in the clothier's practices, an omniscient God sees the deceits of the trade. May suggests that by bringing the corruption "to light," God will figuratively illuminate the obscured cloth to "shame" the perpetrators.

Until that day of judgment, which Middleton dramatizes at the end of *Michaelmas Term* when Shortyard and Falselight are banished, the shame of the cloth industry must land upon the shoulders of the nation, its leader, and its subjects. May turns away from heavenly punishment to the worldly woes that arise from falsity in wool cloth when he describes the "inconveniences" of an industry besieged by fraudulence: "first, indignitie to our king, whose seale is fixt on this cloth, injurie to our nation that workes abuse on this cloth, infamie to ourselves that weare some part of this Cloth, and utter ruine of all benefits which should arise by this cloth" (39). When cloth is well made, nearly everyone in England, from the weaver, to the wearer, to the king "benefits." When it is adulterated, everyone suffers and the "nation" is defamed. As cloth goes, so goes the nation.

"Indignitie ... injurie ... infamie ... utter ruine." While May's words might seem hyperbolic, his language resonates with other "official" texts that treat the abuses in the cloth industry. A 1590 proclamation regulating cloth manufacture describes the "impoverishment and utter undoing" of poor clothworkers ("A Proclamation Mitigating Statutes," 53). The "great loss ... of her majesty's subjects" is noted as the result of weaving "deceivable things" into wool in a proclamation of 1596 ("A Proclamation Enforcing Statutes for Winding," 162). In a 1606 act for the "punishing and correcting of deceipt and frauds" on the part of wool workers, Parliament claims that when corrupt practices are allowed to exist "true Cloth making is much hindred, and Idleness doth daylie increase ... to the greate Damage and Hinderance of the Common wealth" ("An Act for the Punishinge," 1164). As in May's document, these official texts describe the triple threat of corrupt cloth: damage to workers, subjects, and the nation. The local problems associated with faulty clothmaking practices, increased poverty, and individual loss when a person buys cloth that shrinks or falls apart, are directly tied to the nation's problems. May's text, along with these government generated texts, suggest that poverty and vagrancy exist because other nations will not buy English cloth if it is seen to be of poor quality. And England's own subjects will reject faulty cloth in favor of foreign imported fabrics. John May argues that the problems associated with bad English cloth have truly become a national crisis: "In our owne Countrie, where much of our Wooll may be vented, the falshood of clothing is so common, that everie one striveth to weare any thing rather than cloth" (38).[3] Foreign markets for English cloth have declined as a result of corrupt wool and the home market, which should be the primary market for English wool, has followed suit. May's text then, while describing the "estate of cloth" in

---

3   May seems to imply that English people are turning away from their domestic product in favor of foreign fabrics such as silks and velvets. I discuss the threat to the domestic wool industry brought on by foreign imported textiles in Chapter 4.

England is also doing much more: he describes the state of English wool in the eyes of the world. By demonstrating the declining international reputation of English cloth, May necessarily points to what was at the heart of James's interest in the industry: the recuperation and advancement of the overseas cloth trade.

In what now seems prophetic language, May concludes that the venerable cloth industry can only be salvaged by the greatest of efforts and diligence: "Extraordinarie means and panes must be applied to the cause, which may be recovered by good industrie" (39). What May implies, and what his document goes on to describe, is stricter governmental control over cloth made in England in the form of more searches of the cloth's quality as well as more regulations regarding length and weight. Indeed, in a 1613 proclamation, most likely written after May's report,[4] King James apparently heeded May's warnings and mandated that because "the trade of clothing hath been much discredited by the corrupt desires and practices" of various members of the cloth community, stricter regulations and searching were to be employed in the industry ("A Proclamation for the True Working and Dying of Cloth," 301). While this proclamation seems simply to reinforce and sanction May's findings, it was the first step in a project that would significantly change the course of England's cloth industry.

The Cockayne Debacle

When May called for "extraordinarie meanes" by which the integrity of the cloth industry might be recovered, he probably did not imagine the extreme measures to which James would go. James, perhaps understanding the gravity of May's assessment, saw the national crisis which had arisen due to the poor quality of English cloth. But James was little concerned with how this quality affected the average English citizen who was forced to wear faulty cloth; rather, he wanted to alter the quality of English cloth primarily for its overseas trade. Although history has generally acknowledged James's ineptitude regarding complex financial matters, he embraced the opportunity to intervene in the sluggish English cloth trade. In preparation for what is now famous as the Cockayne project, named for the London Alderman who came up with the scheme, James endorsed several proclamations putting manufacture and export reforms into law.[5]

---

4   I can only speculate about dates here. The language of the proclamation, which includes phrases very similar to those of May, and the late calendar date of 7 December 1613, suggest that it was written after May's document.

5   William Cockayne was a wealthy and successful Eastland Merchant, trading specifically to the Baltic. During the conflicts with Ireland, Cockayne was purveyor to the English forces sent to suppress the Irish rebellion. Further, Cockayne was a moneylender; in 1610 James owed him the staggering sum of £6, 000 and, as a result, "he naturally gained James's favour" (Friis, 236). The seminal study on the Cockayne project remains Friis, *Alderman Cockayne's Project*, in which the author provides a thorough background of the business of the Merchant Adventurers. It is not clear whether Friis had access to May's document when writing. Other studies include Davies, "Intervention in the Cloth Trade"; Supple, *Commercial Crisis and Change in England*; and Brenner, *Merchants and Revolution*.

Prior to 1614 over half of London's cloth exports were undyed and undressed broadcloths, England's so called "old draperies." The Merchant Adventurers, the guild that dealt primarily with exporting this product, sent the unfinished cloth to be dyed and dressed to the Netherlands and Germany (Supple, 33).[6] It was proposed that the finishing and dyeing of cloths in England would promote the domestic industry by putting more English to work, thereby alleviating poverty and promoting the overseas trade of a purely domestic product. The regulations in quality of cloth and frequency in searching of cloth that May had called for six months earlier had been greatly expanded. Despite very reasonable arguments against the success of the endeavor, not the least of which was the lack of knowledgeable workers to finish and dye the cloth and the poor quality of English dyes, Cockayne and the projectors, with the support of the crown, managed to convince the Privy Council that there was enough manpower and means of production to uphold this radically altered form of export. And in response to the Merchant Adventurers' argument that the nations to which the cloth would be exported would greet the project with hostility and turn to other sources for cloth, Cockayne countered that the European countries could not thrive without English cloth. Merchants, who for years had sent cloth abroad to be dyed and dressed before reaching foreign markets, were instructed to send only cloth that had been dyed and finished in England.[7]

The background of Cockayne's project is complicated to be sure.[8] But it is important to iterate the basic narrative so as to understand that one of the nation's most devastating economic debacles, and one that was directly responsible for the precipitous decline of the cloth trade, was based largely on corrupt political scheming. In 1612 the Commissioners of the Treasury sought projects that would improve state revenue. One of the schemes, by William Cockayne on behalf of the Clothworkers' Company, proposed the prohibition of the export of undyed and undressed cloths. The stranglehold that the Merchant Adventurers had over exports would be broken (benefiting Cockayne and the Eastland Merchants) and the crown would profit greatly (benefiting the King). The proposal was sent to the commissioners and the King directly who, having been in prior debt to Cockayne, wholeheartedly supported the scheme. The project was passed on to the Privy Council. Although the council

---

6   In 1602 the Merchant Adventurers had the sole rights to a license for the unlimited export of white cloth (Supple, 34).

7   Between 1604 and 1614 English merchants sent two thirds of the textile exports to the Netherlands and Germany, four-fifths of which were undyed and undressed broadcloths (Davis, 24). In 1606 Alderman Cockayne and the London Clothworkers supported an unsuccessful effort to enforce the finishing of cloths that were dyed in England. The effort failed and was greatly expanded several years later in the 1614 scheme (Supple, 34). In *A Declaration*, May reminds his reader of the days when England exported raw wool rather than wool cloth, perhaps as a warning of the danger of relying too much on foreigners for the finishing of cloth: "For when it [raw wool] converted from the sheeps backe, fit for mans back, it was returned by them to this realm at a treble rate, only increased by their [the foreigners'] industrie; which shameful course brought great scandal of our idlenesse" (2). See Schneider, "Fantastical Colors," for a succinct discussion of England's domestic dyeing industry and its efforts to expand it.

8   My narrative draws largely from Friis's Chapter 4.

expressed skepticism at the success of the plan, the King's keen interest in the project kept the proposal alive and in spring 1613 a commission was set up to review the project. Around this time, May's text was also likely published. No details are known of the outcome of this committee meeting, although Friis asserts that "there can hardly be any doubt ... that the majority were unwilling to promote the clothworkers' petition" (241). Clearly unsatisfied at this turn of events, the King replaced the first commission with a new one, on which no member of the reluctant Privy Council sat. The two members of the previous commission who did remain were known supporters of the scheme, one of whom was Sir Edward Coke, who would soon go on to be appointed to the Privy Council; another member was Cockayne himself.[9] By December, Coke, learned in the history of English legislation, went before the Privy Council to report on the Commission's findings. Principally, he attacked the validity of the Merchant Adventurers' charter, basing his arguments on past statutes and proclamations, some of which were remote and obscure, which promoted the production and trade of domestic products rather than unfinished or partially finished commodities.[10] Throughout the next several months, the Privy Council heard arguments against Cockayne's project and ultimately put the decision into the hands of the King. James found the Merchant Adventurers' argument against the project "too weake" and agreed "to putt in execution the dying and dressing of all broadclothes before they be transported" (qtd. in Friis, 265).

In the space of a year—December 1613 to December 1614—there were no less than five royal proclamations gradually putting Cockayne's project into place. The first proclamation, "for the True Working and Dying of Cloth" (December 1613), was clearly a response to May's document and continued to acknowledge the rampant corruption among manufacturers and sellers of cloth. The proclamation assured that cloth would be carefully inspected at Blackwell Hall, implored neither subject nor stranger to sell or export cloths that had not been "Searched and Sealed," and promised that offenders would be fined (302). Although the proclamation offers no explicit connection to Cockayne's proposal, according to James F. Larkin and Paul L. Hughes "this text is the first public step in the Cockayne Project ... to increase employment in England, to prevent fraudulent making of cloth by enforcing older laws against exporting undyed and undressed cloth, and to make a profit for the King [and Cockayne's supporters] in the process" (n. 1, 301). Another significant

---

9   Despite Coke's antagonism towards monopolies—and therefore his criticism of the Merchant Adenturer's practices—Prestwich finds Coke's "enthusiasm" for the project "difficult to account for" since he was a fastidiously "acute lawyer" (168). Similarly, one would expect to find antagonism to the project on the part of Parliament. However, as Brenner notes, "the House of Commons was simply unalterably opposed, both by interest and principle, to the chartered commercial companies." Although the scheme was attacked by Robert Middleton, an MP and Merchant Adventurer, the other MPs "could muster little sympathy for the Adventurers; in fact, some of them used the occasion to attack the company once again" (Brenner, *Merchants and Revolution*, 210–11). In effect, then, the unlikeliness of success of the new scheme was subordinated to the distaste for the monopolistic structure of the Merchant Adventurers.

10 Coke also cited the argument that foreigners were corrupt in their cloth finishing practices, apparently ignoring that this practice was rampant among domestic cloth producers.

stipulation of the proclamation was that the charter of the Merchant Adventurers would be revoked so that James could create his own company of cloth exporters—the New Merchant Adventurers—resulting in profits for the crown, rather than the citizens. Larkin and Hughes assert that "to get on with their plan," supporters of the scheme "had to take the cloth trade away from the Merchant Adventurers; and this they were able to do by lavish bribery and holding out to James (then £600, 000 in debt) the prospect of £300, 000 income for himself each year" (n. 1, 301).

The second proclamation, issued in July 1614 "against the Exportation of Cloathes, undyed and undressed," pressed the first even further and combined reforms in cloth production with a radical reorganization of export practices. The proclamation's initial demand was that, as of 2 November 1614, "all Broad Clothes may be Died & Dressed within our Kingdome, before they be exported." This will be "for the further good of Our loving Subjects, in whose riches & good estate Wee shall always thinke our selves rich & happie" (312–313). The proclamation stresses the benefit that such a radical reorganization of cloth production would have on the English subjects. The commonwealth's "good estate" allows for the King's "riches." In order to justify such a bold move, the crown must argue that—despite decades of successful dyeing and dressing of English cloth on the part of foreign nations—the foreigners have actually been debasing the English product: "the Strangers ... have usually practiced both to set false Colours upon Our said Clothes, and also to Tenter them in length," which results in the "extreame damage of the wearer, and the intolerable discredite of this Noble and Staple commoditie" (313). It is this vilification of the foreign manufacturer that sets the groundwork for the second major element of the proclamation. If the foreigners are mishandling "white" broadcloths, and the Merchant Adventurers are the guild responsible for exporting undyed and undressed cloths, then the the Merchant Adventurers, those at the root of the "problem," must be prohibited from conducting business.

The proclamation ordered that after 2 November, "all Our loving Subjects of what qualitie soever ... shall be admitted to Ship, and Export the same to any staple Townes beyond the seas," allowing for "a Free Trade for all Our loving Subjects" (313, 314). This proposed freedom of trade seemingly enabled a democratization of what had largely been an export monopoly held by the Merchant Adventurers and, as such, appeared to be a magnanimous gesture on the part of the King. However, what becomes clear is that the crown rather than the King's subjects would benefit the most and that only a handful of men would be able to participate in the "free trade":

> [A]ll and singular persons which shall shippe or export any such Dyed and Drest Cloathes into the Territories aforesaid shall first subscribe their names, with such summes of Money, as they will yearly employ during the space of three yeeres next ensuing, in a Register Booke, which shall be kept by William Cockaine Alderman of our Citie of London ... And that all others, which refuse or neglect so to doe, shall forever bee excluded from using and exercising the Trade of Exportation of Dyed and Drest Clothes into the places and dominions aforesaid. (314)

What initially seemed like an earnest effort to increase domestic manufactures and create equity among exporters, emerges by the end of the proclamation as a strictly controlled money making scheme for the crown. Although "all" subjects, which presumably included members of the Merchant Adventurers, were initially invited to participate in the exportation of cloth, it is clear that only the richest merchants would be able to do so.[11] In addition to paying traditional levies on the cloth, the exporters would have to dole out an undisclosed amount to Cockayne, the man behind the scheme and he who convinced James to go along with the project with the promise of royal profits.[12]

The entire scheme began to collapse even as it was officially put into place. Most of the prominent members of the old Merchant Adventurers declined to be part of the new guild.[13] Further, James did not predict that the Dutch, who made much of their profits in the dyeing and dressing of wool, would be so angered by this affront to their industry that they would immediately ban the import of all English cloth, resulting in the "utter ruin" of cloth exportation for several years. While the July Proclamation was an official effort to squeeze out the old guild of Merchant Adventurers, this effort was greatly expanded five months later when the crown officially revoked their charter and licenses.[14] However, the new company did not have the experience or ability to take over such a massive trade. The English, who relied on Dutch ships to carry English cloth to other continental markets, were not equipped to take over the shipping, and in the early months of 1615 the export of undressed broadcloths decreased by over 50 percent (Supple, 39). By May 1615, dyeing and dressing was at a standstill. Within three years the Merchant Adventurers had to be recalled and have their licenses reissued, though not all of their privileges were restored. Everyone involved in the domestic broadcloth industry, from country weavers and spinners—who relied on London clothiers to buy their cloth—to drapers, to merchant adventurers, was financially devastated.[15]

---

11 See Davies, pp. 120–21, for a discussion of Cockayne's role in shaping the New Merchant Adventurers.

12 The third proclamation issued within 1614 was a reinstitution of an Act made during the early years of Elizabeth's reign. The proclamation prohibited "the Exportation of Sheepe, Woolls, Wool-fells [sheepskins] and Fullers Earth," a naturally occurring clay sediment that was used to extract oils from sheep's wool. This was an extension of the other proclamations previously issued relating to Cockayne's project. The proclamation thwarts those who would export live sheep and raw wool as an attempt to circumvent the laws prohibiting undyed and undressed cloth. The punishment for those who flouted the law exporting sheep included imprisonment and "the loss of the offenders left hand" (318). The fourth proclamation was "against the Transporting of Woollen Yarne, &c" to foreign countries. The fifth was the official revocation of the Merchant Adventurers' charter.

13 As Supple suggests, it was the reluctance on the part of the important members of the old company to join with the new that was "the principal reason for the ultimate failure of Cockayne's company to handle the trade in undressed cloth" (37).

14 According to Larkin and Hughes, the Merchant Adventurers were supposed to have relinquished their charter on 9 October 1614. On 14 October they agreed to surrender the charter as long as the King would reinstate it if the New Merchant Adventurers failed. They also requested that they continue to be allowed to collect debts owed to them. They did not, however, formally surrender their charter until February 1615.

15 Cockayne's notorious posthumous reputation was perhaps somewhat tempered by John Donne, who wrote Cockayne's funeral sermon in 1626. For a deft discussion of the sermon vis-à-vis Coackyne's involvement in the debacle, see Freer. Prestwich also attends to this.

May's "Declaration," a document designed to alert the government to the abuses in the cloth industry and to suggest ways to remedy the situation through an increase in regulation, was ironically the seed of the Cockayne project, which caused the largest depression in the cloth trade that England had ever seen and from which it never recovered. Of course, May could not have imagined this would be the case and in fact ends his document by assuring his readers that the government will step in to work to repair the industry: "It was never known that true government did at any time decay any trade, but rather caused it to increase and flourish, by this meanes much more Cloth will be made, better sould, and more desired and sought for" (50). Rather than assisting in the recovery of the trade, James and Alderman Cockayne did what May asserted was unthinkable; that is they precipitated the "decay" of the cloth industry.

The Golden Fleece

In October 1614, three months after Cockayne's project was put into place and even as it was proving to be disastrous, the guild companies elected a draper as London's Lord Mayor. The following October they did the same. That citizens involved in the production or sale of cloth were elected Lord Mayor twice in a row was not alone remarkable—several guilds that made up the 12 "great" companies from which Lord Mayors were elected were involved in the textile industry.[16] But that they were elected at a time when the broadcloth industry was in serious turmoil suggests the widespread concern for the state of the cloth among London merchants.[17] As Muriel Bradbrook has suggested, the civic pageants of 1614 and 1615, written by the draper Anthony Munday to celebrate the inauguration of the new Lord Mayors, "are concerned with the City's struggle against [the] particular menace" of the Cockayne project (103). While Bradbrook rightly refers to the socioeconomic crisis taking place in England at this time, I would press the point further to argue that the civic pageants written for these two Lord Mayors are an effort to overcome the debacle of Cockayne's project. That is to say, by looking to the venerable past of English cloth, Munday's two civic pageants, *Himatia-Poleos* (1614) and *Metropolis Coronata* (1615), take significant pains to triumph over James's disastrous attempt to expand the broadcloth industry. The pageants associate the new Lord Mayors with famous traditions and figures of the "ancient" cloth industry and place the new City representatives within that history. This has a twofold effect: first, the present state of the cloth industry that John May so painstakingly and regretfully laid out is placed in relation to the decades and centuries in which the cloth industry was valued by those

---

16 While most of London's companies had the good fortune of having one of their own elected as Lord Mayor, those companies connected to the production and sale of cloth were particularly well represented since many of the 12 Great Companies of London—the Drapers, Clothworkers, Haberdashers, Mercers, and Merchant Taylors—were associated with the production of cloth (Bradbrook, 96).

17 It is possible that drapers rather than members of other companies associated with the cloth trade were elected as Lord Mayors in these years because, as sellers rather than manufacturers or traders of cloth, the drapers were not significantly involved in the project and thus escaped blame. See Girtin, *The Triple Crowns*, p. 214.

who produced, sold, and regulated it. Second, by associating the two Lord Mayor drapers with the glorious history of English cloth, Munday distinguishes them from the King who would not respect that past. Recalling the past becomes, for Munday, a radical act where current policies can be challenged.

The civic pageants, which celebrated the inauguration of the new Lord Mayor on October 29th, during Michaelmas Term, were elaborate and expensive affairs.[18] Similar to their courtly counterparts, the royal masque, these civic pageants were a fantastic display of unproductive consumption in that they were generally performed just once and then dismantled.[19] In celebrating the King (or Queen) and Lord Mayor, both the masque and pageant, furthermore, underscored the authority of a politically crucial individual (Tumbleson, 54). The similarities, however, might be said to end there.[20] While the court masque was performed in an enclosed architectural space, usually at a Banqueting Hall, in front of a limited and largely aristocratic audience invited to view the display, the Lord Mayor's show traveled down the streets of London, before thousands of spectators across the socio-economic strata. As Thomas Dekker writes in a preface to one of his own pageants, "[s]o inticing a shape they carry, that *Princes* themselves take pleasure to behold them; they with delight; common people with admiration" (*Troia Nova*, 230). While the sovereign's coffers paid for the masques, the mayoral pageants were fully funded by the craft guilds of London, who also orchestrated the productions (Bergeron, "Actors," 24).[21] While both genres of performance highlighted the triumph of virtuous behavior and flattered the individual for whom the play was performed, they did so in highly disparate ways: the court masque generally presented an imaginative vision of an ordered England "outside the world bound by sense and time" (Paster, *The Idea of the* City, 145), while the Mayor's pageant was absolutely tied to the city, and indeed the nation, surrounding its stage in its emphasis on England's history and the

---

18 The first Lord Mayor's show was performed in 1535 and the last in 1701. Tumbleson argues that the beginning and ending dates for the Lord Mayor's Pageants coincide with the growth of London as a global force. See p. 54.

19 I borrow this term from Georges Bataille. Bataille defines consumption as "unproductive" if it includes expenditures associated with "luxury, mourning, war, cults, the construction of sumptuary monuments, games spectacles, arts, perverse sexual activity ... activities which ... have no end beyond themselves" (118). See Paster, "The Idea of London," p. 48, for a discussion of how civic pageants imitated the masques. For a thorough comparison between the Stuart masque and the Lord Mayor's pageants, see Nancy Wright.

20 The Lord Mayors' shows had more in common with other civic processions, which were performed much less frequently, such as Royal entrances. Dekker's *The Magnificent Entertainment*, a script for King James, Queen Anne, and Prince Henry's entrance into London in 1603, acknowledged the role of the commoner as audience member in writing the script in the vernacular: "The multitude is now to be our Audience, whose heads would miserably runne a wool-gathering, if we doo but offer to breake them with hard words" (255). For a detailed discussion of the route of the procession, see Manley, *Literature and Culture*, Chapter 5.

21 In this respect, the civic pageants share a connection to medieval cycle drama, which was largely funded by the craft guilds. Several mayoral shows prominently portray the patron saint of the particular guild. For a further discussion of civic pageantry's indebtedness to medieval drama, see Bergeron, "Civic Pageants." See Lancashire for a discussion of the Draper' Company's involvement in plays throughout the Middle Ages and early Renaissance.

guilds' place within this history. Further, while the purpose of the mayoral pageant was ostensibly to honor the new Lord Mayor, in so doing the pageants honored the company from which he came and all the members of that company from the richest merchant to the lowest apprentice. Paid for by London's trade companies, honoring the Lord Mayor, an esteemed member of a company, performed by children from the Company's schools (Bergeron, "Actors" 18) as well as stage companies, and often written by guild members who were also professional writers, the Lord Mayor's pageant decidedly emphasized and celebrated the mercantile class. In this sense, the pageants were antithetical to court masques which glorified the sovereign and high-born. As Gail Paster asserts, "the pageants ministered to the city's self-esteem by challenging aristocratic assumptions that birth, courtly grace, and royal favor matter most of all" (*The Idea of the* City, 149).[22] On the day of the pageant what mattered most of all was that a man who had ascended through the ranks of his own beloved company had become its representative and the triumphant governor of London.[23]

For the literary critic, the Lord Mayor's shows pose a special problem since the pageants were largely visual spectacles. Further, it is difficult to make a claim about what cultural work the pageants did for the audience since their experience must have been, at best, fragmentary. Speeches given by individual actors would have been difficult to discern, even by those in the vicinity. And aside from the key participants, no one would have likely seen the show in its entirety. What we do have to go by, though, are the scripts, which were printed with increasing frequency in the Jacobean period.[24] As Bergeron argues, the proliferation of printed pageant texts is concordant with a general increase in the printing of other playscripts, which "suggests an ever-increasing reading public, a market for playtexts, and an emerging self-consciousness that drama might become a book" ("Stuart Civic Pageants," 163). Indeed, often the scripts were entered into the Stationer's Register prior to Lord Mayor's Day, which indicated an assumed printing.[25] The textual incarnation of the pageant, however, was certainly distinct from the initial script written for the parade. For one thing, the printed texts are self-consciously *textual*. That is to say, they have a frontispiece, which includes details of the performance (the name of the new Lord Mayor, the date of the pageant), the author of the script, and the imprint. Additionally, the printed scripts contained a fair bit of front matter, usually providing some family history of the new Lord Mayor or lauding the company from whose ranks he was elected. Lawrence Manley notes that "all of the surviving Jacobean and Caroline shows printed not only the spoken verses but also an elaborate prose commentary

---

22 Responding to Mullaney's claim that "ceremony is a way in which the city defines itself," Garrett Sullivan asserts that "it is not the only way, and we must understand that much of what the city contains—for example, foreign born workers, nonguild industry, and a seasonally employed workforce—is not registered within its rituals" (201).

23 The Lord Mayor's pageants borrowed the term "Triumph" from the reward given to a Roman conqueror. The correlation between a Roman ruler and a London citizen further suggests the confusion of social order that might have been shored up with the pageants. See Kipling for a comparison between the London civic processions and the Roman triumph.

24 For a discussion of the pageants as *texts*, see Paula Johnson.

25 An example of this is Dekker's *Troia-Nova Triumphans*, which was entered into the Stationer's Register on 21 October 1612, more than a week before the pageant.

describing the devices and incidentally reviewing the history and function of the ceremony, its various customs and liturgical features" (*Literature and Culture*, 275). The printed texts for the Lord Mayor's pageants written by Thomas Middleton all offer formal dedications to the mayor. The initial text is largely extra-theatrical, giving the reader more and new information than would have been allowed the spectator. The texts also provide the entire speeches given by the actors (one presumes with some revisions), offer a narrative of each of the spectacles, and announce transitions between "scenes." While the scripts give a thorough sense of the day's spectacle, as Bergeron explains, they also do more:

> [T]hese texts become commemorative books that both capture and immortalize the event and add to it. They assume an expository and narrative function that sets them apart from the typical dramatic text ... they exhibit a growing self-consciousness as books and ... do not obliterate theatrical performance or displace it so much as they complete it. ("Stuart Civic Pageants," 163)

Since the theatrical performance can never be recaptured, our understanding of what transpired during any given parade must remain speculative. However, if we take the scripts to be generally accurate in their description of the order of events and the details of the shows, we have a good point of departure for discussion. Because the texts provide the extra-theatrical matter, they also give us more in the way of content and context than the shows themselves ever could. Further, and importantly for our purposes, they give their author a voice.[26]

Anthony Munday, the chief writer for the Lord Mayor's shows in the early Stuart period, was particularly conscientious in preparing the pageant scripts for printing.[27] Like many Jacobean authors, Munday did not survive by only one type of writing or even by only one profession. He was a regular contributor to the Jacobean stage while also writing prose fiction, pamphlets, and translations, as well as a revision of Stow's *Survey of London*.[28] He began his professional life as a printer, although

---

26 As Paula Johnson notes, no Lord Mayor's pageant script that was printed was done so anonymously and all but one was written by an established London writer (158).

27 There are only two full-length studies devoted entirely to Anthony Munday, those by Celeste Turner Wright and Tracey Hill. Wright's book is magisterial in its biographical detail (although scholars have offered correctives to specific matters since the time of publication). Hill's recent text, published over seventy-five years after Wright's, is a thorough—and long overdue—study of Munday in his London context, and therefore goes far beyond the bounds of "biography."

28 See Celeste Turner Wright and Eccles for details of Munday's biography found in official records. See Merritt for a discussion of his involvement in the revision of Stow's *Suvey*. Munday was at least partly responsible for fifteen pageants and was the premier writer until Middleton came on the scene. See Tumbleson, p. 56 and Bradbrook, p. 100. For a discussion of the ostensible rivalry between Middleton and Munday (or lack thereof), see Bergeron, "Middleton and Munday." Munday was neither educated at university nor the Inns of Court, which may—as Beer argues of Stow—put him "closer to the ordinary men and women of Tudor England than to the political elite" (Beer, *Tudor England*, 18).

he was a freeman of the Drapers' Company.[29] The extent to which he practiced the trade of the draper is unclear, although he did apparently provide the drapery for the 1602 Lord Mayor's pageant sponsored by the Merchant Taylors, for which he wrote the script (Tracey Hill, 28). In 1611, he seemed to combine all three of his trades in his involvement with the pageant for the Lord Mayor from the Goldsmiths' Company, *Cruso-Thriambos*. The company records indicate that Munday required remuneration for the drapery he provided "'for all the persons and children in the orpherie' ... 'to make fit and apt speeches for expressing of the shew'" that he himself wrote. He also demanded "'500 books thereof to be made and printed, '" which were presumably the textual scripts of the pageant (qtd. in Tracey Hill, 28).

When in two succeeding years (1614 and 1615), a draper rose to be Lord Mayor of London, Munday was the logical choice to compose the Triumph. Not only was he skilled in writing pageants, but he was one of the drapers' own and could properly praise the company and glorify the new Lord Mayor.[30] He would also have understood the damage inflicted on the cloth industry by the King and Cockayne. While neither *Himatia-Poleos: The Triumphs of Olde Draperie, or the Rich Cloathing of England* nor *Metropolis Coronata: The Triumphs of Ancient Drapery, or the Rich Cloathing of England* explicitly criticize the sovereign or his policies, the emphasis on the "old" and "ancient" cloth industry as England's "richness" indicate that the *present* state of the cloth industry is impoverished. As Garrett Sullivan has argued about the pageants in general, "[t]he Lord Mayor's show is a guild production that in its form represents the primacy of the guilds to the city, but that primacy is threatened by the emergence of industries that lie outside the guilds' influence, just as they often lie outside the city's wall" (205). As Munday's two shows for the Drapers' Company attempt to consolidate a vision of the cloth industry that is whole and wholesome, the repeated references to the beleaguered state of affairs reveal the very fissures facing the industry from forces outside the guild itself.

Himatia-Poleos, Munday's first pageant for Lord Mayor Thomas Haynes, highlights Haynes's place in London's civic history and also in the history of the Drapers' Company.[31] Here, Munday is as interested in glorifying the company from which the Lord Mayor comes as he is in celebrating the Mayor himself. To this end, Munday takes great pains to argue that the first Mayor of London, Henry Fitz-Alwine, appointed by Richard I in the late twelfth century, was in fact a draper. Despite Munday's earlier claims that Fitz-Alwine was a member of the Goldsmiths'

---

29 Munday gained freedom from the Drapers by "patrimony." His father was a member of the Drapers' guild, although he also worked as a stationer (Tracey Hill, 28–9).

30 Bergeron tells us that "scant company records provide little supplementary material" to the pageants of 1614 and 1615 (*English Civic Pageantry*, 150–51).

31 As Munday explains, the phrase "Himatia-Poleos" is a Greek term for the walls of a city: "Intimating thereby, that as garments and cloathing doe ingirt the body, defending it continually from the extremities of cold and heat: so walles, being the best garments of any Citie, do preserve it from all dangerous annoyances" (74–5). The 1614 pageant paid for by the Drapers meant that "a score of new freemen had to be admitted, and assessments of £5 per bachelor had to be made" (Celeste Turner Wright, 161).

Company,[32] and the Mercers' and Fishmongers' own claim that he was a member of their companies, Munday assures the new Lord Mayor that, as a draper, he has descended from London's first Mayor: "having perused more assured authority in the Drapers Hall, that one ... named ... *Henrie Fitz-Alwine*, a brother of the olde Drapers, was Lord Maior of *London*, foure and twentie yeares and a half (by yerely election) and longer had been if he had longer lived" (74).[33] By establishing that Fitz-Alwine was most certainly a draper, when actually there is no firm evidence to prove that he was (Girtin, 3), Munday places Haynes in a distinguished line of citizens who were elected to represent the City. Like all Mayors, Thomas Haynes is associated with the venerable City of London. His status as a draper, however, underscores his importance not only to the city, but to the nation as well. As Munday asserts, the "best advantages" of cities is that they are "ever ensued by making of woolled Clothes, for the continuall maintenance of England's Draperie" (75). Here Munday reminds us that the arms of the trade companies define the City, but perhaps more importantly, the activities of the companies—specifically those involved in the production of wool—maintain England's product, which is national in its importance.

While *Himatia-Poleos* is comprised of tableaux celebrating the glory of the Mayor's profession—such as a pageant featuring "Himatia" as the mother of clothing surrounded by actors performing "services to woollen Cloathes" (75)—the show is dominated by characters who are crucial to the specific traditions and actual history of the Drapers Company.[34] Munday's Lord Mayor's shows are singularly preoccupied with the gravity of the past. His pageants, which "habitually emphasized the historical over the contemporary" (Tracey Hill, 153), also brought that history to bear on the present. If Munday "constantly relies on the presence of Former Lord Mayors in his pageants," for example, their inclusion is always in service to making connections between past and present, in service of demonstrating the "continuity" of history (Bergeron, *English Civic Pageantry*, 159), rather than its distance.[35] For Munday, London's history is also *England's* history: by harkening back to a glorified mayoral past, he simultaneously calls up an idealized England. Paster asserts that the "idealized city history takes on particular significance once we realize the extent

---

32 Munday attempts to cover over this factual error on his part: "it may appear as a blemish on my own browe, because in my Booke in the worthie Company of Goldsmiths, I did set downe *Henrie Fitz-Alwine*" as a goldsmith and the first Mayor of London (73). Munday blames this mistake on information in John Stow's *Survey of London*. Withington dismissively says this slip is one of the only two "noteworthy things in Munday's 1614 show." The other is the figure of Richard I "surrounded by many personified cities" (36).

33 The traditional date assigned to the inauguration of Fitz-Alwine is 1189 (Hope, 10).

34 Munday wrongly claims that the Drapers' Company, rather than the Mercers, was "the first Companie of all others in this Citie" (73). See Bergeron, *Pageants and Entertainments*, 99.

35 Merrit sees this interest in the continuity of history as pervading Munday's other written work as well: "Like the pageants that Munday composed, in which the appointment of new lord mayors was celebrated by the parading of medieval mayors, Munday's *Survey* is largely a celebration of the continuity and achievements of London's governors and people. If there is a triumphalism here, then it is a triumphalism that is based on *continuity* with the past—a glorious civic past which has reached its apotheosis in the present" (Merritt, 63).

to which the civic entertainments identify London's past with that of the nation as a whole" (*The Idea of the* City, 143). And Bergeron asserts that "the emphasis on history was of course commensurate with a rising nationalism" (Bergeron, "Anthony Munday," 345). I would argue that nowhere is this nationalism—the emphasis on London history to celebrate England's glory days—more readily seen than in the pageants of 1614 and 1615, which take up the product most closely tied to England's understanding of itself.

The first spectacle of *Himatia-Poleos*, a performance presented on a barge on the Thames headed for Westminster, is a chariot drawn by lions and wolves carrying an actor playing Richard I who was on the throne when Fitz-Alwine was elected mayor. The first character to speak is Sir John Norman, elected Lord Mayor in 1453, and a member of the Drapers' Company.[36] Harkening back first to the late twelfth century and then to the mid-fifteenth century, Munday underscores just how ancient the eminence of cloth is. Indeed, Munday seems to suggest that the glory of the Drapers' Company precedes even itself: the charter was not granted until 1364, nearly two hundred years *after* Fitz-Alwine was elected Lord Mayor. The confusion of facts (that Fitz-Alwine was a draper) and the inexactitude of dates (when the drapers were granted their charter) underscores the company's legendary status.[37] Like the cloth industry itself, the Drapers' Company is practically, in May's words, "beyond the memory of man." Also like the cloth industry, the Drapers' Company is vital to England's *present*. This continuity of history is seen in the celebrating of Lord Mayor Haynes himself. He is at once a descendent of Henrie Fitz-Alwine and is crucial to London in October 1614.

Directly following the appearance of John Norman, and performed at Westminster where the barge has landed and the Lord Mayor officially would be inaugurated, a Cotswold shepherd—or, likely, somebody playing one—accompanied by "a goodly Ramme or Golden Fleece" speaks directly to the Lord Mayor and the other audience members: "Why gaze yee so upon me? Am I not a man, flesh, bloud, and bone, as you are? Or in these silken satin Townes, are poore plaine meaning Shepheards woondred at, like Comets or blazing Starres? Or is it this goodly beast by me, that fills your eyes with admiration?" (77) Whether or not the audience members were actually "gazing" in amazement at the spectacle before them, the lines suggest that the presence of a humble shepherd and his sheep would have been a noteworthy, if not a remarkable, sight in the metropolis. Wondering if the Lord Mayor is put off by the incongruity of the man's plainness, the shepherd, in a democratizing gesture, equates the Mayor with himself: they—like those commoners who are watching the pageant—are all made of "flesh, bloud, and bone." Despite the similarities between them, the shepherd, who would no doubt have been wearing plain, homespun wool, draws attention to his modest attire and plain speech and wonders if it is his rural humility that elicits such attention. His presence in "silken satin" London makes

---

36 Munday stages the speech of John Norman on the barge because he was purportedly the first Lord Mayor to go to Westminster by these means. This fact has since been discredited (Bergeron, *Pageants and Entertainments*, 82).

37 For a thorough discussion of Munday's confusion surrounding Fitz-Alwine, see Tracey Hill, Chapter 5.

him look like an oddity in a sea of sumptuousness. However, in a pageant that has as its primary purpose the honoring of a Mayor drawn from the ranks of the Drapers' Company, whose primary product is wool, his apparel is perhaps more appropriate than that of some of the audience members. Thus, his "poor" appearance is figured as remarkable as the brilliant "Comets or blazing stars."

Turning to the sheep by his side, the probable object of the city spectators' "admiration," the shepherd takes us from one of God's wonders, the heavenly comets and stars, to another, the earthly ovine. While the shepherd is not a part of the Lord Mayor's lineage, he does represent a specific tradition associated with drapers who become Lord Mayor: "when any worthy Brother of [the Drapers'] Society comes to be Lord Maior of this City, the very fairest Ram in all their flocks is sent to them as a solemne offring" (77). The ceremonious presentation of the ram is followed by the shepherd repeating a Cotswold saying:

From the Ramme
    We have the Lambe
From both our finest
    woolles are shorne
Wool had thus from
    the Ramme and Lambe,
Makes the best Cloath,
    That can be worne.
Thanke then the Draper
    That began:
To make such Cloathing,
    Meete for man. (77–8)

The "finest" wool makes the "best" cloth and the sheep are originators of such fine stuffs. However, the fame of the "ramme" and "lambe" is entirely reliant on the skill of the draper who, although now primarily responsible for selling cloth, "first began" to produce the cloth that is now held in high esteem. If the logical progression of how commendation should be assigned was not made clear in the saying, the shepherd subsequently does so: "For if we have no ram, we are sure to have no lamb; no lamb, no wool; no wool, no cloth; no cloth, no draper" (78). The pageant symbolically and literally links sheep—the drapers' raw material—to the City's governing body. The gift of the best sheep in the flock correlates to the recipient of the gift, the most worthy draper of the Company. The shepherd's ditty becomes an association of crucially linked entities where the ram, the gift presented to the Lord Mayor, is the originary object of importance. The ceremony of giving the ram to the Lord Mayor completes the association: no draper, no Lord Mayor.[38]

---

38 In *Taylors Pastorall*, John Taylor the Water Poet borrows the words "of an ingenious and well affected Poet of our time, Master T.M. where he truly saith, No Ram, no Lambe, no Lambe no Sheepe, no Sheepe no Wooll, no Wooll no Woolman, no Woolman no Spinner, no Spinner no Weaver, no Weaver no Cloth, no Cloth no Clothier, no Clothier no Clothworker, Fuller, Tucker, Shearman, Draper, or scarcely a rich Dier" (D2r). "T.M." might be Taylor's mistake for A.M, Anthony Munday, or perhaps a misremembrance that Thomas Middleton wrote the ditty. Regardless, Taylor's text goes on to provide "names of many worthy men, who

The spectacular celebration of the Lord Mayor and the labor of the company from which he came did not, though, exclude participation by the King himself. During the pageant, the monarch held a prominent position as he gave the Lord Mayor a sword or scepter to carry in front of the sovereign throughout the procession (Manley, *Literature and Culture*, 220). On a day meant to honor the citizens of London, the monarch's presence was never forgotten. As Manley asserts, the "special status of London and the mayoralty was affirmed" by this consolidating act of the King or Queen (*Literature and Culture*, 220). But despite the King's presence, or perhaps because of it, the difference between the two figures of authority was pitched into high relief:

> such ceremonies always negotiated distance and difference ... the pageants of the Lord Mayor's Shows frequently extolled the precedents, charters, and liberties London had wrested from English kings. The neo-feudal ethos of the pageants only thinly concealed a rivalrous relationship, in which merchants liked to represent themselves as the peers of kings. (Manley, *Literature and Culture*, 221)

The presence of the monarch in the pageant procession was a visible yet silent indication of the distinction between the two. On one hand this image might be seen as an act of the King's power: It is he who enables and props up the Lord Mayor. At the same time, the spectator—who may or may not have been present to see the monarch give the Lord Mayor the scepter—would see that the Lord Mayor actually precedes the sovereign and thus is the figure of prominence. Even if the spectators could not hear the procession, they would only have to turn to the text of the pageant to reconcile what they saw before them: the Mayor walking in prominence before the King.[39] The pageants were, after all, immediately printed for purchase by whoever could afford them (Bergeron, "Pageants, Politics, and Patrons," 139). On the written page, then, the King is physically absent and the Lord Mayor rules in prominence.[40]

The celebration of Thomas Haynes's rise to Lord Mayor, however, is not all golden. The pageant also includes a critique of the decline to which English cloth had succumbed. In a speech given by the character of Fitz-Alwine at the Guild Hall, the first Lord Mayor denounces the present by glorifying the past, when he was Mayor and English cloth was as robust as the men who made and wore it:

> In times of olde Antiquitie,
> When men liv'd long and healthfully,
> Detesting sloth and idlenesse,
> Which breeds but surfet and excesse.

---

have been free of London, of such trades and mysteries whereof the *Sheepe* is the originall under God." He first begins with the Drapers who have become Lord Mayors, and starts his list with "Sir *Henrie Fitz Allen* Draper" (D2r). See my Chapter 1 for a discussion of *Taylors Pastorall*.

39 Of course, while the pageant was seen by hundreds of spectators, the actual words said on any of the given "stages" would have hardly been audible. See Bradbrook, p. 96, and Paster, *The Idea of the City*, pp. 138–9.

40 See Lobanov-Rostovsky, p. 881, for a discussion of the Lord Mayor's dual role of audience and actor in the procession.

When yea and nay was greates Oath,
And mens best weare, good woollen Cloth,
Ycleped *England's Draperie*
More worth then gaudie braverie,
Of silken twine, Silver and Golde,
Nere knowen in those blest daise of olde. (78)

Munday distinguishes the venerable past by comparing it to the present, when men are slothful, idle, excessive, and surfeited. This comparison is presented through "*England's*" cloth. Under the current conditions of the numerous vices associated with the time, "good woollen cloth" is impossible to maintain. And perhaps the most biting criticism we have here is in the statement that the good old days were a time when a man's word was his "oath." While John May might have promised the cloth producers and sellers of England that their government would not cause "decay" in the industry, James's policies regarding cloth went decidedly against those words. By reciting these lines to the Lord Mayor directly, Fitz-Alwine seems to warn him of the current conditions of which he as a draper would be acutely aware. The public and histrionic manner in which these words are uttered makes all those listening (and reading), possibly including the King, also aware of the troubled times.

And this, Munday seems to say, is where the Lord Mayor can be of use. In lines that carry subversive potential, especially considering that the King was probably present, Fitz-Alwine explains the power vested in the position of Lord Mayor:

Therefore as God had given [the King] place,
Solely to rule, and judge each case,
So would he plant a deputie,
To figure his authoritee
In the true forme of Monarchie,
Then which, no better soveraigntie,
Which office being imposed upon me,
By such a gracious Majestie. (79)

Fitz-Alwine explains that just as God has divinely placed the King on the earth "to rule," so did the King choose a Lord Mayor to "figure" the King's "authority." The chain of command here seems clear: God to King to Lord Mayor. The Lord Mayor exists on the authority of the King and is held up by that king who is upheld by God. But just as the Lord Mayor physically walking ahead of the King in the procession has a curious duality, this ballad also seems to have the authority going both ways. That Munday emphasizes that the Lord Mayor "figures" the authority of the King potentially disrupts the hierarchy. According to the multiple contemporaneous uses of "figure," this phrase could mean that the Lord Mayor is "planted" on the earth a) to "form" or "shape" the King's authority, b) to "portray or represent" the King's authority "by speech or action," or c) to "be an image" or "symbol" of the King's authority.[41] Each of the second two possible meanings seems to indicate that the Lord Mayor is something of a civic substitute for the King. He will be the King's representative in London. In the Mayoral pageants, the Lord Mayor as

---

41 *OED* "figure" (entries 1a, 4, and 6).

King's substitute is not simply one of representative or mouthpiece: the pageants "regularly establish the idea of the mayor as the king's 'substitute' ... the mayor in the pageants devoted to him often rivaled the king in symbolic importance" (Bergeron, "Pageants, Politics, and Patrons," 142). While the Lord Mayor was serving as the King's representative, he was also crucially a citizen of London and represented the men of his company and looked out for their interests. If by "figuring" the King's authority, he is "forming" or "shaping" it, at least in civic matters, then he truly can act for his fellow drapers, those who, along with clothworkers in England, so desperately needed new policies to be "figured." Spoken by the first Lord Mayor to Haynes, Fitz-Alwine seems to be reminding the new Lord Mayor of his authority at this crucial time in the history of English cloth.

After a long day parading through London, on water and through streets, the 1614 Lord Mayor's show ended with—in the printed text, if not in actuality—the bright stars acting "as so many bright flaming Torches to grace our worthy Magistrate home" (80). The final performance is a "speech delivered to the Lord Maior at parting," the recitation of which is given by an unnamed actor, and indicates the challenges before the Mayor and the promise that he holds in meeting the challenge:

> To doubt of your ensuing care,
> Or to advise yee, to prepare
> For envies storm, or soothing smiles,
> That wait upon such place some whiles:
> Longs not to me. For in your eie
> Such true Charracters I espie
> Of vertue, zeale, and upright heed,
> That you will prove the man indeed,
> Meet such a charge to undergoe:
> Whereto heavens hand hath raised you so. (81–2).

As a newly planted Lord Mayor, Haynes can expect the fawning "soothing smiles" and "envie" that attend those who are in positions of power. However, the speaker underscores that the Lord Mayor's virtuous enthusiasm will "prove" him a fit man to "undergoe" the "charge" that he must face.[42] Although the "charge," is not explicitly here defined, I would suggest that the challenge that Haynes must attend to is the resuscitation of the beleaguered cloth industry to its former state. The 1614 pageant as a whole is a triumph of "Olde Draperie," and the glorious past of the industry cannot be resurrected without the "true character" of the Lord Mayor who is able to withstand "envies storm" and defend the cloth industry from—as the walls of the city defend its citizens from—"dangerous annoyances" (75). And finally, in an astonishing reversal of the sentiment previously expressed by Fitz-Alwine, the speech confirms that the Lord Mayor has been raised to his position not by the King,

---

42 "Traditionally, the shows temper praise with moral didacticism, reminding the new mayor of the virtues necessary for good government" (Lobanov-Rostovsky, 882). Also, the pageants often offered a charge to the new Lord Mayor: "Mayor's Triumphs are particularly characterized by such dramatic revelations of the *triumphator's* future duties" (Kipling, 53).

but by "heavens hand" itself. James has been extirpated not only from the text itself, but also from the solution to the cloth industry's woes.

The next year, when the cloth industry had fully felt the disastrous effects of the Cockayne project, John Jolles, draper and stapler, was elected as Lord Mayor and again Munday was hired to write the inauguration pageant in his honor.[43] Munday spends far less time in this pageant linking the new Lord Mayor to historical predecessors and does not concentrate so heavy-handedly on the glorious traditions of the cloth industry. The author in fact self-consciously eschews tradition in favor of fashion when he asserts that the new pageant will not merely repeat the devises of the previous year; rather, he will "jumpe with the time, which evermore effecteth novelty, in a new forme of this second yeeres triumph" (87). While *Metropolis Coronata* does see the return of the reincarnated mayor/draper Fitz-Alwine, most of the spectacle presents the stories of two legends: Jason and the Golden Fleece and Robin Hood and his merry men.[44] While these myths may seem to dehistoricize the events of the day by presenting a timeless past which has little to do with the Drapers' Company or John Jolles' place in it, as with *Himatia-Poleos*, Munday brings the world of legends into the present. In so doing, these myths—especially the legend of Jason—become didactic warnings against the continued depression in the cloth industry as well as a celebration of what cloth once had been and perhaps again could be.

The inclusion of the myth of Jason and the Golden Fleece was not necessarily an original gesture on the part of Munday. The story had been popular in other literary texts and remained prevalent in early modern pageantry. In addition to playing a central role in Munday's 1615 pageant, Jason was a prominent figure in Thomas Middleton's 1621 Lord Mayor's show, *The Sun in Aries* (Bergeron, "Anthony Munday," 358) and in Thomas Heywood's 1639 show, *Londini Stats Pacatus*, also for the Drapers. Greek and Roman legends, particularly those that involved heroic feats, provided fertile ground for the pageant writers who often used the legendary heroes as means to celebrate the Lord Mayors. Bergeron is correct in asserting that "[t]he use of mythology in these civic entertainments is also consonant with an age which was busily rediscovering the classical writers and myths" (Bergeron, "Anthony Munday," 346). However, as with Munday's use of England's historical

---

43 Although the Staplers, who primarily bought wool from manufacturers and sold it to Drapers or Merchant Adventurers, were once a part of the Drapers Company, they had formed their own guild. Bradbrook links the pageant to the current economic context: *Metropolis-Coronata* celebrates "the election of another member of the Drapers Company as Lord Mayor, doubtless to meet the growing trade crisis. This was largely a water show (it was the exports that had been hit)" (104). Celeste Turner Wright notes that the show cost the Drapers upwards of £688 plus £66 8 s. 4 d. for the painting of Jolles house (161). Given the enormous expense in putting on the pageants, one has to wonder if the Drapers saw the election of two Mayors in a row from their company as much a curse as a blessing.

44 Munday links Robin Hood to the pageant by claiming erroneously that he was the "Sonne in Law (by Marriage) to old *Fitz-Alwine*" (91). Bergeron points out that Munday had portrayed Robin Hood in two of his earlier plays (*Pageants and Entertainments*, 98). While I do not discuss here the implications of including the legend of Robin Hood, also known as Robert, Earl of Huntington, the commonplace understanding that he stole from the rich to give to the poor seems to have relevance to the charge that the Mayor rescue "ancient drapery."

past, the inclusion of classical myth works to illuminate contemporaneous social and political circumstances. As Tracey Hill argues,

> Greek mythology is thus valuable only to the extent to which it is possible to transfer it as a metaphor to illuminate its London setting, in the process of which, naturally, it loses its original meaning ... For Munday, all forms of classical and other ancient mythology are subordinated to the extraordinary and primordial history of the City and its dignatories. (Tracey Hill, 158).[45]

Thus, Jason's quest to seek out the Golden Fleece from Colchos must be mapped onto the matters of the day: the necessity of the Lord Mayor to recover England's own "ancient draperie."

On the Thames headed towards Westminster, the first tableau of the pageant finds Jason, the Argonauts, Medea, and a host of servants on the Argo, returning triumphant from Colchos after attaining the Golden Fleece.[46] In a nearby "Sea Chariot," Fitz-Alwine approaches the Lord Mayor's barge and greets him, as he did Haynes in *Himatia-Poleos*, as a fellow Draper/Stapler/Lord Mayor and reminisces about the glory of the ancient cloth industry:

> In those grave times when woollen Cloth
> Serv'd best for King and Subject both.
> The Draper and the Stapler then
> I tell yee were right worthy men,
> And did more needy soules maintain,
> Then I feare will be seene again.
> But times must have their revolution,
> And each their several execution. (89)

In a comparison that highlights how low the cloth industry has fallen (wool *was* the best cloth for both kings and men, but no longer holds that same position), Munday here underscores the fault of the profession of Draper and Stapler—those involved in the manufacture and sale of cloth. In the ancient days of England's industry, cloth makers were philanthropists through their very profession. By simply practicing honest business, they "maintained" the "soules" of the "needy" because the thriving industry included so many of the working poor. The "feare" that these worthy men will never again exist is directed at the drapers, whose profession has been compromised by the various abuses practiced among them.[47] But this "feare" is also directed at the King whose policies once encouraged the "best" wool. Fitz-Alwine's expression is despairing in tone. Those glorious days will never be "seen again." The following lines, though, point to cautious optimism: Each era must come to an end,

---

45 Tracey Hill further asserts that "[t]he use of Roman terminology such as 'senator' also alludes to a republican rather than monarchal form of government, in the context of which London could be represented as self-ruling and largely independent of Royal subjection" (155).

46 According to Bergeron, this water show was Munday's "most elaborate to date" (*English Civic Pageantry*, 151).

47 See my Chapter 5 for a discussion of these abuses.

revolving into the next. And solutions must be carried out, or "executed," according to the circumstances and challenges of the times. The lines also seem to suggest that the fame of the cloth industry might be recovered if there can be a "revolution," or turning around, of the state of the industry. One might even press the point so far to see that the industry as it is known *today* must be "executed"—or killed under order of law—in order to recover the past and best serve the industry.

Fitz-Alwine explains to the Lord Mayor that the tableau of Jason is meant to bring to mind the history of the cloth industry: the Golden Fleece is "the crest / Of ancient Drapery" (89). But it is from the retelling of the legend that Jolles is supposed to take his lessons:

> The story of the Golden Fleece,
> Fetched by the *Argonautes* of Greece
> From *Cholchos* in resemblance here,
> Where *Jason* and those Greeks appeare,
> Which in that travaile did partake
> Both for his love and honours sake.
> *Medeas* powerfull charmes prevailde,
> And all those dreadfull Monsters quailed,[48]
> That kept the Fleece in their protection,
> Which then was won by her direction.
> By way of Morall application,
> Your Honour may make some relation
> Unto your selfe out of this storie,
> You are our *Jason*, London's glorie,
> Now going to fetch that fleece of Fame,
> That ever must renowne your name. (89)

The story of the Golden Fleece becomes an allegorical impetus, if not an overt didactic imperative, for Jolles who is named early in the pageant as "our *London's Jason*" to "make some relation" of himself to the legend of the Golden Fleece (88).[49] Munday, however, leaves it up to the Lord Mayor, the audience members, and the reader to decode the "moral application." Although one can imagine multiple interpretations of the allegorical significance for Jolles, in the context of the crisis in the cloth industry, one particular reading stands apart: Colchos, which as an island "resembles" England, is the home of the Golden Fleece, the wool that is the "rich cloathing of England."[50] The Golden Fleece, then, resides at home rather than far away. The dreadful monsters that have "kept" the Fleece and whom the new Lord Mayor needs to "quail" to capture it are those who have taken the cloth industry hostage. The ever-watchful dragon, which Jason must lull to sleep in order to seize the fleece, may be seen as the King, whose policies had overtaken the cloth industry

---

48 "To decline from a natural or flourishing condition" (*OED* "quail" 1).

49 Bergeron asserts that by calling Jolles "London's Jason," he is "linked with the mythical Jason and may draw strength from that association" (*English Civic Pageantry*, 152). What "strength" he is supposed to draw remains unexplored.

50 See my Chapter 1 for a discussion of how England and its sheep are represented as Colchos and the Golden Fleece.

in order to increase his own hoard.[51] In the Greek legend, in order to gain access to the monster, Jason first had to sow the teeth of a slain dragon. In so doing, he would reap a field of armed men, whom Jason would in turn have to fight. To extend the allegory, we may see this army, the dragon's brood, as Cockayne, Coke, and the members of the Privy Council who approved unwise laws.

The allegory fits nicely enough until we attempt to explain who Jolles' Medea is. Whose "powerful charmes" must "direct" the Lord Mayor to rescue the cloth industry? Although the pageant does not conclusively answer this query, the tableau immediately following Fitz-Alwine's speech might be some indication of the female entity that will assist Jolles in his undertaking. On the river is "a faire and beautifull Shippe ... called the *Joell*, appearing to bee lately returned, from trafficking Wool and Cloth with other remote Countryes." Accompanying the ship is "*Neptune*, who hath been auspicious to all her adventures, and *Thamesis*, by bringing her alwaies safely within her owne bounds" (90–91). If London's Jason requires a Medea to assist him in claiming the famous fleece/wool, then this can be achieved through the "powerful charmes" of the ship, gendered female here, which is represented as "trafficking" abroad in woolen goods. Following the wool cargo ship is another smaller vessel carrying a "goodly Ramme or Golden Fleece," attended on either side by two virgins "serious imployed in Carding and Spinning Wooll for cloth, the very best commoditie that ever this Kingdome yielded" (91).[52] The significance of the capture of the Golden Fleece must be seen in relation to the uses of the ram: the animal is valuable not only for its symbolic meaning, but perhaps even more so for the quality of the "commoditie" that it produces. At a time when overseas trade "with other remote Countryes" had all but been halted by James's policies, the directive to the Lord Mayor seems clear: open up the cloth trade again, and the Fleece can be yours.[53]

Munday's two pageants for the Drapers' Company dramatize the salvific act of reconstructing the cloth trade by encouraging the City governor to enact the necessary changes in trade relations with foreign countries. Like the conclusion of *Michaelmas Term*, the Lord Mayor's shows create a fantasy whereby the cloth industry may be restored and cloth may again "triumph" in England as it had before.

---

51 Manley points to the complex dynamic between the intense nostalgia of the pageants' mythological aspects and their celebration of London's mercantile community. See "Sites and Rites," p. 48. In putting the matter into Jolles's hands, the pageant suggests a new understanding of who is most apt to advance the economy.

52 Munday's point that the virgins are working on "the very best commoditie that ever this Kingdome yielded" is only a textual one, not a spoken line. This demonstrates how the printed text allowed room for the sort of moralizing commentary that Munday could only hope would come across in the visual spectacle of the pageant.

53 As Lobanov-Rostovsky underscores, "considering that a primary duty of the Lord Mayor was the regulation of markets, civic office allowed these wealthy traders to manipulate the trade in commodities and impose the terms upon which they dealt with craftsmen and competitors." And although the pageants point to an antagonistic relationship between the Mayor and the King, this by no means suggests that the Lord Mayor was without riches and status: "As a celebration of the wealth and power of the guild oligarchs, the pageants served to legitimize the political structure from which this wealth was derived" (890).

While the pageants of 1614 and 1615 are not particularly notable for their artistic achievements, and are not counted among Munday's best, they in many ways are Munday's most personal pageants, if such a term may be attached to such a public spectacle. Imbued with historical gravity and exposing the troubles facing the Drapers, Munday's works reveal a deep connection to the guild company and his hope for their future, as well as that of all guilds affected by the disintegrating cloth trade. Cautiously optimistic in their tone, the pageants suggest a faith in the power of civic government to enact change.

The material reality of the ensuing months, however, was not to be so triumphant. The King insisted on carrying out his policies for more than a year, despite the precipitous decline in cloth sales. In addition to a serious drop in export revenue, the Cockayne project brought on a widespread depression in the western cloth producing counties once famous for their broadcloth manufactures. In December of 1616, the New Merchant Adventurers handed back the bruised and battered cloth trade to the old Merchant Adventurers. While the pageants themselves spectacularly play out the optimism on the London streets, the printed texts, lasting far beyond October 1615, become an ironic reminder of both the promise and failure of civic government to stand up to hostile government policies.

Among the many genres in which concerns for England's cloth industry were aired, the Lord Mayors' pageants were certainly the most public. Thousands of spectators, illiterate and literate alike would have been able to see the drama of the wool trade played out on London's streets. Yet more individuals, and perhaps some of the same spectators, would have been able to purchase the printed versions of the scripts to read about the plight of and the remedy for the industry. The print trade thus expanded the audience beyond London's walls, thus reasserting the expansive nature of the cloth trade and its attendant problems. The scripts for the Mayors' pageants were one among many modes that worked to construct the cloth industry as both the history and future of England's success as a nation in print. As I have been arguing throughout *The Culture of Cloth*, the pervasive sense that the industry was largely responsible for defining English national identity was articulated through several decades of textual output by authors and for audiences across the social spectrum. If this object—wool cloth—held the interest of so many of England's subjects, this was primarily achieved through the circulation of a stunning array of printed texts: didactic verse, prose romance, pastoral poetry, popular ballads, royal proclamations, propaganda, topical satire, city drama, *and* civic pageants. Cloth and print, warp and weft, were the materials comprising the fabric of English nationalism.

Bibliography

Manuscript Sources

British Library, Landsdowne MS 81.30.

Printed Primary Sources

Adams, Thomas. *The White Devil.* 1612. *In God's Name: Examples of Preaching in England from the Act of Supremacy to the Act of Uniformity, 1534–1662.* Ed. John Chandos. Indianapolis: The Bobbs-Merrill Company, 1971. 162–88.

"An Act Agaynst Pullyng Doun of Tounes." 1489. 4 Henry VII c. 19. *Tudor Economic Documents.* Vol. 1. Eds. R.H. Tawney and Eileen Power. 4–6.

"An Act for the Maintenance of Husbandry and Tillage." 1597–1598. 39 Eliz. c. 2. *Statutes of the Realm*, Vol. IV, Part II. 893–6.

"An Act for the Punishinge and Correctinge of Deceipte and Fraudes Committed by Sorters Kembers and Spinners of Wooll and Weavers of Woollen Yarne." 1609–1610. *Statutes of the Realme.* London: Dawsons of Pall Mall, 1810–1828, 1963.

"The Aftermath of Ket's Rising, 1550–53." *Tudor Economic Documents.* Vol. 1. Eds. R.H. Tawney and Eileen Power. 47–53.

Barnfield, Richard. "The Shepherd's Content." 1594. *Richard Barnfield: The Complete Poems.* Ed. George Klawitter. Selinsgrove, PA: Susquehanna University Press, 1990. 98–106.

Bastard, Thomas. *Chrestoleros.* London, 1598.

Becon, Thomas. *Workes.* Vol. 2. London, 1564.

Beverly, Robert. *The History and Present State of Virginia.* 1705. Ed. Louis B. Wright. Chapel Hill: University of North Carolina Press, 1947

Boorde, Andrew. *The Fyrst Boke of the Introduction of Knowledge.* London, 1562(?).

Brathwait, Richard. *The English Gentleman and Gentlewoman.* London, 1641.

———. *The Shepherds Tales.* London, 1626.

Cannon, Nathanaell. *The Cryer.* London, 1613.

Carleill, Christopher. *A Brief and Sommerie Discourse Upon the Entended Voyage to the Hethermoste Partes of America.* 1583. *New American World: A Documentary History of North America to 1612.* Vol. 3. Ed. David B. Quinn. New York: Arno Press, 1979. 27–34.

Cheke, John. *The Hurt of Sedition.* 1549. Menston, UK: Scolar Press, 1971.

Churchyard, Thomas. "A Matter Touching the Journey of Sir Humfrey Gilbarte Knight." 1578. *The Voyages and Colonising Enterprises of Sir Humphrey Gilbert.* Ed. David B. Quinn. Vol. 1. London: The Hakluyt Society, 1940.

"Complaint of the Yeomen Weavers against the Immigrant Weavers." *The London Weavers' Company.* Vol. 1, Appendix 22. Ed. Frances Consitt. Oxford: Clarendon Press, 1933. 312–16.

Cooke, J. *Greene's Tu Quoque or, The City Gallant.* 1611. Ed. Alan J. Berman. New York and London: Garland Publishing, 1984.

Coryate, Thomas. *Coryat's Crudities.* 1611. Vol. 1. Glasgow: James Mac Lehose & Sons, 1905.

Crowley, Robert. *The Way to Wealth.* 1550. *The Select Works of Robert Crowley.* 1872. Ed. J.M. Cowper. Millwood, New York: Kraus Reprint, 1987.

"The Decaye of England Only By the Great Multitude of Shepe." 1550–53. *Tudor Economic Documents.* Vol. 3. Eds. R.H. Tawney and Eileen Power. London: Longmans, Green, and Co., 1924. 51–7.

Dekker, Thomas. *The Gull's Horn-Book.* 1609. Ed. R.B. McKerrow. London: De La More Press, 1905.

———. *The Magnificent Entertainment.* 1603. *The Dramatic Works of Thomas Dekker.* Vol. 2. Ed. Fredson Bowers. Cambridge: Cambridge University Press, 1958. 229–309.

———. *The Seven Deadly Sins of London.* 1606. *The Non-Dramatic Works of Thomas Dekker.* Ed. Alexander Grosart. London: The Huth Library, 1885. 1–81.

———. *Troia-Nova Triumphans.* 1612. *The Dramatic Works of Thomas Dekker.* Vol. 3. Ed. Fredson Bowers. Cambridge: Cambridge University Press, 1958. 225–47.

Dekker, Thomas, and John Webster. *Westward Ho.* 1607. *The Dramatic Works of Thomas Dekker.* Vol. 2. Ed. Fredson Bowers. Cambridge: Cambridge University Press, 1955. 311–403.

Deloney, Thomas. *Jack of Newbury.* 1597. *The Novels of Thomas Deloney.* Ed. Meritt Lawlis. Bloomington: Indiana University Press, 1961. 1–87.

Dickenson, John. *The Shepheardes Complaint.* London, ca. 1594.

Drayton, Michael. *Poemes Lyricke and Pastorall.* London, 1606.

Dreyden, John. *King Arthur, or the British Worthy.* 1691. *Dreyden: The Dramatic Works.* Ed. Montague Summers. New York: Gordian Press, 1968. 231–89.

Earle, John. *Microcosmography.* 1633. Ed. Alfred S. West. Cambridge: Cambridge University Press, 1920.

Elizabeth I. "The Letters Patents Graunted by Her Majestie to Sir Humfrey Gilbert Knight, for the Inhabiting and Planting of our People in America." 1578. Richard Hakluyt. *The Principal Navigations, Voyages, Traffiques and Discoveries of the English Nation.* Vol. 8. New York: AMS Press Inc., 1965. 17–23.

Fabian, Robert. "Of Three Savages." 1497. Richard Hakluyt. *The Principal Navigations, Voyages, Traffiques and Discoveries of the English Nation.* Vol. 7. New York: AMS Press Inc., 1965. 155.

Frederick, Lewis, Duke of Wirtemberg. "A True and Faithful Narrative of the Bathing Excursion." 1602. *England as Seen by Foreigners in the Days of Elizabeth and James the First.* 1865. Ed. and Trans. William Brenchley Rye. London: John Russell Smith, 1967. 3–53.

Fuller, Thomas. *The Worthies of England.* 1662. Ed. John Freeman. London: Allen and Unwin, 1952.

Gascoigne, George. *The Steele Glass.* 1576. *The Complete Works of George Gascoigne.* Vol. 2. Ed. John Cunliffe. Cambridge: Cambridge University Press, 1910. 133–74.

Gilbert, Humphrey. "A Discourse of a Discoverie for a New Passage to Cataia." 1576. *New American World: A Documentary History of North America to 1612*. Vol. 3. Ed. David Quinn. New York: Arno Press, 1979. 5–23.

Gosson, Stephen. *Pleasant Quippes for Upstart Newfangled Gentlewomen*. 1595. London, 1841.

Greene, Robert. *Defence of Conny-Catching*. London, 1592.

———. *Menaphon*. 1589. Ed. Brenda Cantar. Ottowa: Dovehouse, 1996.

———. *A Quip for an Upstart Courtier: Or A Quaint Dispute Between Velvet Breeches and Cloth Breeches*. Vol. 11. *Life and Complete Works in Prose and Verse of Robert Greene*. Ed. Alexander Grosart. New York: Russell and Russell, 1964. 209–94.

———. *The Repentance of Robert Greene*. 1592. New York: Barnes and Noble, 1966.

Hakluyt, Richard the Elder. "Inducements to the Lykinge of the Voyadge intended to that Parte of America which Lyeth Betwene 34. and 36. degrees." 1584(?). *New American World: A Documentary History of North America to 1612*. Vol. 3. Ed. David Quinn. New York: Arno Press, 1979. 62–4.

———. "Notes Prepared by Richard Hakluyt the Elder for Sir Humphrey Gilbert." 1578. *New American World: A Documentary History of North America to 1612*. Vol. 3. Ed. David B. Quinn. New York: Arno Press, 1979. 23–6.

Hakluyt, Richard the Younger. *Discourse of Western Planting*. 1584. *New American World: A Documentary History of North America to 1612*. Vol. 3. Ed. David B. Quinn. New York: Arno Press, 1979. 70–123.

———. *Divers Voyages Touching the Discovery of America and the Islands Adjacent*. 1582. Ed. John Winters Jones. New York: Burt Franklin, 1963.

Harriot, Thomas. "A Brief and True Report of the New Found Land of Virginia." 1588. *New American World: A Documentary History of North America to 1612*. Vol. 3. Ed. David B. Quinn. New York: Arno Press, 1979. 138–55.

Hayes, Edward, and Christopher Carleill. "A Discourse Concerning a Voyage Intended for the Planting of Chrystyan Religion and People in the North West Regions of America in Places Most Apt for the Constitution of Our Boddies, and the Spedy Advauncement of a State." 1591(?). *New American World: A Documentary History of North America to 1612*. Vol. 3. Ed. David Quinn. New York: Arno Press, 1979. 156–72.

Hayes, Edward. "A Report of the Voyage ... by Sir Humphrey Gilbert." 1583. *The Principal Navigations, Voyages, Traffiques and Discoveres of the English Nation*. Ed. Jack Beeching. London: Penguin Books, 1972. 231–42.

Hentzner, Paul. "Travels in England." 1598. *England as Seen by Foreigners in the Days of Elizabeth and James the First*. Ed. and Trans. William Brenchley Rye. London: John Russell Smith, 1865.

Heresbach, Conrad. *Four Books of Husbandry*. Trans. Barnaby Googe. London, 1577.

Heywood, Thomas. *Londini Status Pacatus: Or, London's Peaceable Estate*. London, 1639.

———. *Rape of Lucrece*. 1608. Urbana: University of Illinois Press, 1950.

Hic Mulier; Or, the Man-Woman. 1620. *Half Humankind: Contexts and Texts of the Controversy about Women in England, 1540–1640.* Eds. Katherine Usher Henderson and Barbara F. McManus. Urbana: University of Illinois Press, 1985. 265–76.

Holinshed, Raphael. *Chronicles of England, Scotland, and Ireland.* 1578. Vol. 3. Ed. Henry Ellis. London, 1808. AMS Press, 1965.

"Instructions to the Enclosure Commissioners Appointed June 1548." *Tudor Economic Documents.* Vol. 1. Eds. R.H. Tawney and Eileen Power. New York: Barnes & Noble, 1961. 39–44.

Jackson, William. *The Celestiall Husbandrie: Or, The Tillage of the Soule.* London, 1616.

Johnson, Robert. *Nova Brittania: Offering Most Excellent Fruites by Planting in Virginia.* 1609. *New American World: A Documentary History of North America to 1612.* Vol. 5. Ed. David Quinn. New York: Arno Press, 1979. 234–48.

Jonson, Ben. *Every Man Out of His Humor.* 1599. *The Complete Plays of Ben Jonson.* Vol. 1. Ed. G.A. Wilkes. Oxford: Clarendon Press, 1981. 275–411.

———. "On English Monsieur." 1616. *Ben Jonson: A Critical Edition of the Major Works.* Ed. Ian Donaldson, Oxford: Oxford University Press, 1985. 251–2.

"Kett's Demands Being in Rebellion." *Tudor Rebellions.* Anthony Fletcher. London: Longmans, 1968. 142–4.

Lambarde, William. *A Perambulation of Kent.* 1576. London, 1826.

Lane, Ralph. "Ralph Lane to Richard Hakluyt the Elder and Master H— of the Middle Temple." 1585. *New American World: A Documentary History of North America to 1612.* Vol. 3. Ed. David B. Quinn. New York: Arno Press, 1979. 293.

Latimer, Hugh. *The First Sermon of Maister Hugh Latimer.* 1549. Ed. Edward Arber. *Seven Sermons before Edward VI.* London, 1869. 17–43

Lodge, Thomas. *Phillis.* London, 1593.

Lyly, John. *Midas.* London, 1592.

Marston, John. *Certaine Satyres.* 1598. *The Poems of John Marston.* Ed. Arnold Davenport. Liverpool: Liverpool University Press, 1961. 65–92.

Mascall, Leonard. *The First Booke of Cattell.* London, 1587.

May, John. *A Declaration of the Estate of Clothing Now Used Within This Realme of England.* London, 1613.

Middleton, Thomas. *Michaelmas Term.* 1605–1606. Ed. Gail Kern Paster. Manchester: Manchester University Press, 2000.

Middleton, Thomas and William Rowley. *The World Tossed at Tennis.* 1620. *The Works of Thomas Middleton.* Vol. 5. Ed. Alexander Dyce. London: Edward Lumley, 1840. 155–201.

More, Thomas. *Utopia.* 1516. London: Everyman, 1994.

Munday, Anthony. *Himatiapoleos. The Triumphs of Olde Draperie, or the Rich Cloathing of England.* 1614. *Pageants and Entertainments of Anthony Munday.* Ed. David M. Bergeron. New York: Garland, 1985. 71–84.

———. *Metropolis Coronata. The Triumphs of Ancient Draperie: or Rich Cloathing of England.* 1615. *Pageants and Entertainments of Anthony Munday.* Ed. David M. Bergeron. New York: Garland, 1985. 86–99.

Nashe, Thomas. *Have With You to Saffron-Walden.* 1596. *The Works of Thomas Nashe.* Vol. 3. Ed. Ronald McKerrow. London: A.H. Bullen, 1840. 1–139.

Neville, Alexander. *Norfolkes Furies*. Norfolk, 1575.

"Now A Days." 1520 (?). *Ballads from Manuscripts*. Vol. 1. Ed. Frederick J. Furnivall. Hertford: Stephen Austin and Sons, 1868. 1–107.

"Ordinance of the Weaver's Company; 1589 and 1594." The London Weavers' Company. Vol. 1, Appendix 21. Ed. Frances Consitt. Oxford: Clarendon Press, 1933. 311–12.

Peckham, George. "A True Report of the Late Discoveries and Possessions, Taken in the Right of the Crown of Englande, of the Newfound Landes: by that Valiant and Worthy Gentleman, Sir Humphrey Gilbert Knight." 1583. *New American World: A Documentary History of North America to 1612*. Vol. 3. Ed. David B. Quinn. New York: Arno Press, 1979. 34–60.

"The Phantasick Age." 1634. *Satirical Songs and Poems on Costume: From the 13th to the 19th Century*. Ed. Frederick W. Fairholt. London: The Percy Society, 1849. 155–60.

"Presentments Before the Commission of 1548." *Tudor Economic Documents*. Vol. 1. Eds. R.H. Tawney and Eileen Power. 44–6.

Price, Daniel. *The Marchant, A Sermon Preached at Paul's Cross*. Oxford, 1608.

"A Proclamation against the Exportation of Cloathes, Undyed and Undressed Contrary to Law." 23 July 1614. *Stuart Royal Proclamations*. Vol. 1. Eds. James F. Larkin and Paul L. Hughes. Oxford: Clarendon Press, 1973. 312–14.

"A Proclamation Enforcing Statutes against Enclosure." 11 April 1549. *Tudor Royal Proclamations*. Vol. 1. Eds. Paul L. Hughes and James F. Larkin. New York: Yale University Press, 1964. 451–3.

"A Proclamation Enforcing Statutes for Winding of Wool." 29 May 1596. *Tudor Royal Proclamations*. Vol. 3. Eds. James F. Larkin and Paul L. Hughes. New Haven: Yale University Press, 1969. 162–4.

"A Proclamation Enforcing Statutes for Wool Cloth Manufacture." 20 January 1592. *Tudor Royal Proclamations*. Vol. 3. Eds. James F. Larkin and Paul L. Hughes. New Haven: Yale University Press, 1969. 102–4.

"A Proclamation Enforcing Statutes on Tillage and Enclosures." 1 March 1569. *Tudor Royal Proclamations*. Vol. 2. Eds. Paul L Hughes and James F. Larkin. New Haven: Yale University Press, 1969. 310–11.

"A Proclamation for Reformation of Great Abuses in Measure, Published by the King's Commandment." 1 June 1603. *Stuart Royal Proclamations*. Vol. 1. Eds. James F. Larkin and Paul L. Hughes. Oxford: Clarendon Press, 1973. 23–7.

"A Proclamation for the Ordering of the Use of the Hot Presse." 22 March 1620. *Stuart Royal Proclamations*. Vol. 1. Eds. James F. Larkin and Paul L. Hughes. Oxford: Clarendon Press, 1973. 470–72.

"A Proclamation for the True Winding or Folding of Wools." 18 June 1604. *Stuart Royal Proclamations*. Vol. 1. Eds. James F. Larkin and Paul L. Hughes. Oxford: Clarendon Press, 1973. 82–4.

"A Proclamation for the True Working and Dying of Cloth." 7 December 1613. *Stuart Royal Proclamations*. Vol. 1. Eds. James F. Larkin and Paul L. Hughes. Oxford: Clarendon Press, 1973. 300–302.

"A Proclamation Mitigating Statutes for Wool Cloth Manufacture. 13 March 1590. *Tudor Royal Proclamations*. Vol. 3. Eds. Paul L Hughes and James F. Larkin. New Haven: Yale University Press, 1969. 52–4.

"A Proclamation Pardoning Enclosure Rioters; Ordering Martial Law against Future Rioters." 16 July 1549. *Tudor Royal Proclamations.* Vol. 1. Eds. Paul L. Hughes and James F. Larkin. New York: Yale University Press, 1964. 475–6.

"A Proclamation Prohibiting the Exportation of Sheepe, Woolls, Wool-fells, and Fullers Earth." 26 September 1614. *Stuart Royal Proclamations.* Vol. 1. Eds. James F. Larkin and Paul L. Hughes. Oxford: Clarendon Press, 1973. 317–19.

"A Proclamation Prohibiting the Merchant Adventurers Charter from Henceforth to be Put in Practice or Execution, Either within the Kingdome, or Beyond the Seas." 2 December 1614. *Stuart Royal Proclamations.* Vol. 1. Eds. James F. Larkin and Paul L. Hughes. Oxford: Clarendon Press, 1973. 327–9.

Prynne, William. *Histriomastix.* 1632. New York: Garland Publishing, 1974.

"Report of the Lord Mayor on the Weavers' Pamphlet." *The London Weavers' Company.* Vol. 1, Appendix 22. Ed. Frances Consitt. Oxford: Clarendon Press. 317–18.

Rich, Barnabie. *My Ladies Looking Glasse.* London, 1616.

Sabie, Francis. *Pan's Pipe.* London, 1595.

Sandys, George. *A Relation of a Journey.* London, 1637.

———. *Sandys Travels.* London, 1670.

Scott, William. *An Essay on Drapery.* 1635. Cambridge, MA: Harvard University Press, 1953.

Segar, William. *Honor Military and Civil.* 1602. *The Booke of Honor and Armes (1590) and Honor Military and Civil (1602).* Delmar, NY: Scholars' Facsimiles and Reprints, Inc., 1975.

Shakespeare, William. *2 Henry IV. The Riverside Shakespeare.* 2nd ed. Ed. G. Blakemore Evans. Boston: Houghton Mifflin, 1997. 928–73.

———. *2 Henry VI. The Riverside Shakespeare.* 2nd ed. Ed. G. Blakemore Evans. Boston: Houghton Mifflin Company, 1997. 668–709.

———. *The Merchant of Venice. The Riverside Shakespeare.* 2nd ed. Ed. G. Blakemore Evans. Boston: Houghton Mifflin Company, 1997. 288–317.

———. *Much Ado About Nothing. The Riverside Shakespeare.* 2nd ed. Ed. G. Blakemore Evans. Boston: Houghton Mifflin, 1997. 361–98.

Sidney, Philip. *The Countess of Pembroke's Arcadia.* 1580. Ed. Katherine Duncan Jones. Oxford: Oxford University Press, 1985.

———. *The Countess of Pembroke's Arcadia (The New Arcadia).* 1590. Ed. Victor Skretkowicz. Oxford: Clarendon Press, 1987.

———. *The Defence of Poesy.* ca. 1582. *Sir Philip Sidney: The Major Works.* Ed. Katherine Duncan-Jones. Oxford: Oxford University Press, 2002. 212–50.

———. *A Dialogue Between Two Shepherds, Uttered in a Pastoral Show at Wilton.* 1577(?). *Sir Philip Sidney: A Critical Edition of the Major Works.* Ed. Katherine Duncan-Jones. Oxford: Oxford University Press, 1989. 1–2.

———. "Sir Philip Sidney to Sir Edward Stafford." 1584. *New American World: A Documentary History of North America to 1612.* Vol. 3. Ed. David B. Quinn. New York: Arno Press, 1979. 264.

Smith, Thomas. *A Discourse of the Commonweal of this Realm of England.* 1581. Ed. Mary Dewar. Charlottesville: University of Virginia Press, 1969.

Sotherton, Nicholas. "The Commoyson in Norfolk." 1549. *Tudor Rebellions.* Anthony Fletcher. London: Longmans, 1968. 145–6.

Spenser, Edmund. *Amoretti and Epithalamion. Edmund Spenser's Poetry.* Eds. Hugh Maclean and Anne Lake Prescott. New York: W.W. Norton & Company, 1993. 587–637.

———. *The Shepheardes Calendar. Edmund Spenser's Poetry.* Eds. Hugh Maclean and Anne Lake Prescott. New York: W.W. Norton, 1993. 500–542.

Stow, John. *A Survey of the Cities of London and Westminster.* 1603. Ed. John Strype. London, 1720.

———. *A Survey of London.* 1603. Ed. Charles Lethbridge Kingsford. Oxford: Clarendon Press, 1908.

Strype, John, ed. *A Survey of the Cities of London and Westminster.* 1603. London, 1720.

Stubbes, Philip. *The Anatomie of Abuses.* 1583. Ed. Margaret Jane Kidnie. Tempe, AZ: Arizona Center for Medieval and Renaissance Studies, 2002.

———. *The Second Part of the Anatomie of Abuses.* 1583. New York: Garland Publishing, 1973.

Thynne, Francis. *The Debate Between Pride and Lowliness.* 1577. Ed. J. Payne Collier. London: Shakespeare Society, 1841.

Townshend, Hayward. "Hayward Townshend's Journals." Eds. A.F. Pollard and Marjorie Blatcher. *Bulletin of the Institute of Historical Research* 12 (1934): 1–31.

Trigge, Francis. *The Humble Petition of Two Sisters; The Church and Commonwealth.* London, 1604.

Tusser, Thomas. *Five Hundred Points of Good Husbandry.* 1573. London, 1812.

Vergil, Polydore. *The Anglica Historia.* 1537. Trans. and Ed. Denys Hay. London: Offices of the Royal Historical Society, 1950.

"Vox Populi Vox Dei, A Complaynt of the Commons against Taxes." ca. 1547. Reprinted by G. Woodfall London, 1821.

Webster, John. *The Duchess of Malfi.* 1614. *Three Plays.* Ed. D.C. Gunby. London: Penguin, 1972. 167–292.

Secondary Sources

Ackroyd, Peter. *The Life of Thomas More.* New York: Doubleday, 1998.

Agnew, Jean-Christophe. *Worlds Apart: The Market and the Theater in Anglo-American Thought, 1550–1750.* Cambridge: Cambridge University Press, 1986.

Allen, Robert C. *Enclosure and the Yeoman.* Oxford: Clarendon Press. 1992.

Allison, J.K. "Flock Management in the Sixteenth and Seventeenth Centuries." *Economic History Review* 2nd ser. 11.1 (1958): 98–112.

Alpers, Paul. *What is Pastoral?* Chicago: University of Chicago Press, 1996.

Anderson, Benedict. *Imagined Communities: Reflections on the Origin and Spread of Nationalism.* New York: Verso, 1983.

Andrews, Kenneth R. *Trade, Plunder, and Settlement: Maritime Enterprise and the Genesis of the British Empire, 1480–1630.* Cambridge: Cambridge University Press, 1984.

Armitage, David. "The New World and British Historical Thought: From Richard Hakluyt to William Robertson." *America in European Consciousness, 1493–1750.*

Ed. Karen Ordahl Kupperman. Chapel Hill, NC: University of North Carolina Press, 1995. 52–75.

Atkins, J.W.H. "Elizabethan Prose Fiction." *Cambridge History of English Literature*. Vol. 3. Eds. A.W. Ward and A.R. Waller. Cambridge: Cambridge University Press, 1909. 339–73.

Bailey, Amanda. "'Monstrous Manner': Style and the Early Modern Theater." *Criticism* 43.3 (2001): 249–84.

———. *Flaunting: Style and the Subversive Male Body in Renaissance England*. Toronto: University of Toronto Press, 2007.

Baker, David J. *Between Nations: Shakespeare, Spenser, Marvell, and the Question of Britain*. Stanford: Stanford University Press, 1997.

Baldwin, Frances. *Sumptuary Legislation and Personal Regulation in England*. Baltimore: Johns Hopkins University Press, 1926.

Barthes, Roland. *Mythologies*. 1957. Trans. Annette Lavers. New York: Hill and Wang, 1972.

Bartolovich, Crystal. "Consumerism, or the Cultural Logic of Late Cannibalism." *Cannibalism and the Colonial World*. Eds. Francis Barker, Peter Hulme, and Margaret Iversen. Cambridge: Cambridge University Press, 1998. 204–37.

Baskin, Richard. "'Prince am I none, yet am I princely born': The Confused Hero of the Commons." *Critical Approaches to English Prose Fiction, 1520–1640*. Ed. Donald Beecher. Ottowa: Dovehouse Editions Inc., 1998. 341–54.

Bataille, Georges. "The Notion of Expenditure." *Visions of Excess: Selected Writings, 1927–1939*. Ed. and Trans. Allan Stoekl. Minneapolis: University of Minnesota Press, 1985. 116–36.

Baumlin, James S. "Generic Contexts of Elizabethan Satire: Rhetoric, Poetic Theory, and Imitation." *Renaissance Genres: Essays on Theory, History, and Interpretation*. Ed. Barbara Kiefer Lewalski. Cambridge, MA: Harvard University Press, 1986. 444–67.

Beecher, Donald. Introduction. *Critical Approaches to English Prose Fiction, 1520–1640*. Ed. Donald Beecher. Ottowa: Dovehouse Editions Inc., 1998. 11–44.

Beeching, Jack. Introduction. *The Principal Navigations, Voyages, Traffiques and Discoveries of the English Nation*. Ed. Jack Beeching. London: Penguin Books, 1972. 9–29.

Beer, Barrett L. *Tudor England Observed*. Stroud: Sutton Publishing, 1998.

———. *Rebellion and Riot: Popular Disorder in England during the Reign of Edward VI*. Kent State University Press, 1982.

Beer, George Louis. *The Origins of the British Colonial System: 1578–1660*. Gloucester, MA: Peter Smith, 1959.

Beier, A.L. *Masterless Men: The Vagrancy Problem in England, 1560–1640*. London: Methuen, 1985.

Bergeron, David M. "Actors in English Civic Pageants." *Renaissance Papers*. Eds. Dennis Donovan and A. Leigh Deneef. Durham, NC: Southeastern Renaissance Conference, 1973. 17–28.

———. "Anthony Munday: Pageant Poet to the City of London." *Huntington Library Quarterly* 30.4 (1967): 345–68.

———. "Civic Pageants and Historical Drama." *Journal of Medieval and Renaissance Studies* 5.1 (1975): 89–105.

————. *English Civic Pageantry, 1558–1642*. Rev. ed. Tempe: Arizona Center for Medieval and Renaissance Studies, 2003.

————. "Pageants, Politics, and Patrons." *Medieval and Renaissance Drama in England*. Vol. 6. Ed. Leeds Barroll. New York: AMS Press, 1993. 139–52.

————. "Stuart Civic Pageants and Textual Performance." *Renaissance Quarterly* 51.1 (1998): 163–83.

————. "Thomas Middleton and Anthony Munday: Artistic Rivalry?" *Studies in English Literature: 1500–1900*. 36.2 (1996): 461–79.

————. *Twentieth-Century Criticism of English Masques, Pageants, and Entertainments: 1558–1642*. San Antonio, TX: Trinity University Press, 1972.

————. "Urban Pastoralism in English Civic Pageants." *The Elizabethan Theatre VIII* 14 (1982): 129–43.

Bergeron, David M., ed. *Pageants and Entertainments of Anthony Munday*. New York: Garland, 1985.

Berlin, Michael. "Civic Ceremony in Early Modern London." *Urban History Yearbook*. Ed. David Reeder. Leicester: Leicester University Press, 1986. 15–27.

Bertram, Claire. "Social Fabric in Thynne's *Debate Between Pride and Lowliness*." *Clothing Culture, 1350–1650*. Ed. Catherine Richardson. Aldershot, Hampshire: Ashgate, 2004. 137–49.

Bess, Jennifer. "Hakluyt's *Discourse of Western Planting*." *Explicator* 55.1 (1996): 3–6.

Bhabha, Homi K. "DissemiNation: Time, Narrative, and the Margins of the Modern Nation." *Nation and Narration*. Ed. Homi K. Bhabha. New York: Routledge, 1990. 291–322.

Bindoff, H.C. *Tudor England*. England: Penguin, 1950.

Bindoff, S.T. *Ket's Rebellion, 1549*. London: The Historical Association, 1968.

Blayney, Peter. W.M. *The Bookshops in Paul's Cross Churchyard*. London: The Bibliographic Society, 1990.

Bogel, Frederic V. *The Difference Satire Makes: Rhetoric and Reading From Johnson to Byron*. Ithaca: Cornell University Press, 2001.

Bowden, Peter J. *The Wool Trade in Tudor and Stuart England*. London: Macmillan, 1962.

Bradbrook, M.C. *Shakespeare in his Context: The Constellated Globe. The Collected Papers of Muriel Bradbrook*. Vol. 6. Totowa, NJ: Barnes & Noble Books, 1989.

Bradley, Harriett. *The Enclosures in England: An Economic Reconstruction*. New York: Columbia University Press, 1918.

Bradley, Peter T. *British Maritime Enterprise in the New World from the Late Fifteenth to the Mid-Eighteenth Century*. Lewiston, NY: The Edwin Mellen Press, 1999.

Brennan, Timothy. "The National Longing for Form." *Nation and Narration*. Ed. Homi K. Bhabha. New York: Routledge, 1990. 44–70.

Brenner, Robert. *Merchants and Revolution: Commercial Change, Political Conflict, and London's Overseas Traders, 1550–1653*. Princeton: Princeton University Press, 1993.

————. "The Social Basis of English Commercial Expansion, 1550–1650." *Journal of Economic History* 32.1 (1972): 361–84.

Bridges, Margaret. "The Reinvention of the Medieval Traveller as Cultural Colonization in Richard Hakluyt's *Principal Navigations, Voyages, Traffiques and Discoveries of the English Nation.*" *Zeitsprunge; Forschungen zur Fruhen Neuzeit* 7.2–3 (2003): 317–33.

Bright, James W., and Wilfred R. Mustard. "*Pan's Pipe, Three Pastoral Eclogues with Other Verses*, by Francis Sabie." *Modern Philology* 7.4 (1910): 433–64.

Brissenden, Alan. "Middletonian Families." *Plotting Early Modern London: New Essays on Jacobean City Comedy*. Eds. Dieter Mehl, Angela Stock, and Anne-Julia Zwierlein. Aldershot, Hampshire: Ashgate, 2004. 27–39.

Bruster, Douglas. *Drama and the Market in the Age of Shakespeare*. Cambridge: Cambridge University Press, 1992.

Burnett, Mark Thornton. *Masters and Servants in English Renaissance Drama and Culture: Authority and Obedience*. New York: St. Martin's Press, 1997.

Cady, Diane. "Linguistic Dis-Ease: Foreign Language as Sexual Disease in Early Modern England." *Sins of the Flesh: Responding to Sexual Disease in Early Modern Europe*. Ed. Kevin Siena. Toronto: Centre for Reformation and Renaissance, 2005.159–86.

Capp, Bernard. "Popular Literature." *Popular Culture in Seventeenth-Century England*. Ed. Barry Reay. London: Croom Helm, 1985. 198–243.

Carroll, William C. "'The Nursery of Beggary': Enclosure, Vagrancy, and Sedition in the Tudor-Stuart Period." *Enclosure Acts: Sexuality, Property, and Culture in Early Modern England*. Eds. Richard Burt and John Michael Archer. Ithaca: Cornell University Press, 1994. 34–47.

Chakravorty, Swapan. "Middleton's *Michaelmas Term*, Inductio 13–19." *Explicator* 51.4 (1993): 209–10.

———. *Society and Politics in the Plays of Thomas Middleton*. Oxford: Clarendon Press, 1996.

Chapman, S.D. "The Genesis of the British Hosiery Industry." *Textile History* 3 (1972): 7–50.

Chatterji, Ruby. "Unity and Disparity in *Michaelmas Term*." *Studies in English Literature, 1500–1900* 8.2 (1968): 349–63.

Cheney, Edward P. *Social Changes in England in the Sixteenth Century as Reflected in Contemporary Literature*. Boston: Ginn & Company, 1895.

Clark, Alice. *The Working Life of Women in the Seventeenth Century*. New York: A.M. Kelley, 1968.

Clark, Peter. "A Crisis Contained? The Condition of English Towns in the 1590's." *The European Crisis of the 1590's: Essays in Comparative History*. Ed. Peter Clark. London: George Allen & Unwin, 1985. 23–43.

Clark, Steve. Introduction. *Travel Writing and Empire: Postcolonial Theory in Transit*. Ed. Steve Clark. London: Zed Books, 1999. 1–28.

Coleman, D.C. "An Innovation and Its Diffusion: The 'New Draperies.'" *Economic History Review* 2nd ser. 22.3 (1969): 417–29.

Connery, Brian A. and Kirk Combe. "Theorizing Satire: A Retrospective and Introduction." *Theorizing Satire: Essays in Literary Criticism*. Eds. Brian A. Connery and Kirk Combe. New York: St. Martin's Press, 1995. 1–15.

Cornwall, Julian. *Revolt of the Peasantry, 1549*. London: Routledge, 1977.

Corvatta, Anthony. *Thomas Middleton's City Comedies*. Lewisburg, PA: Bucknell University Press, 1973.

Cressy, David. *Bonfires and Bells: National Memory and the Protestant Calendar in Elizabethan and Stuart England*. Berkeley: University of California Press, 1989.

Crockett, Bryan. *The Play of Paradox*. Philadelphia: University of Pennsylvania Press, 1995.

Croft, Pauline. "English Commerce with Spain and the Armada War, 1558–1603." *England, Spain, and the* Gran Armada, *1585–1604*. Eds. M.J. Rodriguez-Salgado and Simon Adams. Savage, MD: Barnes & Noble Books, 1991. 236–63.

———. "Libels, Popular Literacy and Public Opinion in Early Modern England." *Historical Research* 68 (1995): 266–85.

Crupi, Charles W. *Robert Greene*. Boston: Twayne, 1986.

Davies, Rosalind. "Intervention in the Cloth Trade: Richard Hakluyt, the New Draperies and the Cockayne Project of 1614." *The Crisis of 1614 and the Addled Parliament: Literary and Historical Perspectives*. Eds. Stephen Lucas and Rosalind Davies. Aldershot, Hampshire: Ashgate, 2003. 113–24.

Davis, Ralph. *English Overseas Trade, 1500–1700*. London: Macmillan, 1973.

de Certeau, Michel. *Heterologies: Discourse on the Other*. Trans. Brian Massumi. Minneapolis: University of Minnesota Press, 1986.

de Grazia, Margreta, Maureen Quilligan, and Peter Stallybrass, eds. *Subject and Object in Renaissance Culture*. Cambridge: Cambridge University Press, 1996.

Dillon, Janette. *Theatre, Court, and City, 1595–1610: Drama and Social Space in London*. Cambridge: Cambridge University Press, 2000.

Donaldson, Ian, ed. *Ben Jonson: A Critical Edition of the Major Works*. Oxford: Oxford University Press, 1985.

Dorsinville, Max. "Design in Deloney's *Jack of Newbury*." *PMLA* 88.2 (1973): 233–9.

Dutton, Richard, ed. *Jacobean Civic Pageants*. Staffordshire: Keele University Press, 1995.

Eccles, Mark. "Anthony Munday." *Studies in the English Renaissance Drama: In Memory of Karl Julius Holzknecht*. Eds. Josephine W. Bennett, Oscar Cargill, and Vernon Hall Jr. New York: New York University Press, 1959. 95–105.

Edwards, Philip. "Edward Hayes Explains Away Sir Humphrey Gilbert." *Renaissance Studies* 6.3–4 (1992): 270–286.

———. *Last Voyages: Cavendish, Hudson, Ralegh*. Oxford: Clarendon Press, 1988.

Escobedo, Andrew. *Nationalism and Historical Loss in Renaissance England: Foxe, Dee, Spenser, Milton*. Ithaca: Cornell University Press, 2004.

Everitt, Alan. "Common Land." *The English Rural Landscape*. Ed. Joan Thirsk. Oxford: Oxford University Press, 2000. 210–35.

Fisher, F.J. "The Development of London as a Centre of Conspicuous Consumption in the Sixteenth and Seventeenth Centuries." *Transactions of the Royal Historical Society*. Ser. 4. Vol. 30. London, 1948. 37–50.

———. "London's Export Trade in the Early Seventeenth Century." *The Growth of English Overseas Trade in the Seventeenth and Eighteenth Centuries*. Ed. W.E. Minchinton. London: Methuen, 1969. 64–77.

Fitzmaurice, Andrew. "Classical Rhetoric and the Promotion of the New World." *Journal of the History of Ideas* 58.2 (1997): 221–43.

——. "'Every man, that prints, adventures': The Rhetoric of the Virginia Company Sermons." *The English Sermon Revised: Religion, Literature, and History 1600–1750.* Eds. Laurie Anne Ferrell and Peter McCullough. Manchester: University of Manchester Press, 2000. 24–42.

Fletcher, Anthony. *Tudor Rebellions.* London: Longmans, 1968.

Franklin, Wayne. *Discoverers, Explorers, Settlers: The Diligent Writers of Early America.* Chicago: University of Chicago Press, 1979.

Freer, Coburn. "John Donne and Elizabethan Economic Theory." *Criticism* 38.4 (1996): 497–520.

Friis, Astrid. *Alderman Cockayne's Project and the Cloth Trade: The Commercial Policy of England in its Main Aspects.* Copenhagen: Levin & Munksgaard, 1927.

Fuchs, Barbara. "Imperium Studies: Theorizing Early Modern Expansion." *Postcolonial Moves: Medieval Through Modern.* Eds. Patricia Clare Ingham and Michelle R. Warren. New York: Palgrave MacMillan, 2003. 71–90.

Fuller, Mary. "'Ravenous Strangers': The Argument of Nationalism in Two Narratives from Richard Hakluyt's *Principal Navigations.*" *Studies in Travel Writing: Papers from the Essex Symposium of "Writing Travels"* 6 (2002): 1–28.

——. *Voyages in Print: English Travel to Amercia, 1576–1624.* Cambridge: Cambridge University Press, 1995.

Fumerton, Patricia. *Cultural Aesthetics: Renaissance Literature and the Practice of Social Ornament.* Chicago: University of Chicago Press, 1991.

Fumerton, Patricia, and Simon Hunt, eds. *Renaissance Culture and the Everyday.* Philadelphia: University of Pennsylvania Press, 1999.

Gibbons, Brian. *Jacobean City Comedy: A Study of Satiric Plays by Johnson, Marston, and Middleton.* Cambridge, MA: Harvard University Press, 1968.

Girtin, Thomas. *The Golden Ram: A Narrative History of the Clothworkers' Company, 1528–1958.* UK: Worshipful Company of Clothworkers, 1950.

——. *The Triple Crowns: A Narrative History of the Drapers' Company, 1364–1964.* London: Hutchinson, 1964

Goose, Nigel. "The 'Dutch' in Colchester: The Economic Influence of an Immigrant Community in the Sixteenth and Seventeenth Centuries." *Immigrants and Minorities* 1.3 (1982): 261–80.

Greenblatt, Stephen J. "Learning to Curse: Aspects of Linguistics Colonialism in the Sixteenth Century." *First Images of America: The Impact of the New World on the Old.* Eds. Fredi Chiappelli, Michael J.B. Allen, Robert L. Benson, and Robert S. Lopez. Berkeley: University of California Press, 1976. 561–80.

——. Introduction. *New World Encounters.* Ed. Stephen Greenblatt. Berkeley: University of California Press, 1993. vii–xviii.

——. *Marvelous Possessions: The Wonder of the New World.* Chicago: University of Chicago Press, 1991.

——. "Murdering Peasants: Status, Genre, and the Representation of Rebellion." *Representing the English Renaissance.* Ed. Stephen Greenblatt. Berkeley: University of California Press, 1988. 1–29.

Griswold, Wendy. *Renaissance Revivals: City Comedy and Revenge Tragedy in the London Theatre, 1576–1980.* Chicago: Chicago University Press, 1986.

Haaker, Ann. "Anthony Munday." *The Popular School: A Survey and Bibliography of Recent Studies in English Renaissance Drama.* Eds. Terence P. Logan and Denzell S. Smith. Lincoln: University of Nebraska Press, 1975. 122–36.

Hadfield, Andrew. *Shakespeare, Spenser and the Matter of Britain.* New York: Palgrave Macmillan, 2004.

Hamlin, William M. "Imagined Apotheoses: Drake, Hariot, and Ralegh in the Americas." *Journal of the History of Ideas* 57.3 (1996): 405–28.

Harris, Jonathan Gil. *Foreign Bodies and the Body Politic: Discourses of Social Pathology in Early Modern England.* Cambridge: Cambridge University Press, 1998.

Hart, Jonathan. *Representing the New World: The English and French Uses of the Example of Spain.* New York: Palgrave, 2001.

———. "Strategies of Promotion: Some Prefatory Matter of Oviedo, Thevet, and Hakluyt." *Imagining Culture: Essays in Early Modern History and Literature.* Ed. Jonathan Hart. New York: Garland Publishing, 1996. 73–92.

Harte, N.B. Introduction. *The New Draperies in the Low Countries and England, 1300–1800.* Ed. N.B. Harte. Oxford: Oxford University Press, 1997. 1–6.

Heinemann, Margot. *Puritanism and Theatre: Thomas Middleton and Opposition Drama under the Early Stuarts.* Cambridge: Cambridge University Press, 1980.

Helfers, James P. "The Explorer or the Pilgrim? Modern Critical Opinion and the Editorial Methods of Richard Hakluyt and Samuel Purchase." *Studies in Philology* 94.2 (1997): 160–86.

Helgerson, Richard. *Forms of Nationhood: The Elizabethan Writing of England.* Chicago: University of Chicago Press, 1992.

———. "Langauge Lessons: Linguistic Colonialism, Linguistic Postcolonialism, and the Early Modern English Nation." *Yale Journal of Criticism: Interpretation in the Humanities* 11.1 (1998): 289–99.

Heller, Herbert Jack. *Penitent Brothellers: Grace, Sexuality, and Genre in Thomas Middleton's City Comedies.* Newark: University of Delaware Press, 2000.

Hentschell, Roze. "Clothworkers and Social Protest: The Case of Thomas Deloney." *Comitatus* 32 (2001): 43–67.

———. "Luxury and Lechery: Hunting the French Pox in Early Modern England." *Sins of the Flesh: Responding to Sexual Disease in Early Modern Europe.* Ed. Kevin Siena. Toronto: Centre for Reformation and Renaissance, 2005. 133–57.

———. "A Question of Nation: Foreign Cloth on the English Subject." *Clothing Culture: 1350–1650.* Ed. Catherine T. Richardson. London: Ashgate, 2004. 49–62.

———. "Treasonous Textiles: Foreign Cloth and the Construction of Englishness." *Journal of Medieval and Early Modern Studies* 32.3 (2002): 543–70.

Herr, Alan Fager. *The Elizabethan Sermon: A Survey and Bibliography.* Philadelphia: Alan Fager Herr, 1940.

Hill, Christopher. "The Many-Headed Monster in Late Tudor and Early Stuart Political Thinking." *From the Renaissance to the Counter-Reformation: Essays in Honor of Garrett Mattingly.* Ed. Charles H. Carter. New York: Random House, 1965. 296–324.

Hill, Tracey. *Anthony Munday and Civic Culture: Theatre, History and Power in Early Modern London, 1580–1633.* Manchester: Manchester University Press, 2004.

Hindle, Steve. *On the Parish? The Micro-Politics of Poor Relief in Rural England, c. 1550–1750*. Oxford: Clarendon Press, 2004.

Holderness, B.A. "The Reception and Distribution of the New Draperies in England." *The New Draperies in the Low Countries and England, 1300–1800*. Ed. N.B. Harte. Oxford: Oxford University Press, 1997. 217–44.

Hope, Valerie. *My Lord Mayor: Eight Hundred Years of London's Mayoralty*. London: Weidenfeld and Nicholson, 1989.

Howard, Jean E. and Phyllis Rackin, eds. *Engendering a Nation: A Feminist Account of Shakespeare's English Histories*. London: Routledge, 1997.

Howarth, R.G. *Two Elizabethan Writers of Fiction: Thomas Nashe and Thomas Deloney*. South Africa: Rustica Press, 1956.

Hughes, Paul L., and James F. Larkin. *Tudor Royal Proclamations*. Vols. 1 and 2. New Haven: Yale University Press, 1964.

Hulme, Peter. *Colonial Encounters: Europe and the Native Caribbean, 1492–1797*. London: Routledge, 1986.

Hunter, G.K. *Dramatic Identities and Cultural Tradition: Studies in Shakespeare and His Contemporaries*. Liverpool: Liverpool University Press, 1978.

Hunting, Penelope. *A History of the Drapers' Company*. London: The Drapers' Company, 1989.

Jardine, Lisa. *Still Harping on Daughters: Women and Drama in the Age of Shakespeare*. 2nd ed. New York: Columbia University Press, 1989.

———. *Worldly Goods: A New History of the Renaissance*. New York: W.W. Norton, 1996.

Jaster, Margaret Rose. "Of Bonnets and Breeches: Sumptuary Codes in Elizabethan Popular Literature." *Proceedings of the PMR Conference* 16/17 (1992–93): 205–11.

Johnson, A.H. *The History of the Worshipful Company of the Drapers of London*. 2 Vols. Oxford: Clarendon Press, 1915.

Johnson, Paula. "Jacobean Ephemera and the Immortal Word." *Renaissance Drama* ns 8 (1977): 151–71.

Jones, Ann Rosalind, and Peter Stallybrass. *Renaissance Clothing and the Materials of Memory*. Cambridge: Cambridge University Press, 2000.

Jones, Howard Mumford. "The Image of the New World." *Elizabethan Studies and Other Essays in Honor of George F. Reynolds*. Boulder, CO: University of Colorado Press, 1945. 62–84.

Jones, Whitney R.D. *The Mid-Tudor Crisis, 1539–1563*. London: Macmillan Press, 1973.

Jordan, Constance. "The 'Art of Clothing': Role-Playing in Deloney's Fiction." *ELR* 11 (1981): 183–93.

Joughin, John J., ed. *Shakespeare and National Culture*. Manchester: Manchester University Press, 1997.

Kathman, David. "Grocers, Goldsmiths, and Drapers: Freemen and Apprentices in the Elizabethan Theater." *Shakespeare Quarterly* 55.1 (2004): 1–49.

Keene, Derek. "Material London in Time and Space." *Material London, ca. 1600*. Ed. Lena Cowen Orlin. Philadelphia: University of Pennsylvania Press, 2000. 55–74.

Kernan, Alvin. *The Cankered Muse: Satire of the English Renaissance.* New Haven: Yale University Press, 1959.

Kerridge, Eric. "Agriculture c. 1500–1793." *Victoria History of the Counties of England: Wiltshire.* Vol. 4. Ed. Elizabeth Crittall. London: University of London Institute of Historical Research, 1962. 43–64.

———. *Textile Manufactures in Early Modern England.* Manchester: Manchester University Press, 1985.

Kinney, Arthur F. "Sir Philip Sidney and the Uses of History." *The Historical Renaissance: New Essays on Tudor and Stuart Literature and Culture.* Eds. Heather Dubrow and Richard Strier. Chicago: University of Chicago Press, 1988. 293–314.

Kinney, Jane M. "Rewriting History: Thomas Deloney's *Jack of Newbury* and Elizabethan Politics." *Philological Papers* 44 (1998–9): 50–57.

Kipling, Gordon. "Triumphal Drama: Form in English Civic Pageantry." *Renaissance Drama* ns 8 (1977): 37–56.

Kistner, A.L., and M.K. Kistner. "Heirs and Identity: The Bases of Social Order in *Michaelmas Term.*" *Modern Language Studies* 16.4 (1986): 61–71.

Knapp, Jeffrey. *An Empire Nowhere: England, America, and Literature from* Utopia *to* The Tempest. Berkeley: University of California Press, 1992.

Knight, W. Nicholas. "Sex and Law Language in Middleton's *Michaelmas Term.*" *"Accompaninge the Players": Essays Celebrating Thomas Middleton, 1580–1980.* Ed. Kenneth Friedenreich. New York: AMS Press, 1983. 89–108.

Knights, L.C. *Drama and Society in the Age of Johnson.* London: Chatto & Windus, 1962.

Knowles, James. "The Spectacle of the Realm: Civic Consciousness, Rhetoric and Ritual in Early Modern London." *Theatre and Government under the Early Stuarts.* Eds. J.R. Mulryne and Margaret Shewring. Cambridge: Cambridge University Press, 1993. 157–89.

Kuchta, David. "The Semiotics of Masculinity in Renaissance England." *Sexuality and Gender in Early Modern Europe: Institutions, Texts, Images.* Ed. James Grantham Turner. Cambridge: Cambridge University Press, 1993. 233–47.

Kupperman, Karen Ordahl. "Fear of Hot Climates in the Anglo-American Experience." *William and Mary Quarterly* 41.2 (1984): 213–40.

———. *Settling With the Indians: The Meeting of English and Indian Cultures in America, 1580–1640.* Totowa, NJ: Rowman and Littlefield, 1980.

Kussmaul, Ann. *Servants and Husbandry in Early Modern England.* Cambridge: Cambridge University Press, 1981.

Ladd, Roger A. "Thomas Deloney and the London Weavers' Company." *Sixteenth Century Journal* 32.4 (2001): 981–1001.

Lancashire, Anne. "Medieval to Renaissance: Plays and the London Draper's Company to 1558." *The Centre and its Compass: Studies in Medieval Literature in Honour of Professor John Leyerle.* Eds. Robert A. Taylor, James F Burke, Patricia J. Eberle, Ian Lancashire, and Brian S. Merrilees. Kalamazoo, MI: Western Michigan University Press, 1993. 297–313.

Land, Stephen K. *Kett's Rebellion: The Norfolk Rising of 1549.* Ipswich: The Boydell Press, 1977.

Larkin, James F., and Paul L. Hughes, eds. *Stuart Royal Proclamations*. Vol. 1. Oxford: Clarendon Press, 1973.

Lawlis, Merritt E. *Apology for the Middle Class: The Dramatic Novels of Thomas Deloney*. Bloomington: Indiana University Press, 1960.

Lawlis, Merritt E., ed. *The Novels of Thomas Deloney*. Bloomington: Indiana University Press, 1961.

Leggatt, Alexander. *Citizen Comedy in the Age of Shakespeare*. Toronto: University of Toronto Press, 1973.

Leggett, William F. *The Story of Wool*. Brooklyn, NY: Chemical Publishing, 1947.

Lehr, John. "Two Names in Middleton's *Michaelmas Term*." *English Language Notes* 18 (1980): 15–19.

Leinwand, Theodore B. *The City Staged: Jacobean Comedy, 1603–1613*. Madison: University of Wisconsin Press, 1986.

———. "London Triumphing: The Jacobean Lord Mayor's Show." *CLIO* 11.2 (1982): 137–53.

———. "Redeeming Beggary/Buggery in *Michaelmas Term*." *ELH* 61 (1994): 53–70.

Levin, Carol. *The Heart and Stomach of a King: Elizabeth I and the Politics of Sex and Power*. Philadelphia: University of Pennsylvania Press, 1994.

Levin, Harry. "Notes toward a Definition of City Comedy." *Renaissance Genres: Essays on Theory, History, and Interpretation*. Ed. Barbara Kiefer Lewalski. Cambridge, MA: Harvard University Press, 1986. 126–46.

Levin, Richard. "Quomodo's Name in *Michaelmas Term*." *Notes and Queries* 20 (1973): 460–61.

Levin, Richard, ed. *Michaelmas Term*. Thomas Middleton. 1605–1606. Lincoln: University of Nebraska Press, 1966

Linthicum, M. Channing. *Costume in the Drama of Shakespeare and His Contemporaries*. Oxford: Clarendon Press, 1936.

Linton, Joan Pong. *The Romance of the New World: Gender and the Literary Formations of English Colonialism*. Cambridge: Cambridge University Press, 1998.

Lipson, E. *The History of the Woollen and Worsted Industries*. 1921. London: Frank Cass, 1965.

———. *A Short History of Wool and Its Manufacture Mainly in England*. Melbourne: William Heinemann Ltd., 1953.

Lobanov-Rostovsky, Sergei. "*The Triumphes of Golde*: Economic Authority in the Jacobean Lord Mayor's Shows." *ELH* 60.4 (1993): 878–98.

Mackerness, E.D. "Thomas Deloney and the Virtuous Proletariat." *The Cambridge Journal* 5.1 (1951): 34–50.

Maclure, Millar. *The Paul's Cross Sermons, 1534–1642*. Toronto: University of Toronto Press, 1958.

Maley, Willy. *Nation, State, and Empire in English Renaissance Literature: Shakespeare to Milton*. New York: Palgrave Macmillan, 2003.

Mancall, Peter C. Introduction. *Envisioning America: English Plans for the Colonization of North America, 1580–1640*. Ed. Peter C. Mancall. Boston: Bedford Books, 1995. 1–30.

Manley, Lawrence. *Literature and Culture in Early Modern London*. Cambridge: Cambridge University Press, 1995.

———. "Of Sites and Rites." *The Theatrical City: Culture, Theatre, and Politics in London, 1576–1649.* Eds. David L. Smith, Richard Strier, and David Bevington. Cambridge: Cambridge University Press, 1995. 35–54.

Manning, Roger B. *Village Revolts: Social Protest and Popular Disturbances in England, 1509–1640.* Oxford: Clarendon Press, 1988.

———. "Violence and Social Conflict in Mid-Tudor Rebellions." *Journal of British Studies* 16.2 (1977): 19–40.

Margolies, David. *Novel and Society in Elizabethan England.* London: Croon Helm, 1985.

Martin, Luc. "The Rise of the New Draperies in Norwich, 1550–1622." *The New Draperies in the Low Countries and England, 1300–1800.* Ed. N.B. Harte. Oxford: Oxford University Press, 1997. 245–74.

Martin, Matthew. "'[B]egot between tirewomen and tailors': Commodified Self-Fashioning in *Michaelmas Term.*" *Early Modern Literary Studies* 5.1 (1999): 21–36.

Marx, Leo. *The Machine in the Garden: Technology and the Pastoral Ideal in America.* New York: Oxford University Press, 1964.

McCoy, Richard. *Sir Philip Sidney: Rebellion in Arcadia.* New Brunswick, New Jersey: Rutgers University Press, 1979.

McEachern, Claire Elizabeth. *The Poetics of English Nationhood, 1590–1612.* Cambridge and New York: Cambridge University Press, 1996.

McKeon, Michael. *The Origins of the English Novel, 1600–1740.* 1987. Baltimore: The Johns Hopkins University Press, 2002.

McRae, Andrew. *God Speed the Plough: The Representation of Agrarian England, 1500–1660.* Cambridge: Cambridge University Press, 1996.

———. *Literature, Satire and the Early Stuart State.* Cambridge: Cambridge University Press, 2004.

———. "The Verse Libel: Popular Satire in Early Modern England." *Subversion and Scurrility: Popular Discourse in Europe from 1500 to the Present.* Eds. Dermot Cavanagh and Tim Kirk. Aldershot, UK: Ashgate, 2000. 58–73.

Merritt, J.F. "The Reshaping of Stow's *Survey*: Munday, Strype, and the Protestant City." *Imagining Early Modern London: Perceptions and Portrayals of the City from Stow to Strype, 1598–1720.* Ed. J.F. Merritt. Cambridge: Cambridge University Press, 2001. 52–88.

Mesa-Pelly, Judith Broome. "Fantasy and Social Change in Thomas Deloney's *Jack of Newbury* and *Thomas of Reading.*" *Studies in the Humanities* 23.1 (1996): 84–98.

Miller, Shannon. "Consuming Mothers/Consuming Merchants: The Carnivalesque Economy of Jacobean City Comedy." *Modern Language Studies* 26.2/3 (1996): 73–97.

———. *Invested with Meaning: The Raleigh Circle in the New World.* Philadelphia: University of Pennsylvania Press, 1998.

Money, Walter. *A History of Newbury.* 1887. Maidenhead, UK: Thames Valley Press, 1972.

Montrose, Louis. "Of Gentlemen and Shepherds: The Politics of Elizabethan Pastoral Form." *ELH* 50.3 (1983): 415–59.

196   *The Culture of Cloth in Early Modern England*

Munro, John H. "The Origins of the English 'New Draperies': The Resurrection of an Old Flemish Industry, 1270–1570." *The New Draperies in the Low Countries and England, 1300–1800*. Ed. N.B. Harte. Oxford: Oxford University Press, 1997. 35–127.

Neeson. J.M. *Commoners: Common Right, Enclosure and Social Change in England, 1700–1820*. Cambridge: Cambridge University Press, 1993.

Netzloff, Mark. *England's Internal Colonies: Class, Capital, and the Literature of Early Modern English Colonialism*. New York: Palgrave MacMillan, 2003.

Neuberg, Victor E. *Popular Literature: A History and Guide from the Beginning of Printing to the Year 1897*. Harmondsworth, UK: Penguin Books, 1977.

Neville-Sington, Pamela. "'A very good trumpet': Richard Hakluyt and the Politics of Overseas Expansion." *Texts and Cultural Change in Early Modern England*. Eds. Cedric C. Brown and Arthur F. Marotti. New York: St. Martin's Press, 1997. 66–79.

Newcombe, Laurie Humphrey. *Reading Popular Romance in Early Modern England*. New York: Columbia University Press, 2002.

Newman, Karen. *Fashioning Femininity and English Renaissance Drama*. Chicago: University of Chicago Press, 1991.

Orlin, Lena Cowen, ed. *Material London, ca. 1600*. Philadelphia: University of Pennsylvania Press, 2000.

Outhwaite, R.B. "Dearth, the English Crown, and the 'Crisis of the 1590s'." *The European Crisis of the 1590's: Essays in Comparative History*. Ed. Peter Clark. London: George Allen & Unwin, 1985. 23–43.

Paster, Gail Kern. *The Idea of the City in the Age of Shakespeare*. Athens, GA: University of Georgia Press, 1985.

———. "The Idea of London in Masque and Pageant." *Pageantry in Shakespearean Theater*. Ed. David M. Bergeron. Athens, GA: University of Georgia Press, 1985. 48–63.

———. Introduction. *Michaelmas Term*. Ed. Gail Kern Paster. Manchester: Manchester Universty Press, 2000. 1–51.

———. "Quomodo, Sir Giles, and Triangular Desire: Social Aspiration in Middleton and Massinger." *Comedy from Shakespeare to Sheridan: Change and Continuity in the English and European Dramatic Tradition*. Eds. A.R. Braunmiller and J.C. Bulman. Newark: University of Delaware Press, 1986. 165–78.

Patterson, Annabel. *Censorship and Interpretation: The Conditions of Writing and Reading in Early Modern England*. Madison: University of Wisconsin Press, 1984.

Payne, Anthony. "'Strange, Remote, and Farre Distant Countreys': The Travel Books of Richard Hakluyt." *Journeys through the Market: Travel, Travellers, and the Book Trade*. Eds. Robin Myers and Michael Harris. New Castle, DE: Oak Knoll Press, 1999. 1–37.

Pelling, Margaret. "Appearance and Reality: Barber-Surgeons, the Body, and Disease." *London 1500–1700: The Making of the Metropolis*. Eds. A.L. Beier and Roger Finlay. London: Longman, 1986. 82–112.

Peter, John. *Complaint and Satire in Early English Literature*. 1959. Folcroft, PA: The Folcroft Press Inc., 1969.

Ponting, K.G. *The Wool Trade Past and Present.* Manchester: Columbine Press, 1961.

Prescott, Anne Lake. "Humour and Satire in the Renaissance." *The Cambridge History of Literary Criticism.* Vol. 3. Ed. Glyn P. Norton. Cambridge: Cambridge University Press, 1999. 284–91.

Prestwich, Menna. *Cranfield: Politics and Profits under the Early Stuarts; The Career of Lionel Cranfield, Earl of Middlesex.* Oxford: Clarendon Press, 1966.

Priestly, Ursula. *The Fabric of Stuffs: The Norwich Textile Industry from 1565.* Norwich: University of East Anglia, 1990.

Quilligan, Maureen, ed. "Special Issue: Renaissance Materialities." *Journal of Medieval and Early Modern Studies* 32.3 (2002).

Quinn, David B. *Explorers and Colonies: America, 1500–1625.* London and Ronceverte: The Hambledon Press, 1990.

———. "Sir Thomas Smith and the Beginnings of English Colonial Theory." *Proceedings of the American Philosophical Society* 89.4 (1945): 543–60.

Quinn, David B., ed. *New American World: A Documentary History of North America to 1612.* Vols. 3 and 5. New York: Arno Press, 1979.

Rabb, Theodore K. *Enterprise and Empire: Merchant and Gentry Investments in the Expansion of England, 1575–1630.* Cambridge, MA: Harvard University Press, 1967.

Raleigh, Walter. *The English Voyages of the Sixteenth Century.* Glasgow: James MacLehose and Sons, 1906.

Ramsay, G.D. "Clothworkers, Merchant Adventurers and Richard Hakluyt." *English Historical Review* 92 (1977): 504–21.

———. *The English Woollen Industry, 1500–1750.* London: MacMillan, 1982.

———. *The Wiltshire Woollen Industry in the Sixteenth and Seventeenth Centuries.* London: Frank Cass & Co., 1965.

Relihan, Constance C. *Fashioning Authority: The Development of Elizabethan Novelistic Discourse.* Kent, OH: Kent State University Press, 1994.

———. Introduction. *Framing Elizabethan Fictions: Contemporary Approaches to Early Modern Narrative Prose.* Ed. Constance C. Relihan. Kent, OH: Kent State University Press, 1996. 1–15.

Richardson, Catherine. Introduction. *Clothing Culture, 1350–1650.* Ed. Catherine Richardson. Aldershot, Hampshire: Ashgate, 2004. 1–25.

Rosenheim, Edward W. *Swift and the Satirist's Art.* Chicago: University of Chicago Press, 1963.

Rowe, George. "Prodigal Sons, New Comedy, and Middleton's *Michaelmas Term.*" *English Literary Renaissance* 7.1 (1977): 90–107.

Rye, William Brenchley. *England as Seen by Foreigners in the Days of Elizabeth and James the First.* London: John Russell Smith, 1865.

Salzman, Paul. *English Prose Fiction, 1558–1700: A Critical History.* Oxford: Clarendon Press, 1985.

Sampson, Martin W., ed. *Michaelmas Term.* Thomas Middleton. 1605–06. New York: American Book Company, 1915.

Scanlan, Thomas. *Colonial Writing and the New World, 1583–1671: Allegories of Desire.* Cambridge: Cambridge University Press, 1999.

Schneider, Jane. "Fantastical Colors in Foggy London: The New Fashion Potential of the Late Sixteenth Century." *Material London, ca. 1600.* Ed. Lena Cowen Orlin. Philadelphia: University of Pennsylvania Press, 2000. 109–27.

Scholz, Susanne. *Body Narratives: Writing the Nation and Fashioning the Subject in Early Modern England.* New York: St. Martin's Press, 2000.

Schwyzer, Philip. *Literature, Nationalism, and Memory in Early Modern England and Wales.* Cambridge: Cambridge University Press, 2004.

Selden, Raman. *English Verse Satire: 1590–1765.* London: Allen & Unwin, 1978.

Shammas, Carole. "English Commercial Development and American Colonization." *The Westward Enterprise: English Activities in Ireland, the Atlantic, and America, 1480–1650.* Eds. K.R. Andrews, N.P. Canny, and P.E.H. Hair. Liverpool: Liverpool University Press, 1978. 151–74.

Sharp, Buchanan. *In Contempt of All Authority: Rural Artisans and Riot in the West of England, 1586–1660.* Berkeley: University of California Press, 1980.

Siemon, James R. "Landlord Not King: Agrarian Change and Interarticulation." *Enclosure Acts: Sexuality, Property, and Culture in Early Modern England.* Eds. Richard Burt and John Michael Archer. Ithaca: Cornell University Press, 1994. 17–33.

Simons, John. "Realistic Romance: The Prose Fiction of Thomas Deloney." *Contexts and Connections: Winchester Research Papers in the Humanities* 12 (1983): 1–26.

Simpson, W. Sparrow. *Chapters in the History of Old S. Paul's.* London: Elliot Stock, 1881.

———. *Gleanings from Old S. Paul's.* London: Elliot Stock, 1889.

Spufford, Margaret. *Small Books and Pleasant Histories: Popular Fiction and its Readership in Seventeenth Century England.* Cambridge: Cambridge University Press, 1981.

Stallybrass, Peter. "Worn Worlds: Clothes and Identity on the Renaissance Stage." *Subject and Object in Renaissance Culture.* Eds. Margreta De Grazia, Maureen Quilligan, and Peter Stallybrass. Cambridge: Cambridge University Press, 1996. 289–320.

Steele, Robert. *A Bibliography of Royal Proclamations of Tudor and Stuart Sovereigns, 1485–1714.* Vol. 1. Oxford: Clarendon Press, 1910.

Steggle, Matthew. "Charles Chester and Richard Hakluyt." *SEL Studies in English Literature 1500–1900* 43.1 (2003): 65–81.

Stemmler, Theo. "The Rise of a New Literary Genre: Thomas Deloney's Bourgeois Novel *Jack of Newbury*." *Telling Stories: Studies in Honour of Ulrich Broich on the Occasion of His 60th Birthday.* Eds. Elmar Lehmann and Bernd Lenz. Amsterdam: B.R. Grüner, 1992. 47–55.

Stevenson, Laura Caroline. *Praise and Paradox: Merchants and Craftsmen in Elizabethan Popular Literature.* Cambridge: Cambridge University Press, 1985.

Stock, Angela, and Anne-Julia Zwierlein. Introduction. *Plotting Early Modern London: New Essays on Jacobean City Comedy.* Eds. Dieter Mehl, Angela Stock, and Anne-Julia Zwierlein. Aldershot, Hampshire: Ashgate, 2004. 1–24.

Stone, Lawrence. "Elizabethan Overseas Trade." *Economic History Review* 2nd ser. ii (1949): 30–58.

Sullivan, Ceri. *The Rhetoric of Credit: Merchants in Early Modern Writing.* Madison, NJ: Fairleigh Dickinson University Press; London; Cranbury, NJ: Associated University Presses, 2002.

Sullivan, Garrett A., Jr. *The Drama of Landscape: Land, Property, and Social Relations on the Early Modern Stage.* Stanford: Stanford University Press, 1998.

Supple, B.E. *Commercial Crisis and Change in England, 1600–1642: A Study in the Instability of a Mercantile Economy.* Cambridge: Cambridge University Press, 1964.

Sussman, Anne. "Histor, History, and Narrative Memory in Sidney's *Arcadia.*" *Sidney Journal* 21.2 (2003): 39–49.

Sutton, John L. Jr. "A Historical Source for the Rebellion of the Commons in Sidney's *Arcadia.*" *English Language Notes* 23.4 (1986): 6–11.

Suzuki, Mihoko. *Subordinate Subjects: Gender, the Political Nation, and Literary Form in England, 1588–1688.* Aldershot, Hampshire: Ashgate, 2003.

Sweet, Timothy. "Economy, Ecology, and *Utopia* in Early Colonial Promotional Literature." *American Literature* 71.3 (1999): 399–427.

Taussig, Michael. *Mimesis and Alterity: A Particular History of the Senses.* New York: Routledge, 1993.

Tawney, R.H. *The Agrarian Problem in the Sixteenth Century.* 1912. Oxford: Harper Torchbooks, 1967.

Thirsk, Joan. *Economic Policy and Projects: The Development of a Consumer Society in Early Modern England.* Oxford: Clarendon Press, 1978.

———. "Enclosing and Engrossing." *The Agrarian History of England and Wales: Volume IV, 1500–1640.* Ed. Joan Thirsk. Cambridge: Cambridge University Press, 1967. 200–255.

———. "'The Fantastical Folly of Fashion': The English Stocking Knitting Industry, 1500–1700. *The Rural Economy of England: Collected Essays.* Ed. Joan Thirsk. London: Hambledon Press, 1984. 235–57.

———. "Tudor Enclosures." *The Tudors.* Ed. Joel Hurstfield. London: Sidgwick & Jackson, 1973. 104–27.

Thrupp, Sylvia L. Introduction. *An Essay on Drapery.* 1635. William Scott. Cambridge, MA: Harvard University Press, 1953. 1–13.

Tribble, Evelyn B. "'We Will Do No Harm with Our Swords': Royal Representation, Civic Pageantry, and the Displacement of Popular Protest in Thomas Deloney's *Jack of Newberie.*" *Place and Displacement in the Renaissance.* Ed. Alvin Vos. Binghamton, NY: Medieval and Renaissance Texts & Studies, 1995. 147–57.

Tumbleson, Raymond D. "The Triumph of London: Lord Mayor's Day Pageants and the Rise of the City." *The Witness of Time: Manifestations of Ideology in Seventeenth Century England.* Eds. Katherine Z. Keller and Gerald J Schiffhorst. Pittsburgh, PA: Duquense University Press, 1984. 53–68.

Van der Wee, Herman. "The Western European Woollen Industries, 1500–1750." *The Cambridge History of Western Textiles.* Vol. 1. Ed. David Jenkins. Cambridge: Cambridge University Press, 2003. 397–472.

Vincent, Susan. *Dressing the Elite: Clothes in Early Modern England.* Oxford: Berg, 2003.

Wallace, Nathaniel. "The Darkened Vision of Renaissance Satire." *Pennsylvania English* 14.2 (1990): 36–53.

Walter, John and Keith Wrightson. "Dearth and Social Order in Early Modern England." *Past and Present* 71 (1976): 22–42.

Watts, Sheldon. *Epidemics and History: Disease, Power and Imperialism*. New Haven: Yale University Press, 1997.

Wells, Susan. "Jacobean City Comedy and the Ideology of the City." *ELH* 48 (1981): 37–60.

White, Helen C. *Social Criticism in Popular Religious Literature of the Sixteenth Century*. New York: The MacMillan Company, 1944.

Williams, Penry. *The Tudor Regime*. Oxford: Oxford University Press, 1979.

Williams, Raymond. *The Country and the City*. Oxford: Oxford University Press, 1973.

Withington, Robert. *English Pageantry: An Historical Outline*. Vol. 2. New York: Benjamin Blom, Inc., 1926.

Wolf, William. "Anthony Munday as Popular Artist." *Journal of Popular Culture* 13.4 (1980): 658–62.

Woolf, Daniel. *The Social Circulation of the Past: English Historical Culture, 1500–1730*. Oxford: Oxford University Press, 2003.

Worden, Blair. *The Sound of Virtue: Philip Sidney's Arcadia and Elizabethan Politics*. New Haven: Yale University Press, 1996.

Wright, Celeste Turner. *Anthony Munday: An Elizabethan Man of Letters*. Berkeley: University of California Press, 1928

Wright, Eugene. *Thomas Deloney*. Boston: Twayne, 1981.

Wright, Louis. *Middle Class Culture in Elizabethan England*. 1935. Ithaca: Cornell University Press, 1958.

Wright, Nancy E. "'Rival Traditions': Civic and Courtly Ceremonies in Jacobean London." *The Politics of the Stuart Court Masque*. Eds. David Bevington and Peter Holbrook. Cambridge: Cambridge University Press, 1998. 197–217.

Wrightson, Keith. *Earthly Necessities: Economic Lives in Early Modern Britain*. New Haven: Yale University Press, 2000.

Yachnin, Paul. "Social Competition in Middleton's *Michaelmas Term*." *Explorations in Renaissance Culture* 13 (1987): 87–99.

Yates, Julian. *Error, Misuse, Failure: Object Lessons from the English Renaissance*. Minneapolis: University of Minnesota Press, 2003.

Youings, Joyce. "Did Raleigh's England Need Colonies?" *Raleigh in Exeter 1985: Privateering and Colonisation in the Reign of Elizabeth I*. Ed. Joyce Youings. Exeter: University of Exeter Press, 1985. 39–57.

Zeeveld, Gordon W. "The Uprising of the Commons in Sidney's *Arcadia*." *Modern Language Notes* 48.4 (1933): 209–17.

Zell, Michael. "Credit in the Pre-Industrial English Woollen Industry." *Economic History Review*. New ser. 49.4 (1996): 667–91.

———. *Industry in the Countryside: Wealden Society in the Sixteenth Century*. Cambridge: Cambridge University Press, 1994.

Index

159–62, 163, 166, 170, 171–3, 174, 175, 176, 177
Jardine, Lisa 105n. 6, 115n. 33
Jason and the Argonauts 13, 24, 24n. 9, 173–6
Jaster, Margaret Rose105n. 6, 120n. 45
Johnson, A.H. 131, 142n. 28, 150
Johnson, Paula 164n. 24, 165n. 26
Johnson, Robert 2, 98–100
Jolles, John 173–6
Jones, Ann Rosalind 7, 8, 63, 105, 106n. 8, 113, 113n. 27
Jones, Howard 81n. 16
Jones, Whitney R.D. 32n. 22, 40, 40nn. 38, 39, 41, 41n. 43, 42, 42n. 48
Jonson, Ben 103–4, 111, 112, 149n. 43
Every Man Out of His Humour 104n. 4
"On English Monsieur" 103–4, 111, 112
Volpone 149n. 43
Jordan, Constance 64n. 35
Joughin, John 9n. 18

Keene, Derek 4n. 8, 78n. 6
Kent 2, 23
Kernan, Alvin 106n. 11
kersies 30, 63n. 30, 124, 142
Kerridge, Eric 3nn. 1, 2, 20n. 1, 44, 53n. 6, 62, 63n. 30
Kett, Robert 40–49
Kett's Rebellion 40–49
Kinney, Arthur 44n. 52
Kinney, Jane 52n. 4
Kipling, Gordon 164n. 23, 172n. 42
Kistner, A.L. and M.K. 132, 143n. 32, 146
Knapp, Jeffrey 92n. 41
Knight, W. Nicholas 142n. 27
Knights, L.C. 132n. 8
Kuchta, David 123, 123n. 47
Kupperman, Karen Ordahl 84n. 20, 96n. 53, 97, 99
Kussmaul, Ann 27n. 12

labor 4nn. 5, 6, 7, 10–11, 14–15, 21, 25–7, 31n. 18, 32–3, 39, 45, 47, 49, 52, 55–8, 61–4, 66, 67, 70, 88–9, 91–2, 115, 117, 170
Ladd, Roger A. 52n. 4, 61n. 25, 67n. 39, 70n. 43
Lambarde, William 1, 2, 23, 23n. 8
Lancashire, Anne 163n. 21
Land, Stephen K. 32n. 21, 42n. 49

landlords 6, 10, 21, 31, 32, 34, 37–9, 40, 41, 42n. 48, 44, 47, 49–50, 51, 64, 91; *see also* landowners
landowners 3, 6, 11, 21, 32n. 21, 33, 35, 39, 40, 45, 142n. 26, 146
Lane, Ralph 96n. 51
Larkin, James F. 159
Latimer, Hugh 36n. 29
Lawlis, Merritt 52n. 3, 53n. 5, 54n. 10, 65
Leggett, William F. 3n.1, 89n. 35, 99n. 59, 100n. 59
Lehr, John 147n. 38
Leinwand, Theodore 132, 139n. 20, 140n. 23, 141n. 25, 142n. 26, 151
Levant Company 6, 79, 131n. 5
Levin, Carol 55
Levin, Harry 132, 150n. 47
Levin, Richard 147n. 38
Linthicum, M. Channing 117n. 40
Linton, Joan Pong 63n. 33, 81n. 14, 90, 90n. 38, 92n. 43, 98, 99, 100, 101
Lipson, E. 3n. 1, 62
Lobanov-Rostovsky, Sergei 170n. 40, 172n. 42, 176n. 53
Lodge, Thomas 25, 58
London 4, 5n. 9, 7, 12–14, 31n. 18, 42, 51, 52n. 4, 53–5, 56, 57, 65, 70, 78n. 6, 80n. 12, 96, 104, 105n. 5, 111–12, 115, 116n. 36, 117, 118, 120, 122, 123, 124, 129, 130–36, 137n. 16, 138–9, 141–3, 145–9, 151, 153, 157, 158, 160, 161, 162, 163–77
London's Lord Mayor 2, 13, 53, 54, 55, 153, 162–4, 166–7, 168–77
Lord Mayors' pageants 2, 12, 13, 154, 162–77; *see also* civic pageants
Low Countries 4, 5, 69, 79, 80, 131n. 5, 143n. 31, 148; *see also* Netherlands *and* Dutch Provinces
luxury textiles 6, 12, 82n. 17, 93, 105, 108, 113, 117–19, 122–3, 124n. 49, 129, 130n. 2, 138; *see also* silk *and* velvet
Lyly, John 115

Mackerness, E.D. 52
Maclure, Millar 36n. 29, 116n. 36, 117n. 39, 138
Maley, Willy 9n. 18
Mancall, Peter C. 77n. 3, 92n. 44

Peckham, George 77, 91–3, 91n. 40, 92n.
 42, 94, 95, 96–8, 100
Pelling, Margaret 113
Perkins, William 138n. 18
Persius 106
Peter, John 107nn. 14, 16
"The Phantastick Age" 110–11, 113, 122
Ponting, K.G. 3n. 1
Portugal 88
pox 112–13; *see also* venereal disease
Prescott, Anne Lake 107n. 17
Prestwich, Menna 159n. 9, 161n. 15
Priestly, Ursula 53n. 6, 66n. 38
Privy Council 148, 154n. 1, 158–9, 176
prose 2, 9, 10, 11, 12, 21, 44, 52, 58–60,
 65n. 36, 106, 107, 114, 164, 165, 177
Prynne, William 104

Quilligan, Maureen 7n. 14
Quinn, David B. 84n. 22, 85, 86, 87nn. 27,
 28, 93

Rabb, Theodore 77
Rackin, Phyllis 9n. 18
Raleigh, Walter 75–6, 82, 82n. 17, 85n. 24,
 86–7, 92n. 43, 93, 99
Ramsay, G.D. 3, 4, 91, 136n. 14, 137n. 16,
 142n. 29, 144n. 33,
religious texts 9, 12; *see also* sermons
Relihan, Constance C. 58n. 19, 59
Richard I 166, 167n. 32, 168
Richardson, Catherine 134
Rosenheim, Edward W. 108, 108n. 18
Rowley, William 141
royal proclamations 2, 3, 9, 12, 32, 36n. 31,
 37n. 33, 38–9, 41, 42n. 46, 55, 130n. 1,
 136n. 13, 137, 138n. 18, 144n. 33,
 151, 154, 156, 157, 159–61, 177;
 see also cloth, legislation of
Russia 79, 80n. 13
Rye, William Brenchley 108n. 19

Sabie, Francis 28–9, 31
St. Paul's Cathedral 104, 108, 115–16, 131,
 140n. 23
Salzman, Paul 59
Sampson, Martin W. 140n. 24, 148n. 40
Sandys, George 79
Satin 4, 6, 105, 106, 118, 119, 123, 124, 168
satire 9, 12, 105n. 5, 106–8, 110
Scanlan, Thomas 77n. 3, 81

Schneider, Jane 5n. 12, 105, 158n. 7
Scholz, Susanne 114n. 28, 115n. 31
Schwyzer, Philip 9n. 18
Scotland 64–5
Scott, William 129, 135
Selden, Raman 106n. 11, 107–8
sermons 9, 36n. 29, 41, 81n. 15, 105, 107,
 108, 115–17, 122, 125, 132, 135,
 138, 151, 161n. 15
Shakespeare, William 23nn 5, 6, 28n. 13,
 39n. 37, 46n. 58, 111n. 22, 138n. 17
 2 Henry IV 138n. 17
 2 Henry VI 23n. 5, 39n. 37, 46n. 58
 Much Ado About Nothing 23n. 6
 Merchant of Venice 111n. 22
 Winter's Tale 28n.13
Shammas, Carole 79n. 10
Sharp, Buchanan 51, 51n. 2, 57
sheep 1, 3, 5n. 12, 6, 10–11, 15, 19–39, 40n.
 48, 41–2, 44, 45, 47, 50, 51, 65, 99,
 100n. 59, 158n. 7, 161n. 12, 168,
 169, 170n. 38, 175n. 50, 179n. 50
sheep farming 6, 11, 13n. 20, 20–21, 23, 26,
 32–4, 36–9, 41, 42n. 48, 51, 76
shepherds 3, 10–11, 19–21, 23, 24–34, 36n.
 29, 38, 42, 45, 47, 49, 168–9
Shropshire 3
Sidney, Philip 9, 10, 11, 19, 21, 25, 29, 29n.
 15, 43, 44–50, 58, 59, 84n. 22, 86n.
 25
 A Dialogue Between Two Shepherds 25
 The Defense of Poesy 19, 45
 New Arcadia 48–50
 Old Arcadia 9, 10–11, 19, 21, 25, 29n.
 15, 43, 44–50
Siemon, James R. 32n. 20
silk 4, 6, 10, 56n. 14, 57, 58n. 18, 66, 82, 89,
 93, 94, 96n. 51, 105, 106, 112–13,
 116, 117, 118, 119, 123, 124n. 49,
 138, 144, 155n. 2, 156n. 3, 168, 171;
 see also luxury textiles
silkweavers 11, 51, 53, 54–7, 64, 69, 70
Silkweavers' Company 69
Simons, John 59n. 20
Simpson, W. Sparrow 104n. 3, 116n. 37
Slany, Stephen 54, 54n. 9, 55
Smith, Thomas 37–8, 37nn. 34, 35
Sotherton, Nicholas 42, 42n. 49, 43, 46, 47, 48
Spain 5–6, 11–12, 51, 53, 57, 68–9, 76–80,
 83, 84, 85, 86–90, 97, 98, 99, 100n.